Playable Bodies

PLAYABLE BODIES

Dance Games and Intimate Media

Kiri Miller

OXFORD
UNIVERSITY PRESS

OXFORD
UNIVERSITY PRESS

Oxford University Press is a department of the University of Oxford. It furthers
the University's objective of excellence in research, scholarship, and education
by publishing worldwide. Oxford is a registered trade mark of Oxford University
Press in the UK and certain other countries.

Published in the United States of America by Oxford University Press
198 Madison Avenue, New York, NY 10016, United States of America.

Library of Congress Cataloging-in-Publication Data
Names: Miller, Kiri, author.
Title: Playable bodies : dance games and intimate media / Kiri Miller.
Description: New York, NY : Oxford University Press, [2017] |
Includes bibliographical references and index.
Identifiers: LCCN 2016032517 | ISBN 9780190257835 (hardcover : acid-free paper) |
ISBN 9780190257842 (pbk. : acid-free paper) | ISBN 9780190257859 (updf) |
ISBN 9780190257866 (epub)
Subjects: LCSH: Dance and technology.
Classification: LCC GV1588.7.M55 2017 | DDC 792.8—dc23
LC record available at https://lccn.loc.gov/2016032517

9 8 7 6 5 4 3 2 1

Paperback printed by Webcom Inc., Canada
Hardback printed by Bridgeport National Bindery, Inc., United States of America

(Every nerve and muscle in Rosamond was adjusted to the consciousness that she was being looked at. She was by nature an actress of parts that entered into her physique: she even acted her own character, and so well, that she did not know it to be precisely her own.)
                    —George Eliot, *Middlemarch* (1871–1872)

CONTENTS

ACKNOWLEDGMENTS

My first thanks must go to the dance game players, designers, and choreographers who shared their time and insight with me over the past five years. To all of these gracious collaborators: I'm still thinking through your ideas and feeling out your choreography every day. Special thanks to the YouTube uploaders whose interviews are remixed in Chapter 6, the volunteers who danced with me and Aleysia at Brown, the participants on the DC player forums, and Matt Boch, Marcos Aguirre, and Chanel Thompson at Harmonix for extended conversations about the nature of virtual dance transmission. I'm also grateful to Denise Plouffe, my childhood dance teacher, for my earliest and most enduring lessons in repetition with a difference— and to Cjaiilon Andrade, my unexpected train companion, for sharing his experience as a young dancer on the rise.

My brilliant and inspiring student research assistants Emily Xie, Aleysia Whitmore, and Tristan Rodman contributed enormously to this book. Their help was made possible through the support of Radcliffe's Research Partnership Program, Brown's UTRA program, and a grant from Brown's Creative Arts Council. I'm also indebted to the students in my courses on Musical Youth Cultures, Digital Media & Virtual Performance, Ethnography of Popular Music, and Music & Technoculture. It has been a special privilege to work closely with students pursuing thesis and dissertation projects on technoculture, popular music, and media circulation topics at Brown; my thanks to Colin Fitzpatrick, Erik-Dardan Ymeraga, Ben Nicholson, Joe Maurer, Yen Tran, Alexander Jusdanis, Tristan Rodman, Rasaan Turner, Liam McGranahan, Aleysia Whitmore, Triin Vallaste, Jordan Bartee, Francesca Inglese, Micah Salkind, Byrd McDaniel, and Cora Johnson-Roberson. Our intellectual collaborations have been the best continuing-education curriculum a scholar could hope for.

Many friends, colleagues, and mentors in the academy discussed this work with me, invited me to present it on their campuses, offered feedback, and generally helped me feel like these ideas might be worth developing and sharing. They include Carol Babiracki, Greg Barz, Jayson Beaster-Jones, Harmony Bench, Harry Berger, Betsey Biggs, Tom Boellstorff, Jim Buhler, Peter Bussigel, Mark Butler, Gianna Cassidy, Theo Cateforis, Will Cheng, Karen Collins, Nick Cook, Tim Cooley, Martin Daughtry, Beverley Diamond, Jeffers Engelhardt, Ana Flavia,

Melanie Fritsch, William Gibbons, Dana Gooley, Matt Guterl, Brian House, Monique Ingalls, Patrick Jagoda, David Kaminsky, Mark Katz, Bevin Kelley, Neil Lerner, Susan Manning, Peter McMurray, Karl Hagstrom Miller, Jim Moses, David Roesner, Susana Sardo, Martin Scherzinger, Rebecca Schneider, Brandon Shaw, Sydney Skybetter, Jason Stanyek, Michael Steinberg, Jonathan Sterne, Jane Sugarman, Tim Taylor, David Trippett, Steve Waksman, Peter Webb, Todd Winkler, and several anonymous peer reviewers.

For collective conversation, thanks to the participants in the 2013 Mellon Summer Seminar on dance studies at Brown, the 2014 CRASSH conference on sonic and visual media at Cambridge, the Mellon Humanities Working Group on mobilizing music at Syracuse, the AHRC Research Network on music games and creativity, UCLA Inertia 2015 (Mike D'Errico!), Post-Ip'15 at the University of Aveiro (Aoife Hiney and Rui Oliveira!), the 2016 North American Conference on Video Game Music (Neil Lerner!), and the 2016 Conference for Research on Choreographic Interfaces (¡¡Sydney Skybetter!!).

For long-term support and much close reading, my deepest gratitude to Kay Kaufman Shelemay, Richard Wolf, Tomie Hahn, and Judith Hamera. And to Jeff Todd Titon, my mentor in birdsong, heirloom vegetables, phenomenology, and department politics: your close listening remains unparalleled.

Norm Hirschy, my OUP editor, has been an encouraging presence and ideal cross-disciplinary reader from the first days of this project—not to mention so responsive to email that I sometimes suspect he's a bot, running AI so sophisticated that it has broken the empathy barrier. (Counterevidence: he's also been present in convincing embodied form at every conference I've ever attended.) Ben Shaykin designed a cover that vividly depicts how dance games ask players to put their bodies on the line and test the edges of their comfort zones. I'm also grateful for the work of Lauralee Yeary, Jeremy Toynbee, Patterson Lamb, and all the OUP editorial, design, production, and promotions staff whose work is still to come. Here at Brown, my thanks to Jen Vieira, Kathleen Nelson, Mary Rego, and Ashley Lundh for the personal and administrative support that made it possible for me to bring this project to completion, and to Ned Quist, Laura Stokes, Nancy Jakubowski, Sheila Hogg, and Harriette Hemmasi for exceptional research support at the Brown University Library. I began this research at the Radcliffe Institute for Advanced Study, and later made great headway during a semester at Brown's Cogut Center for the Humanities; I remain grateful for the material support and collegial conversations afforded by these research fellowships.

Finally, my unending gratitude and love to the friends and chosen family who have seen me through from the difficulty-at-the-beginning to the forking paths of outrageous fortune in this past year: Vanessa Ryan, Victoria Widican, Molly Kovel, Katie Mitchell, Sheryl Kaskowitz, Ben Shaykin, Barb and Joel Revill, Christina Linklater, Jessa Leinaweaver, Joshua Tucker, Carolyn Deacy, Megan Jennings, Te-Yi Lee and Chris Jeris, Aaron Girard, Mary Greitzer, Natalie Kirschstein, Paja Faudree, Chance and Woody Allen, Cypress LaSalle, Jesse Polhemus, Jo Guldi, Zachary

Gates, and James Baumgartner. A toast to the unending process of intimate mis/recognition: may we all find a propitious balance of bitter and sweet in our lives.

This book is dedicated to the numbers 3, 31, 46, and 406.

Earlier versions of some sections of this book have appeared in different form in the following publications:

"Multisensory Musicality in *Dance Central*." In *The Oxford Handbook of Interactive Audio*, ed. Karen Collins, Bill Kapralos, and Holly Tessler. Copyright © 2014 Oxford University Press.

"Gaming the System: Gender Performance in *Dance Central*." *New Media & Society* 17(6):939–957. Copyright © 2015 by the author.

"Virtual and Visceral Ethnography." In *Out of Bounds: Ethnography, Music, History*, ed. Ingrid Monson, Carol Oja, and Richard Wolf. Copyright © 2017 Harvard University Press.

The shape-note scale in Figure I.4 is reprinted from *The Sacred Harp* with the gracious permission of the Sacred Harp Publishing Company, copyright © 1991.

ABOUT THE COMPANION WEBSITE

www.oup.com/us/playablebodies

Oxford has created a website to accompany *Playable Bodies*. It includes links to auxiliary material related to the book's content along with screencaps from the book in full size and color. Using the site will allow readers to continue conversation on- and offline.

Playable Bodies

Introduction

Dance Games and Body Work

What can machines teach us about ourselves? If we reveal ourselves to them, what can they see in us that no one else can see? We ask these questions as we embark on intimate relationships with other humans. Increasingly, we are cultivating similar kinds of intimacy with the machines in our lives. We carry phones and tablets with built-in user-facing cameras and voice-recognition software. We load them up with apps that track and analyze the number of steps we take, our GPS routes through the maps of our daily lives, the music we use to channel our emotions, the relationships we forge and maintain through social networks, our spending patterns and our sleeping patterns. We constantly generate parallel and intersecting streams of data. In return, we only ask: Tell me something I didn't know about myself. And we also worry: What might this machine know and not tell? What might it conceal from me, but sell to someone else? What if it isn't calibrated to recognize me properly—if it can't see me, am I invisible? On the other hand, that invisibility might be a human superpower: It could be deeply reassuring to discover there's something about oneself that a machine can't perceive or feed to its black-box algorithms.

This book is about machines that teach humans to dance, and how the game of learning choreography is also the labor of developing an intimate relationship with interactive surveillance technologies. Dance games took the video game industry by storm between 2009 and 2014, outselling established game franchises and driving sales of newly developed motion-sensing interfaces. Together, the leading dance game franchises *Just Dance, Dance Central,* and *Zumba Fitness* sold nearly 76 million game units over these five years (Lewis 2014, VGChartz 2016). In a period when many argued that digital games were moving out of living rooms and onto mobile phones and social media platforms, dance games demonstrated the deep appeal of an entirely different kind of "casual" and "social" gaming (cf. Juul 2010, Jones and Thiruvathukal 2012). These games can be played in three-minute sessions, yet they offer an immersive multisensory experience. They are accessible to novice gamers, yet their full-body dance routines can be fiendishly challenging. They persuade players to move their bodies in new ways by promising a safe, private space for learning to dance, but they also capitalize on the complex pleasures of embarrassing oneself among trusted friends. While they rely on new interfaces and proprietary motion-capture and motion-tracking technologies, they are also built around already circulating popular music, and they offer players a transferrable skill: When players learn a dance, they are *really dancing*, with their own bodies. They can leave the game console in the living room and take those moves to the club, the prom, the gym, YouTube, and Twitter—and they have. (See Figure I.1.)

I embarked on this project with two broad questions: What happens when players learn an embodied repertoire from a virtual instructor, and what can motion games tell us about the enculturation of new interfaces as technologies of the body? Dance games make it possible for players to learn a physically demanding, minutely codified repertoire without ever interacting with a physically present teacher. They also offer opportunities for players to experiment with movement styles that don't match their own sense of self. The dance styles in these games incorporate performative markers of gender, race, sexuality, class, age, and able-bodied fitness, intertwined with received ideas about discipline, morality, virtuosity, natural talent versus learned skill, and creative agency versus compliant repetition. The private and public pleasures of digital dance games are bound up with their presentation of gendered and racialized kinesthetic repertoires; they invite players to imagine how it might feel to dance in someone else's body.

Figure I.1: A player-produced gameplay video created for YouTube (riffraff67 2012). (Screenshot by the author.)

Playable Bodies explores five major thematic areas: surveillance and control; performativity and embodied difference; kinesthetic listening; the virtual transmission of embodied practice; and choreographic labor. Each of these themes affords different insights into how dance games function as intimate media—that is, how they configure intimate relationships among humans, interfaces, musical and dance repertoires, and social media platforms. In this book, "intimate media" refers not to media texts that present intimate material or media platforms that allow for discussion of intimate subject matter, but to media that choreograph the gradual accrual of intimacy over time, through practice.[1] I proceed from the premise that intimacy is a relational quality, generated by dynamics of recognition and reciprocity as well as control and consent. It is not instant mutual knowledge but rather a form of cumulative understanding that entails deferred agency, vulnerability, and struggles to communicate.

As we will see, dance offers a powerful model for thinking about intimacy in terms of multisensory experience and the materiality of human bodies. Dance games link those sensing, material bodies to interactive technologies that cultivate new techniques of moving, listening, seeing, and being seen. They teach players to regard their own bodies as both interfaces and avatars, a radical change from the established gaming paradigm of using a game controller to direct the actions of an on-screen avatar. Dance games offer object lessons on the affinities of choreography and programming code—as interactive and archival media, as technical practices, and as metaphors that people use to make sense of relationships among humans and machines (Bench 2009, Chun 2011, Galloway 2012). They also continually reassure players that choreography does not function like code, and that playable bodies are not automata. It's easy to deploy choreography as a metaphor as though it were synonymous with puppetry, ventriloquism, programming, or other forms of direct control, but any dance technique class or rehearsal will demonstrate that choreography doesn't actually work that way. Learning someone else's choreography requires active participation, mobilizes cumulative technique, and engages dancers in interpretive work over the course of repeated practice.

Dance games and their player communities illustrate new possibilities for the transmission of performance practice, for converting virtual social connections into visceral common knowledge, and for creating deeply engaging play experiences that bind together sound and physical movement. They offer new channels for teaching and learning embodied knowledge, and for indexing that knowledge through popular music. They make players' living rooms into the staging ground for emergent forms of digital performance and participatory culture (Jenkins 2006). At the same time, they raise questions about "the body as a laboring instrument, a force of production that is actively being displaced, recreated, and reimagined by digital technologies" (Burrill and Blanco Borelli 2014:439), and they draw attention to neoliberal capital investments in methods to measure "the human body and 'life itself' in terms of their informational substrate, such that equivalencies might be found to value one form of life against another, one vital capacity against another"

(Clough 2010:221). Through my research with players and designers, as well as my own gameplay experiences, I have learned that performing this choreography can feel natural or transgressive, liberating or compulsory, playful or laborious.

A BRIEF HISTORY OF DANCE GAMES

Just Dance and *Dance Central*, the two game franchises I discuss in this book, were originally designed for two different motion-sensing game systems: the Nintendo Wii console, purpose-built for motion gaming, and the Xbox Kinect, a peripheral device for the existing Xbox console. As Jones and Thiruvathukal write in their book about the Wii, gaming platforms

> span *multiple* materialities—from microchips to social institutions. . . . As a platform, a video game console is a computing-based foundation for running games, but it's also an example of industrial design, a consumer product, a generator of expectations as well as a media system that mediates between the various layers of hardware, code, interface, game, the screen, the player's body, the peripherals, the living room, the invisible networks of communication technologies and the larger network, and the world. (2012:159–60)

When the Wii came on the market in 2006, it was positioned to compete with existing game consoles across these multiple materialities, in technical, social, and economic terms. The Wii promised an innovative yet accessible gestural interface, an emphasis on casual social gameplay in domestic spaces, and a significantly lower price point than the market-dominating PlayStation and Xbox systems. These other consoles had been engaged in a graphics/processing-power arms race to better support increasingly high-intensity, immersive, rapid-response, action-oriented, long-session gaming. The Wii was intended to support a different kind of gameplay, one that would particularly appeal to casual/social gamers and the all-important and hitherto underexploited "consumer mom" demographic—women who might appreciate the invitation to become players themselves, as well as purchasing games for their children (Jones and Thiruvathukal 2012:31).

The launch games for the Wii emphasized physically co-present social gameplay and vigorous physical activity, handily addressing potential consumers' anxieties about screen time, childhood obesity, how to create opportunities for active play in safely monitored spaces, and how to make consumer choices that properly demonstrate parental fitness (Bozon 2016). As Jones and Thiruvathukal observe, all gaming is social, but "the Wii was the first home video game platform consciously designed as a whole—from initial concept to prototype to shipped product—to first and foremost promote social gameplay out in physical space. . . . Engineering the social space of gameplay is its whole point" (2012:4–5). With its mimetic interface and range of "prop" peripherals—a hand-held remote that can be a tennis racket, sword, or conductor's baton, a balance-board platform that draws attention to the shifting weight of the player's body—the Wii frames the play space as "the center of the action, the place where gaming is meaningfully experienced, where the player's body encounters the materiality of the platform" (Jones and Thiruvathukal 2012:23). *Wii Sports*, the Nintendo-developed launch title that came bundled with the Wii in most countries and was featured in television advertising for the new console, particularly emphasized these affordances. Sports-oriented titles also established a strong link between the Wii and physical fitness, suggesting that the Wii could be a platform for guilt-free productive play, or labor-made-fun.

The *Just Dance* series has its roots in *Rayman Raving Rabbids* (Ubisoft 2006), a Wii launch title comprising a set of mini-games that explored the potential of the Wii Remote as a gestural mimetic interface. A subcategory of dance mini-games was entitled "Shake Your Booty!"—an enthusiastic imperative that tells us a lot about the kind of social dance experience that *Raving Rabbids* aimed to evoke and that indexes a long history of global commercial circulation of African American popular culture. Notably, the Wii could not actually detect booty-shaking in *Raving Rabbids*; it tracked the handheld Wii Remote, not hip or torso movements.[2] Gameplay involved using arm movements to knock out an advancing cavalcade of bunnies in time to the music on a disco dance floor, reframing a boxing game as dance. Two years later, *Rayman Raving Rabbids: TV Party* continued to develop the dancing mini-game category by challenging players to mirror a stream of freeze-frame poses modeled by stick-figure icons. *Just Dance*, released by Ubisoft in 2009, built an entire game around this streaming-icon system and a 32-track playlist of licensed popular songs. Artists ranged from the Beach Boys and Anita Ward to Fatboy Slim and Katy Perry, with song selections evincing a mix of nostalgia, silliness, and anthemic bravura that became a signature of the franchise—the same bring-everyone-to-the-floor strategy that drives the work of successful wedding DJs.

As Harmony Bench observes, media formats choreograph bodies in highly specific ways: "Media represent bodily motion according to their protocols and parameters, and then compel dancers to fit themselves into the bodies that have been imagined for them" (2009:279). At the same time, "in the process of adapting and conforming to media formats, [dancing bodies] make new movement strategies available, render choreographies apparent, and reveal cultural assumptions regarding motion, labor, and corporeality" (6). Judging by its commercial success, *Just Dance* offered players compelling corporeal experiences and imaginative possibilities. Developed by Ubisoft's flagship Paris studio, its built-in cultural assumptions derive partly from contemporary Europe's robust and diverse dance-club cultures and warm embrace of dance-pop musical genres, ritually marked as public culture through the nationalist spectacle of the annual Eurovision song contest (see, e.g., McRobbie 1993, Thornton 1996, Redhead et al. 1997, Raykoff and Tobin 2007, Garcia 2011). *Just Dance* was initially marketed with the expectation of greater sales in Europe than the United States; despite lukewarm critical reviews that dubbed it "technically and graphically crude," the game was the top-selling title in the United

Kingdom within a month of its holiday 2009 release (MacDonald 2014). In the United States, *Just Dance 2* was the seventh-bestselling game across all platforms in 2010, and took second place among Wii titles (Reilly 2011a). By the fall of 2014, the series had sold over 50 million copies worldwide (Lewis 2014).

When we consider the enormous and sustained commercial success of the *Just Dance* series, we would do well to step back and ask some basic questions about the nature of dance. *What is dance for?* Some will immediately protest that it doesn't have to be for anything; it is an art form, intrinsically valuable on aesthetic grounds, without recourse to utility. Dance has nothing to prove. Others might nimbly side-step the question by explaining some special capacities of dance, without explicitly stating what ends these capacities might serve: Dance is a mode of expressive communication, of "corporeal orature" (DeFrantz 2004:67), of narrating, remembering, and archiving bodily experiences. It is a way of being in the world with one's own body and other bodies, a way of structuring one's sensorium, a way of seeing and being seen, feeling and being touched, whether skin-to-skin or at a distance bridged by kinesthetic empathy (Foster 2011). When we dance to music, we make sense of sound through the pattern and flow of gesture. When we listen to the sound of feet striking the floor, joints creaking, breath quickening in counterpoint with heart rate, we make sense of bodily structure through the pattern and flow of sound. Dance mediates sensory relations and social relations. With these principles in mind, the question might take a new form: If we have some idea of what dance can do, then what do we want it to do? What is dance *good for*?

If you wanted to design a successful commercial videogame about dance, you would have to engage with these questions. You would be in the business of persuading people that dance is good for something and that your game can bring out those qualities. You would have to make a game that offers pleasure and challenge, delivered through a dance experience. So you would have to ask yourself: What are the specific pleasures and challenges of various kinds of dance? How can we map them onto the structure of a game, with rules and rewards? And who are our players? Do they have experience as dancers, as gamers, both or neither? How will we teach them to dance, and to regard dance as play? What kinds of dance will they be willing to do? How will we convince them to engage with their bodies as the latest playable interface, easily plugged into a game system? How do we harness our dance game to other domains that matter to players: their music, their social networks, their self-image, even their physical fitness? And how do we stay in business? How do we make dance work as a consumable product that players can keep consuming, spending money on new games, dances, or songs? How do we tie our game to existing systems of production and consumption: celebrity, fashion, lifestyle products? Players need to know what this game is for: They have to recognize and accept its invitation to the dance floor.

The developers of the games I discuss in this book took different approaches to these questions while working at the same cultural moment and targeting the same consumers. *Just Dance* posits joyful disinhibition as the core function of social dance. *Dance Central*'s central value is authenticity, generated through cycles of mastery-oriented rehearsal and performance undertaken in culturally specific dance contexts. Both also follow the lead of the Zumba dance-fitness craze by conjoining exoticist pleasure with responsible self-care: Discipline your body by freeing your hips. (The *Zumba Fitness* game series has also been enormously popular; it is not a focus of this book because it falls squarely in the tradition of home aerobics videos, with a light overlay of interactive game elements and minimal motion-tracking capacities [Pipeworks Software 2010]).) Dance games are part of a broader trend in which popular music circulates in connection with both moving images and specific kinesthetic practices—that is, music is not something you absorb through your ears but something you encounter in connection with a playable interface that cultivates multisensory engagement. In recent years the *Guitar Hero* series offered a highly visible example of this phenomenon in the gaming world, but we could also look to YouTube dance crazes, karaoke, remix practices, and online music lessons (see Miller 2012).

In terms of core gameplay mechanics and game design lineage, dance games generally fall into the "rhythm game" genre: They involve haptic/kinetic interaction with an interface in time with audiovisual cues. This description also applies to the vast majority of video games across all genres; as Karen Collins argues, game audio design typically relies on "kinesonic synchresis," or the binding of action and sound (2013:27). Collins's term combines "kinesonic"—a portmanteau of "kinesthetic" and "sonic" that describes "the mapping of sound to bodily movements" (Wilson-Bokowiec and Bokowiec 2006:47)—with Michel Chion's "synchresis," referring to the perceptual phenomena generated by co-occurring sound and image in film (1994). In rhythm games, kinesonic synchresis is the main event: Gameplay explicitly revolves around forging haptic/audio/visual relationships and generating novel perceptual experiences through multisensory integration.

The electronic memory game *Simon*, first released by Milton Bradley in 1978, is one important antecedent for contemporary rhythm games (Knoblauch 2016). The original *Simon* was a round device about the size of a dinner plate, with its face divided into sectors by four large colored buttons. It integrated audio and visual cues by pairing these four buttons with distinctive sounds. *Simon* presented players with a series of audio tones, visually reinforced by flashing lights in each button. Players repeated the series by pressing the buttons; *Simon* then presented a longer series, gradually building up the difficulty level. The game thus bound together interface-specific motor skills, audiovisual engagement, and challenges to memory and attention span. In a broad sense these are common features of virtually all videogames—as Torben Grodal puts it, they are "stories for eye, ear and muscles" based on "learning processes and rehearsals" (2003:147). However, *Simon*'s explicit emphasis on listening, repetition, and linking button presses to audio outputs makes it a distinctly musical game. *Simon* engages players in the cognitive process of organizing sounds into meaningful units, while also cultivating motor-kinetic skills that highlight the affinities of haptic computing interfaces and musical instruments (Blaine 2005, Miller 2012).

The many rhythm games released over the next 35 years continued to build on this model. As game sound technology developed beyond the domain of 8-bit synthesis, rhythm-game designers increasingly integrated contemporary popular music and dance styles into their games. These direct connections to popular culture helped make rhythm games both more conceptually accessible and more affectively complex, linking them to other domains of players' everyday lives (see Collins 2008b, 2013; Austin 2016). Three major game franchises released over a 10-year period exemplify these developments: *Dance Dance Revolution* (Konami Corporation 1998), *Guitar Hero* (Harmonix Music Systems 2005), and *Rock Band* (Harmonix Music Systems 2007). All three clearly influenced the design and reception of *Just Dance* and *Dance Central*.

Dance Dance Revolution (DDR) was the dominant dance game series of its era. Historical accounts of game development circulating in academic and industry circles often highlight three "revolutionary" qualities of DDR: its use of an alternate interface, its reliance on popular music as a driver of affective experience, and its staging of digital gameplay as a competitive performance genre that could attract an audience (Smith 2004, Demers 2006). DDR was initially released as an arcade game in Japan in 1998, where it integrated some of the public performance conventions of arcade culture and karaoke culture (Konami Corporation 1998). The first home version of DDR was released for the PlayStation in Japan in 1999, with additional home versions released around the world starting in 2001. Whether on a large arcade machine with a metal stage area or on a foam dance pad at home, DDR's dance gameplay revolves around footwork: Players are pressing buttons with their feet. As with the *Simon* game, both audio and visual cues play a role in directing their movements. A continuous stream of multidirectional arrows scrolling up the screen corresponds to arrows printed on the floor pad. Players move to the rhythms of a wide selection of pop electronica tracks, many of which were produced specifically for the game series and attracted a cult following. As is the case with many music/rhythm games, it might be technically possible for a player to earn high scores at DDR with the sound turned off, but that does not mean music is incidental to the satisfactions of gameplay. As Joanna Demers observes, "Playing these games can feel like a genuinely musical experience: The controller is no longer a trigger but a percussion instrument, and the player stops thinking in terms of locking on targets and instead tries to feel the groove" (2006:65).

DDR engages players in spectacular full-body performances for both machinic and human audiences. It stages tightly framed episodes of "mixed reality" gaming, "fold[ing] the ephemerality of digital representation and the concrete materiality of physical, embodied presence into a unique hybrid space" (Behrenshausen 2007:340). The game offers encouraging exhortations and playfully insulting feedback on players' dancing in both screen-text and voiceover forms, though it can only assess the accuracy of players' inputs on the floor pad. Human audiences play a key role in arcade and tournament contexts and in social gameplay at home. Demers addresses *DDR*'s "tendency to draw crowds and hence turn game-play into a public performance" (59); following work by karaoke scholar Johan Fornäs, she observes that *DDR* gameplay, like karaoke, "leaves a gap in which the performer . . . restructures the surrounding layers of media. . . . That the gap is filled by a dancing body allows for a particular kind of diverse and global fan culture, while also creating tensions within it" (69). In the *DDR* context this "gap" is partly constituted by the limits of the floor pad interface; many human players and audiences became interested in performances that exceed what the game demands or can evaluate, such as acrobatic moves and feats of agility inserted between the required button presses (Smith 2004).

These deliberately excessive gameplay performances invoked standards for creativity, virtuosity, and authenticity that directly informed the design and reception of the *Guitar Hero* and *Rock Band* games. In pragmatic economic terms, *DDR*'s successful employment of an alternate controller—an extra piece of hardware that players had to be persuaded to purchase, learn how to use, and keep around the house—also provided a major impetus for the development of *Guitar Hero* (Harmonix Music Systems 2005). The game was commissioned by RedOctane, a maker of *DDR* dance pads, with the aim of selling guitar controllers. After Harmonix and RedOctane were acquired by separate parent companies in 2006, Harmonix went on to develop *Rock Band* (Harmonix Music Systems 2007), creating a long-running franchise rivalry driven by competing playlists of licensed popular music tracks, different approaches to balancing score-oriented versus rock-performance-oriented design elements, and related claims to musical and gaming authenticity—in many respects foreshadowing the competition between *Just Dance* and *Dance Central*. The *Guitar Hero* and *Rock Band* games were designed to evoke live rock performance experiences rather than simply functioning as instrument-playing simulators; this distinction drove decisions about how the guitar, bass, and drum controllers should replicate or diverge from traditional instruments in physical form and playing technique (Miller 2009). Similarly, *Just Dance* and *Dance Central* were each designed to evoke particular kinds of dance experience, rather than simply inculcating technical proficiency in controlling one's bodily motions.

In prior research, I showed how *Guitar Hero* and *Rock Band* engaged players in "schizophonic performance," forging a connection between the physical gestures of live musical performance and the reproduction of recorded songs (Miller 2009, 2012). These games proved to be highly effective platforms for schizophonic performance in large part due to some special characteristics of the rock genre. Canonical rock music features at least three distinctive instrumental lines (one or two guitars, bass, and drums), each of which could theoretically be performed live (Auslander 1999:82); each rock instrument also indexes a distinctive embodied performance style (Waksman 1999). With a few careful design cues, the games guided players in picking out one instrumental part from the mix and stitching it to their physical performance with an instrument-shaped game controller. There is no straightforward way to apply these principles to electronic dance music genres (EDM). EDM tracks often feature layered samples that would be difficult to map to a single instrument interface. Even when there are distinctive individual instrumental parts, they might be physically impossible for a human to perform (as in the case of many sample-based drum parts), or they might be too repetitive to make for compelling gameplay. In EDM production, variation often comes in the form of shifting digital effects and the addition or subtraction of sampled layers, rather than showy instrumental solos that could be mapped to feats of manual dexterity on a controller. Activision, publishers of the *Guitar Hero* franchise since 2006, attempted to address these challenges and capitalize on EDM's soaring popularity with *DJ Hero* (FreeStyleGames 2009), a game that featured a controller modeled on a turntable. But players struggled to create a satisfying kinesthetic connection to the musical material using this interface, and the game sold very poorly (Miller 2013b). Dance games represent a different approach to this problem: They still guide players in mapping musical structures to embodied performance, but they do not revolve around virtual musicianship. They cultivate physically active, immersive, performance-oriented engagement with music without recourse to the idea that players are generating sound.

Like *Guitar Hero* and *Rock Band*, *Just Dance* was designed as a platform for selling value-added versions of familiar popular music tracks. Its screen dancers model choreography that kinesthetically amplifies the music, and players dance along in their living rooms (see Chapters 3 and 4). Given *Just Dance*'s simple graphics, limited motion-detection system, and dearth of game-progression elements, many industry reviewers and gamers questioned whether it was a legitimate game at all. The game industry was changing rapidly during this period, as "casual games" for the Nintendo Wii, mobile devices, and social media platforms attracted tens of millions of new players, sparking something of an identity crisis for game industry professionals and longtime players (Juul 2010). Many writers for game industry websites seemed to approach *Just Dance* with suspicion if not outright hostility, addressing it as a collection of cartoon music videos with interactive menus; in the comment threads unspooling below their reviews, players dismissed the game as "shovelware," a derisive term for cheaply produced, technically unsophisticated, and creatively uninspired games designed solely to maximize profit for a publisher (see, e.g., Parkin 2010 and comments).

But although some regarded it as a hoax perpetrated on the masses, *Just Dance* was a runaway commercial hit, and industry writers were duty-bound to review it—not only to solve the mystery of "What made a throwaway party game on Wii a *Modern Warfare*-beater?" (Parkin 2010), but also because coverage of chart-topping games drives page views that in turn drive advertising revenue for web-based publications. As I discuss in Chapter 1, these industry reviews of *Just Dance* and associated player discourse show how the series challenged fundamental assumptions about what counts as authentic interactivity and worthwhile gameplay. *Eurogamer* writer Ellie Gibson summed up the early debate in a review published just as *Just*

Dance was reaching #1 standing on the UK game charts: "Just Dance should be rubbish. It's stupid, shallow, crude and not nearly as technically proficient as it pretends. . . . But despite all that, if you're in the right company and the right frame of mind, it's tremendous fun" (Gibson 2010).

The initial reception of *Just Dance* established some of the terms by which *Dance Central* and the Xbox Kinect interface would be assessed when they came on the market a year later. *Dance Central* was designed as one of the launch titles for the Kinect, the motion-sensing camera peripheral released by Microsoft in 2010 in an effort to upstage the Nintendo Wii (Jones and Thiruvathukal 2012). The advertising slogan for the Kinect, "You are the controller," not only played directly to consumers' anxieties about their agency over technology but also recast the Wii Remote as an outmoded encumbrance, something destined to become obsolete as motion games reached their full potential. But the Kinect also invoked players' experiences with an established technology. Unlike the Wii, the Kinect looks very much like a camera—a fact that called for preemptive reassurance about who would be in control of this new system (see Chapter 1). Following Tarleton Gillespie's work on "the politics of platforms," I suggest that in examining the first-generation games for this newly domesticated interactive surveillance technology, we can see designers and players "making decisions about what that technology is, what it is for, what sociotechnical arrangements are best suited to achieve that and what it must not be allowed to become" (Gillespie 2010:355–56).

The Kinect sensor would sit unobtrusively on top of the TV, ready to facilitate interactive media experiences. It would be integrated into everyday social and domestic spaces, functioning like a mashup of a gaming interface and a domestic surveillance system (Staples 2014). We have grown accustomed to sitting in front of or carrying around devices equipped with user-facing cameras and microphones, but we are also used to activating those technologies for specific activities; we look for the green light, the video monitor window, or the pulsing audio level indicator. The Kinect is different: If it is turned on, its cameras and microphone are always live. Moreover, self-monitoring feedback mechanisms that might give a player insight into exactly what the Kinect is "seeing" or "hearing" are highly variable and idiosyncratic, depending on the particular game or program being used. Accepting the charge of "being the controller" requires learning new forms of bodily self-control and may also entail new forms of self-disclosure. It is difficult to fully understand the perceptual capabilities of devices like the Kinect. They tend to create "information asymmetry" between observer and observed (Staples 2014:4), due in part to the proprietary "black box" status of their layered technologies and in part to the analogous complexity and unknowability of human embodiment. A mass-produced hardware controller with a few buttons offers tremendous communicative clarity: Press X, and you will know that you have pressed X, and the software will generally keep up its side of the bargain by responding to this input in a predictable manner. But as dance games have demonstrated to millions of players, without the mediating constraints of a controller, our bodies move and communicate in ways that we may be ill-equipped to understand, control, or even notice.

Dance Central was meant to help sell the Kinect by engaging players in full-body dance routines that would showcase the device's ability to track the motion of 20 joints on the human body (Pitts 2012). It was also positioned to compete with *Just Dance,* which had sold 10 million units by the end of 2010 (Reilly 2011b). Over the next five years, the two franchises maintained an active competition through regular releases of new game editions and additional downloadable content for existing games. However, *Dance Central* sales were substantially limited by the franchise's exclusive relationship with Microsoft's Xbox platform, and the requirement that players spend an extra $150 on a Kinect sensor. The Kinect entered the marketplace four years after the Wii and never came close to matching its market share. The three main editions of *Dance Central* were released in time for pre-holiday shopping in 2010, 2011, and 2012; as of early 2013, only 24 million Kinect sensors had sold, compared to 99.84 million Wii consoles. Meanwhile, by 2011 *Just Dance* had expanded to three platforms, with simultaneous releases for the Wii, the Xbox Kinect, and the PlayStation Move (though gameplay across all three platforms maintained the hallmarks of the original Wii-oriented design). Despite these structural limitations, the *Dance Central* series was a critical and commercial success, selling about 6 million game units between 2010 and 2015 (Makuch 2013, Nintendo 2013, VGChartz 2016).

Thanks to their work on the *Guitar Hero* and *Rock Band* games, the developers at Harmonix Music Systems had years of experience with licensing popular music tracks and translating them into performance-oriented music games that relied on players' prior cultural knowledge (Miller 2012, Collins 2013). As part of a game industry convention panel in 2012, *Dance Central* project director Matt Boch reflected on the early design process for the series and explained how the team drew on contemporary dance culture:

> We look at what we think are facets of dance in the real world, we have this long, exhaustive list of things we'd like to capture about dance culture within the game, and dance's function in society.... Drawing from things like *America's Best Dance Crew,* drawing from the external world, but also saying, here's what our feature set is.... And trying to get as much of the vocabulary from the established world [as possible] and then also build your own vocabulary, because you are building an approximation of something, not the actual thing. (Boch 2012)

Here Boch recapitulates Ian Bogost's argument that "vividness comes not from immersion, but from abstraction.... [M]eaning in videogames is constructed not through a re-creation of the world, but through selectively modeling appropriate elements of that world" (2007:45–46). Boch described how the Harmonix staff took dance classes together, watched dance television shows, and learned dance terminology from the choreographers hired to create the routines for the game.

This approach situated *Dance Central* as part of a broader music/dance culture and a diverse media ecology (Horst et al. 2010). Both designers and players experience these games alongside dance-oriented music videos, YouTube dance crazes, televised dance competitions, dance classes at the gym, and cosmopolitan dance-club trends.

In highlighting the Kinect's affordances, *Dance Central* privileged particular dance techniques and kinesthetic styles (Foster 2011), incorporating and expanding on the choreographic repertoires in previous digital games. *Dance Dance Revolution* required technically precise footwork on a floorpad, relocating a traditional button interface under the player's feet (Smith 2004). *Just Dance* emphasized upper-body motion and directional gestures, tracking the motion of a handheld Wii Remote. The Kinect's innovative potential lay in its capacity to track torso, hip, and shoulder movements, as well as the simultaneous, coordinated motion of different parts of the body—affordances that made it an excellent match for contemporary hip-hop, Latin dance, and related club dance styles. These types of motion are key elements of gendered, sexualized, and racialized dance vocabularies (see Chapter 2). They also index constructions of dance as natural, sensual, primitive, and authentically human—as opposed to stiff, mechanized, "robot" dancing (see Chapter 4). Harmonix built on these affordances in marketing campaigns that emphasized *Dance Central*'s authenticity, implying that this was the *real* dance game, while games like *Just Dance* could only offer silly escapism. The Kinect's technical limitations also shaped *Dance Central*'s stylistic norms and performance frames. The Kinect privileges a frontal orientation and well-defined two-dimensional silhouette; that is, the sensor can "see" an arm motion out to one side better than an arm motion in front of the torso. The Kinect has trouble tracking overlapping bodies, so two-player choreography couldn't include physical contact or position crossing (both of which occur frequently in *Just Dance* routines). Instead, two dancers perform side by side, maintaining a mirroring relationship with two on-screen characters. However, additional players often dance at the fringes of the play space without being tracked by the Kinect.

As Susan Foster observes,

> Any standardized regimen of bodily training . . . embodies, in the very organization of its exercises, the metaphors used to instruct the body, and in the criteria specified for physical competence, a coherent (or not so coherent) set of principles that govern the action of that regimen. These principles, reticulated with aesthetic, political, and gendered connotations, cast the body who enacts them into larger arenas of meaning where it moves alongside bodies bearing related signage. (1995:8)

Just Dance and *Dance Central* summon players into distinctive "arenas of meaning," where their gameplay experience and reflective discourse enter into interactive feedback loops with other received ideas about music, dance, and embodied/performed identity. While *Just Dance* promises instantly accessible fun—its very title exhorts players to adopt an uninhibited pleasure-seeking orientation—*Dance Central* emphasizes the pleasures of practice and mastery. As in the *Guitar Hero* and *Rock Band* games, the songs in the *Dance Central* repertoire are classified by difficulty level (ranging from "Warmup" to "Off the Hook"); players also choose among multiple difficulty levels for each individual dance routine, working their way from a version that might repeat the same simple step-and-clap four times in an eight-count of music to one that introduces more complex moves at a much faster rate of variation. *Dance Central* offers separate rehearsal and performance modes, allowing players to practice individual moves or small subsets of routines until they receive maximum credit for their performances. Meanwhile, *Just Dance* implicitly prioritizes social relationships among dancers over a dancer's relationship with a repertoire. The *Just Dance* games offer a wider range of multiplayer options, and they convert the Wii's relatively limited motion-tracking capabilities into a social-gaming asset by allowing more leeway for players to turn toward each other and interact on the dance floor, yielding the satisfactions of "coordinated physical activity involving mutual gaze" (Isbister 2016:96).

In addition to structuring different forms of social relations among players, the two series also stage markedly different versions of "avatar relations," my term for the implied relationship between players and game characters. *Just Dance* includes a wide range of fanciful human and animal screen dancers, based on video recordings of elaborately costumed human dancers. These model moving bodies have no voices or names and are depicted with blank faces, prompting players to imagine they are occupying the screen dancers' silhouettes or looking into a mirror. The *Dance Central* screen dancers are more traditional game characters; their performances rely on digital animation and motion-capture technologies. They have distinctive speaking voices, personalities, and relationships with each other, and they address the player directly as a fellow dancer. (See Figures I.2 and I.3.)

Overall, the two series present quite distinct versions of the pleasures of social dance and how they should be achieved—differences that have driven player discourse about the nature of authentic dance and authentic gameplay. Each game series invites players to engage with music and dance in the service of affective experience: complex cocktails of pleasure/challenge/accomplishment/shame, or escape/freedom/constraint/intimacy, often generated by counterposing various forms of risk and reward. The basic design of each series suggests different priorities in selecting, blending, and balancing these elements into distinctive affective profiles. These master recipes for emotional engagement might be likened to the proprietary flavor formulas of rival soft drink brands; while individual players' experiences will differ, each series nonetheless aims for a recognizable "feel." Players actively participate in this process, engaging in comparative work to identity features that differentiate the games, gauge their own preferences, and persuade others of the relative merits of each series.

Just Dance and *Dance Central* also share two crucial attributes that distinguish them from the vast majority of videogames. First, *there are no conventional avatars;*

Figure I.2: The *Just Dance* 2 screen dancer for Outkast's "Hey Ya!" Detail from a player-produced gameplay video (BowserBike 2013). (Screenshot by the author.)

Figure I.3: Angel and Miss Aubrey, two *Dance Central* characters. Detail from a player-produced gameplay video of the *Dance Central* 2 routine for Mary J. Blige's "Real Love" (AverageAsianDude 2012). (Screenshot by the author.)

the player's motions don't control an on-screen character's motions. The screen dancers offer models for the player's performance rather than dancing the way the player dances. Second, *these games evaluate players on the basis of their actions in the actual world, not the virtual world*. To understand this distinction, imagine a more typical gameplay situation: A player controls a character who completes various challenges in the context of a three-dimensional digital gameworld. The game awards points for the character's performance in the gameworld, not the player's performance in the living room. From the standpoint of the scoring mechanism, it doesn't matter whether the player is providing inputs with her fingers or toes, or via programmed shortcuts—"scripts" or "bots" that might complete the challenges automatically. In dance games, motion-tracking technologies are positioned at the traditional fourth-wall boundary line and directed into the player's actual space. The player never crosses that line—except perhaps through identification with the on-screen characters, which may take place despite designers' efforts to the contrary (see Chapter 2). In this version of "avatar relations," the player who faithfully performs the kinesthetic repertoire of an on-screen character is representing that character in the actual world in much the same way that traditional game avatars represent human players in virtual worlds. Moreover, that work of representation can extend into domains far removed from the play space framed by game software and hardware. Human players can take a dance game's kinesthetic repertoire with them wherever they go.

PLAYABLE THEORIES: METHODS AND FRAMEWORKS

The arguments in this book are grounded in qualitative ethnographic research that gives equal attention to interface affordances, game design, player experiences, and game-related discourse. My work on dance games grew out of a series of previous projects on forms of play, performance, and embodied practice that bridge virtual and visceral experience by engaging participants in "playing along" with interactive media (Miller 2012). Broadly speaking, my research investigates digital media, participatory culture, and dispersed communities of practice, with an emphasis on how digital media are brought to bear in the transmission of multisensory embodied knowledge.

This book draws on data from seven complementary research approaches:

(1) Five years of participant observation (2011–2016), including regular gameplay in a variety of social settings, informed by game-related social media, documented via reflective fieldnotes. I characterize this practice-based research as "do it yourself, do it again" ethnography, discussed in more detail below.

(2) Analysis of game-related web materials, including industry-sponsored and player-produced discussion forums, blogs, YouTube videos, game advertising, professional and amateur game reviews, game industry articles about the Wii

and Kinect, player-produced multimedia coverage of game conventions, and published interviews with game development staff. I annotated and keyword-coded these materials, paying special attention to recurring themes, points of conflict, and influential individuals in particular interpretive communities.

(3) Semi-structured interviews with seven dance game players who were especially active and influential on YouTube and Twitter, conducted via recorded telephone conversation, Skype videoconference, or email in 2011, during the period when players were getting to know the recently released *Dance Central* and comparing it to *Just Dance*.

(4) Fieldwork at the PAX East game convention in Boston, Massachusetts, in 2012 and 2013, including observation, casual interaction, and video documentation of players and game company staff at the *Dance Central* stage, as well as recording and transcribing related panel discussions.

(5) Personal interviews and follow-up correspondence with *Dance Central* lead designer/project director Matt Boch and two *Dance Central* choreographers, Marcos Aguirre and Chanel Thompson, conducted between 2012 and 2015. (I was unable to secure interviews with *Just Dance* developers and choreographers so have relied on published interviews when discussing the development history of that franchise.)

(6) Daily drop-in gameplay sessions at Brown University in the summer of 2013. Eleven participants volunteered for hour-long semi-structured interviews that focused on inexperienced players' impressions of gameplay and comparative reflections about their other dance and gaming experiences.

(7) A web-based qualitative survey designed to solicit experienced players' reflections on key themes identified through the other research channels. I received 56 responses, primarily recruited from participants on the *Dance Central* player forums, with some snowball referrals within local player communities. 76 percent self-identified as male, 24 percent as female (no respondents selected an additional non-binary gender option). 50 percent were from outside the United States, including 15 respondents from a player community in the Philippines that also had a very active Facebook group; four others were from Brazil, and single responses came from Ghana, Singapore, Germany, Canada, Argentina, Ireland, Russia, the United Kingdom, and Mexico. The survey asked, "What best describes your racial/ethnic background?"; many respondents checked more than one box from the available options. Including these multiple identifications, 29 percent of respondents identified as White/European, 22 percent as East Asian, 18 percent as South Asian, 16 percent as Hispanic/Latino, 14 percent as African American/Black, 4 percent as Native American, and 4 percent as Native Hawaiian/Pacific Islander. Six respondents entered text into the "Other" box, self-identifying as Southeast Asian (2), Vietnamese, African Brazilian, West Indian, and "Mixed—black and white." These respondents do not constitute a representative sample of dance game players worldwide and across franchises, but the

demographic figures do tell us something about the range of voices involved in *Dance Central* forum discourse by 2013, after the release of the three main games in this franchise. All respondents had played some version of *Dance Central*; 70 percent had also played some version of *Just Dance*. 79 percent of respondents reported using *Dance Central*'s rehearsal mode, and 95 percent reported that their typical play sessions lasted more than 30 minutes, suggesting an investment in mastery of choreographic repertoire.

Pursued in tandem, these research approaches offer overlapping windows into diverse player and industry perspectives, and they provide comparative checks that help distinguish extreme outlier experiences and interpretations from those that are more commonly held or broadly influential (cf. discussions of methodology in Boellstorff 2008, Coleman 2010, Boellstorff et al. 2012, Miller 2012). In the present context, these data support insights into designed and perceived *potential*—the transformative possibilities of virtual and visceral performance, as realized by particular individuals—rather than documenting quantitatively verifiable "effects" on a given population. A multitude of invitations, cultural assumptions, and forms of persuasion are embedded in these games, and individual players engage with them on their own terms as they co-construct emergent game culture (Taylor 2006:126–27).

My arguments here build on a foundation of ethnographic scholarship in popular culture, performance studies, and media studies, informed by Birmingham School cultural studies, anthropological and phenomenological theories of embodied practice, and interdisciplinary approaches to participatory culture and interpretive communities (e.g., Bourdieu 1977 [1972]; Fish 1980; Ortner 1984; Schechner 1985; Sobchack 1992; Berger 1999, 2009; Jenkins 2006; Fischer-Lichte 2008; Noland 2009; Ito et al. 2010). I will introduce and engage with specific theoretical frameworks as they become relevant over the coming chapters, providing "just-in-time information" in a meaningful context—a key principle of learning-oriented game design (Gee 2004:65). Meanwhile, a concise overview of some of the key concepts and areas of inquiry that have structured my research should serve as an orientation aid.

My disciplinary background in ethnomusicology and performance theory has led me to address digital gameplay as a form of expressive culture that relies on cumulative rehearsals of "restored behavior" (Schechner 1985). I also address dance games as music games, attending to how they inculcate specific techniques of listening as well as techniques of moving and looking. Dance gameplay is a form of embodied popular music reception that intersects with other forms of popular music circulation, social media practice, and dispersed participatory culture, raising questions about listening subjectivity and affective circulation (Kassabian 2013). I also investigate the parallels between digital media interfaces and musical instruments: People build up embodied practices based on the designed and perceived affordances of interfaces/instruments, as well as on the "relational infrastructure" offered by communities of practice (Hamera 2007; see also Lave and Wenger 1991, Pearce 2009, Chun 2011, Galloway 2012).

I address video games as "learning machines" (Gee 2004, 2006) but also specifically as teaching machines. Dance games teach players particular choreographic repertoires, using pedagogical methods borrowed from contemporary popular dance classes. The Kinect and Wii rely on sensors—data-gathering devices—but dance games also exemplify "an emerging form of information distribution" (Gillespie 2010:355), using multisensory interactive technology to archive and transmit kinesthetic repertoires in a manner radically different from any previous form of dance inscription. My analysis of these processes of data collection and dance transmission draws on the performance studies/dance studies literature on archive and repertoire (Taylor 2003, Schneider 2011), ethnographies of dance training (Hahn 2007, Hamera 2007, Davida 2012), and theories of kinesthetic empathy and networked bodies (Bench 2009, Foster 2011) as well as scholarship on surveillance and biometrics as disciplining technologies (Marx 1988, Negishi 2013, Staples 2014, Brown 2015, Pham 2015).

Archive and repertoire have long been crucial concepts for performance studies, offering tools for conceiving of live performance as material and enduring rather than defined by ephemerality and disappearance. In an influential formulation, Diana Taylor refers to performances as "vital acts of transfer" and warns of the political risks of "thinking about embodied knowledge and performance as ephemeral, as that which disappears" (2003:2, 36). She associates this stance with histories of epistemic violence and imperial conquest, "the repression of indigenous embodied practice as a form of knowing as well as a system for storing and transmitting knowledge" (18). Rebecca Schneider acknowledges Taylor's work "to situate the repertoire as *another kind of archive*" while also urging theorists to take up "the twin effort of situating the archive as *another kind of performance*," predicated on "live practices of access" (2011:108, emphasis original). Dance games put these theoretical issues into practice through the basic mechanics of studio production and gameplay. They also draw out the connections between "scriptive things"—"items of material culture that prompt meaningful bodily behaviors" (Bernstein 2011:71)—and the digital scripts that drive interactive media. I am particularly interested in how these games archive, script, monitor, and evaluate performances of gendered and racialized bodily repertoires, functioning as Foucauldian "technologies of the self" in a play context that encourages racial masquerade and identity tourism (Foucault 1988; see Balsamo 1996, Nakamura 2002, and Royse et al. 2007).

In the context of game production, the choreographer's body is an archive, from which data can be extracted and repurposed through live encounter: by the choreographers themselves in the course of crafting a dance, and by motion-capture technologies when choreographers perform their own routines to generate the code that will animate a screen dancer. Notably, most of the dance repertoires involved here emerged from African American, Latinx, and/or queer communities of practice, and most of the dancer-choreographers hired to perform them likewise hail from those communities. Their employment as embodied archives who generate game content raises questions about the entanglement of "economic, cultural, and racial capital" in this context, including how these games participate in the racialized power dynamics that have long informed "contests for credit and ownership" in the dance world (Kraut 2009:93–94; see also Manning 2004, DeFrantz 2014). The games themselves are also archives, in the more conventional sense of preserving a selected set of materials and organizing them in ways that facilitate particular kinds of access. Because they are digital archives, accessing their materials requires execution of scripts, a process with striking affinities to performing choreography; as Bench writes, "Like choreography, code's performatives are directives drawn from a repertoire of possible actions. In their execution, display, and navigation functions, computer processors, Web browsers, and computer users all follow the scripted set of behaviors and outcomes—the choreography—in the constitution of an interactive work's unique onscreen performances" (2009:258–59). Dance games make these affinities vivid and visceral, by creating a circuit of scripts and performances that continually cycles across a digital/embodied divide staged by gameplay. As in other interactive media contexts, player inputs prompt the execution of digital code, but in this case that code in turn accesses directives that choreograph players' bodies, with their consenting participation. In this interactive work, it is the player's embodied performance that is figured as unique, while the on-screen performance is stable and repeatable.

I join Bryan Behrenshausen in adopting a performance studies framework for digital gameplay, one that attends to the cumulative embodied experience of players as well as to their constant anticipation of the games' possible responses to their actions. As he notes, "Although we certainly cannot ignore the future orientation of the player's body, we cannot forget that this body also bears the weighty marks of the past—past encounters, past tradition, and past discipline—that materializes in its always-present performative reiteration at the site of engagement with the video game" (2007:336). This imperative to investigate the cumulative effects of repetitive practice has significant methodological implications for ethnographic work on expressive practices and participatory culture. In many ways it has driven the development of my own research orientation, which I have come to think of as DIY/DIA ethnography: do-it-yourself, do-it-again.

DIY/DIA ETHNOGRAPHY: FROM VIRTUAL TO VISCERAL

My first ethnographic research project investigated Sacred Harp singing, an American vernacular hymnody tradition with a strong participatory ethos that brought together singers from widely divergent social backgrounds (for instance, rural conservative Christians and urban liberal folk revivalists). It wasn't difficult to describe this research as ethnographic, even though in some respects it was quite untraditional. My fieldwork was multi-sited and episodic, taking place during weekend trips to singing conventions around the United States. I didn't do a single, continuous "year in the field," and I often didn't know much about the daily lives of the other singers at Sacred Harp conventions. As in many affinity communities, participants' conversations usually focused on their shared experiences with this musical practice rather than their day jobs or potentially divisive subjects like politics or religion (Miller 2008c). But few scholars asked me to explain or defend my methodology, perhaps because Sacred Harp singing came with so many trappings of ethnographic authenticity. It was enough that I traveled long distances to small southern churches in obscure rural locations; I offered sufficient proof of the "being there" of ethnographic authority (Clifford 1988:21–54, Geertz 1988:1–24).

When I began working on video games, a lot more questions started to come up. The anthropologist Tom Boellstorff tells a similar story in his book *Coming of Age in Second Life*, where he describes encountering "skepticism toward the idea of conducting ethnography in virtual worlds on their own terms" (2008:62). In responding to these questions, Boellstorff draws parallels to his previous fieldwork in Indonesia. The comparison helps him identify double standards: For instance, no one expected him to know everything about the lives of every Indonesian person he encountered during his fieldwork or to provide corroborating evidence for every claim his interlocutors made about their own identities and experiences. Yet many people expressed concern that in studying Second Life, "you can't know who the people are offline" (62). Boellstorff makes a strong case that it is redundant and misleading to talk about "virtual ethnography"; he argues that ethnography is always already virtual, that sociality in virtual worlds is as real as sociality anywhere else, and that no anthropologists ever have complete access to their interlocutors' experience (60–86). As he writes, "To demand that ethnographic research always incorporate meeting residents in the actual world for 'context' presumes that virtual worlds are not themselves contexts; it renders ethnographically inaccessible the fact that most residents of virtual worlds do not meet their fellow residents offline. . . . My decision to conduct research wholly within Second Life . . . put into practice my assertion that virtual worlds are legitimate sites of culture" (61).

What does it mean to say that all ethnography is virtual? Boellstorff argues against any binary opposition of "the virtual" and "the real"; instead, he follows a long philosophical tradition of discussing virtuality as a kind of potential, and he characterizes the virtual as that which "approach[es] the actual *without arriving there*" (19). Ethnography is virtual because of its reliance on participant-observation, a method characterized by role-playing, efforts to comprehend other people's perspectives, and frequent shifts between immersion and detachment. Boellstorff draws on Marie-Laure Ryan's writing about virtuality, which offers some clues for thinking about the virtual qualities of the embodied practice of ethnography: Ryan writes, "As for the body, it is virtualized by any practice and technology aiming at expanding its sensorium, altering its appearance, or pushing back its biological limits" (1999:94). Thus when we take up a new instrument, or learn to dance in a new way, or create an avatar in Second Life, we are virtualizing our bodies (see also Miller 2012).

Boellstorff's ethnographic work focuses on the distinctive forms of sociality that develop in virtual worlds and the forms of craft that drive that process. He suggests, "to be virtually human might itself constitute an ethnographic project, in the sense that it involves a dialectic of participation and observation, a self-reflexive crafting of one's point of view" (2008:178). My own ideas about ethnography and virtuality developed along somewhat different lines. My first "virtual" research project investigated the single-player gameworlds of *Grand Theft Auto*, where there was no apparent in-game sociality to discuss, no real-time interaction among physically dispersed players in the course of gameplay (Miller 2007, Miller 2008b). These peculiar fieldwork circumstances led me to engage in an extended thought experiment about what it could mean to treat a single-player gameworld as an ethnographic fieldsite (Miller 2008a). Nevertheless, I knew that most people would assume that the "real" ethnography in this project took place when I was interviewing players, analyzing web-based gamer discussion forums, or sitting on the couch watching someone else play. Ethnography is a social practice; it involves other people. So why did I feel like I was doing ethnography when I played *Grand Theft Auto* alone in my basement? And why didn't I notice the huge chasm between Sacred Harp fieldwork and video game fieldwork that other people kept pointing out?

Reflecting on these questions, I realized that two core methodological principles had governed my own ethnographic practice: *Do it yourself, and do it again.* Ethnography takes repetition seriously. Ethnographers working in ethnomusicology, dance studies, and performance studies are particularly attuned to the importance of repetition, because practice and repertoire are at the heart of how expressive culture works. We observe that repetition can be enlivening, building up thick experience, rather than numbing perception or wearing away individuality and agency. (Think of the patina of use on a much-handled object rather than the patchy surface damage of a flaked-off coating.) Where the lab-based experimental sciences pursue repetition in the name of replicating results, ethnographers and performers engage with repetitions that create different results every time, and over time. I'm not just referring to deliberate, agentive repetition with a difference, like a performer's creative interpretation of a canonical work, or critical Signifyin(g) (Gates 1988), though these are crucial concepts for my research. In this broader methodological discussion, my focus is on practice, the repetition that *makes* a difference through cumulative experience. Practice makes *us* different, by remaking our bodies. It makes our relationships different, by structuring our mutual understanding. It's something gamers have in common with dancers and Sacred Harp singers.[3]

Practice is how you get from virtual to visceral. For me, then, "virtual ethnography" is not ethnography of digitally mediated sociality; rather, it is the first step in the direction of visceral ethnography. I agree with Boellstorff that in some sense ethnography is virtual by nature, but I want to extend and flesh out this idea, to

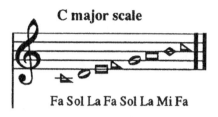

Figure I.4: Shape-note notation (reproduced from McGraw 1991:18, courtesy of the Sacred Harp Publishing Company).

account for how repetition and structuring practice gradually change the quality of experience.

Suppose you are trying to sing from the shape-note notation in *The Sacred Harp* tunebook, translating triangles, squares, and rectangles into fa-sol-la syllables as you sight-read the printed music (McGraw 1991; see Miller 2004 and Figure I.4). Maybe you have heard people do it on recordings for years. The first time you do it yourself, you voice the syllables haltingly, self-consciously. You stumble over your own tongue. You can feel that you aren't actually *doing it*, because you know *doing it* involves practiced fluency. This is virtuality. The virtuality resides partly in your knowledge that this is a practice, that it's "restored behavior," in Richard Schechner's famous terms—"never for the first time," always already "twice-behaved" (1985: 35–36). So if it feels like the first time, then you're not doing it yet—you need to do it again, and again. And it's through doing it again that you come to learn what repetition accomplishes in this practice.

So, once you have achieved effortless proficiency at singing from this notation system and are no longer "reading" the material note-by-note, why keep repeating? Why sing a three-chord song a hundred or a thousand times? It turns out it's not the same every time. This may seem obvious, yet it's a principle still too rarely applied in critical discourse about the three-chord songs that play on the radio a thousand times. Maybe we could find a way to take repetition and practice just as seriously when considering material that is easily labeled disposable, banal, trite, or ephemeral. The re-Tweet, the Facebook "share," the viral video, the radio replay: What happens if we view each of these as practiced repetition that makes a difference rather than as a contagious disease jumping from host to host? (Cf. Jenkins et al. 2013.)

Now, suppose you are trying to learn a dance from a videogame. In *Dance Central*, as in shape-note singing, we have a hybrid notation system: Flashcard icons for each dance move scroll down one side of the screen, while a dancing animated character models the routine. (See Figure I.5.) You try to mirror the animated dancer while also looking ahead at the upcoming flashcards, but it's too much information. You fall behind the beat and earn no points from the game's motion-tracking evaluation system, or you prioritize staying with the rhythm but can only stiffly "hit the frames" that earn you credit for each move, rendering flowing choreography as a series of freeze-frame poses. This is virtual dancing, a form of "marking it"—rehearsing the

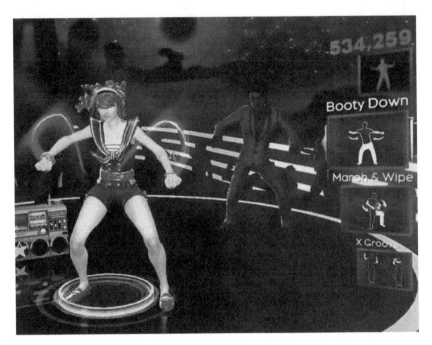

Figure I.5: *Dance Central* notation. Detail from a player-produced gameplay video (AverageAsian Dude 2012). (Screenshot by the author.)

broad outlines of choreography or stage directions. You go through the motions at an abstract level, leaving out the technical detail and interpretive nuance. But even "marking it" is a world away from just watching the character on-screen, or watching someone else attempt the dance. Even if you only do it yourself once, badly, virtually—even if you only do it enough to realize you're not actually doing it at all. If you do it many times over, you might build up a visceral understanding of how dance games engender engagement, how they construct dance technique, why players find them satisfying, and even how you might offer a critical reading of their implications in terms that don't misrepresent how they work.

It might seem obvious that studying video games requires playing them. How could you study games and not play? Would you analyze a symphony after listening to a recording of three minutes of one movement played through tinny laptop speakers? Would you analyze a film with the sound turned off (and never turn it back on)? Would you confidently put forward a close reading of a novel after making one quick skim and never opening the book again? Such approaches might yield some insights, but they wouldn't meet the standards of scholarly rigor in most disciplines; they would be preliminary assays that might help orient a deeper dive into the material. Yet time and again, in question and answer sessions people have asked me whether I actually play these games. I have implied that the answer should be self-evident, but the stakes of the question are different from what my interlocutors might assume. Due to chronic tendon injuries, for many years I have been unable to play games that use a standard handheld controller or a computer keyboard interface, and I have chosen not to study those games. This is a personal choice; I would never tell another scholar that a particular research topic should be off-limits due to a physical disability, or any other aspect of personal identity. Nevertheless, my disciplinary orientation has led me to conclude that I can't do my best work on games that I am physically unable to play. These choices speak to my commitment to a particular kind of participant-observation.

Ethnographers still often focus on fieldwork as *going somewhere*—an expedition to the field, predicated on distance, requiring us to draft maps that chart terrain (Marcus 1995:99). But we also know that once we get to that constructed place, participant-observation is a durational practice. How much time it takes is a mystery—we all struggle to know how long is long enough—but we definitely believe something is happening over time. Recasting this principle using the theme of virtuality, I would suggest that fieldwork-based disciplines rely on an assumption that there is a trajectory from virtual to actual built into ethnographic method. There's an assumption that the virtualized body won't stay virtual. Durational practice gradually materializes into "visceral ethnography," a method for accessing "sensational knowledge" (Hahn 2007).

In a chapter titled "Postmodernism and Posthumanism," Steve Dixon makes a related point when he criticizes work on digital performance that fixates on "how performances reconfigure, challenge or otherwise 'explore' notions of the 'real.'" He observes, "*The real has changed*, as it has always done. The real, and our consciousness of what is real, is subject to *time*. . . . [W]e have quickly become used to and have assimilated the capabilities of the computer and the Web—it is just part and parcel of what today is *real*" (2007:144). As Dixon's larger arguments make clear, it is not simply the passage of time that accomplishes these changes; it is the situated, embodied, practical process of feeling out the affordances of technologies through repetitive use, converting the force of potential to the force of sensational knowledge. This process goes missing in much of the theoretical literature about virtuality. Dixon writes, "In digital performance, one cannot but determine theory and practice frequently moving in opposite and contrary directions. Instilled postmodern belief systems stress fragmentation, split subjectivity, and the rejection of meta-narratives and meanings, whereas in actuality what is *practiced* by digital posthuman performers is commonly the search for the opposite: for cohesion, for meaning, for unity, for intimate cybernetic connections between the organic and the technological" (154–55). This critique suggests that ethnographers have a crucial contribution to make to digital media studies—especially ethnographers of expressive culture and communities of practice. We have been trained to notice transmission, embodiment, repetition, and craft; we can see how people learn to play interfaces like instruments. We know something about how virtuality works.

DIY/DIA ethnography opens a field of inquiry by opening a field of relations and deliberately constructing "relational infrastructure" (Hamera 2007:19). Hamera, Hahn, and other dance ethnographers have offered extraordinary insights into how gesture, technique, training, choreography, and repertoire become the building blocks and tools to construct this infrastructure. In working across the virtual/visceral gap, ethnographers reach for "sensational knowledge" of *why* other people do things through *how* they do things. We aspire to mutual recognition—not of a shared essence that was always there, but of a shared self-fashioning and sensory orientation. We have something in common because we have literally gone through the same motions, have been shaped by the same repertoire, have studied with the same teacher, have learned to explain ourselves using the terms of the same discipline.

DIY/DIA ethnography includes reflection on one's own experience, including accounting for one's subject position. For instance, my encounters with dance games, their repertoires, and my fellow players are structured by my cumulative history as a middle-class white American cisgender woman who grew up in the 1980s in Key West, Florida—a tourist mecca for queer kinesthesia, body work, and escapist identity play—where I took ballet, tap, and jazz lessons and watched clubgoers dance to Latin/Afro-Caribbean music performed by my stepfather's band. But I want to emphasize that a DIY/DIA orientation to ethnography is not reducible to reflexivity, nor transparently equivalent with auto-ethnography. It is not about accounting for how *my story* affects how I tell *your story*, though that is surely an important endeavor. Rather, it is an effort to write us both into *the same story*, or even better, the same virtual world. In this virtual world our experiences are not identical, but we work with common narrative logics, performance conventions, and structural constraints. So, when I ask other people why they play video games or sing Sacred Harp songs, if they reply, "Because it's fun," or "I like the challenge," or "It's just a social thing," or "It's how I relax," perhaps the next step is realizing they're saying they do it because of *how it feels*—and that I have to do it to find out. By doing it myself and then doing it again, maybe I'll learn something about the nature of knowing, the nature of "why," and the process of building relational infrastructure. And then maybe I'll be ready to come back for another conversation, with different questions.

PLAN OF THE BOOK

This book is designed to be read from beginning to end, and many arguments and themes travel and develop across chapters. The order of the chapters roughly tracks the history of the *Just Dance* and *Dance Central* franchises, from interface design, marketing, and early industry reviews to the development of player communities, game choreographers' retrospective reflections on their work, and increasing intersections with other circulating popular media. This structure also corresponds to the experiential trajectory of an individual player, from initial encounters with each game's motion-sensing system, on-screen characters, songs, and choreography to the cultivation of listening and movement techniques through repetitive practice, engagement with behind-the-scenes media about the games, and participation in player communities through the production and circulation of gameplay videos. That said, I have attempted to include enough signage to allow readers some latitude to skip around or read individual chapters without becoming disoriented. The following chapter outline should serve as a helpful road map for those planning to read selectively.

In Chapter 1, I investigate the private/public tensions built into digital dance gameplay, taking as my point of departure an encouraging catchphrase often uttered by *Dance Central*'s voiceover dance teacher: "I see you, I see you!" Dancing to club hits like no one is watching is a high-risk guilty pleasure. But what if only a machine is watching, and the club moves have been choreographed in advance? Dance games offer private dance lessons using surveillance technologies. I explore how this core contradiction drives players' affective experiences and social performances of shame, courage, humor, and intimacy. This chapter also provides an overview of how the Wii and Kinect systems work, and how players test and evaluate each system's perceptual capacities and technical performance. Dance gameplay brings together the performance conventions and technical affordances of videogames, social media platforms, and user-facing cameras integrated into consumer media devices. I address dance games' shifting dynamics of seeing-and-being-seen across multiple contexts, including single-player rehearsal and performance, co-present social play, and gameplay videos posted online.

Chapter 2 shows how dance games invite players to engage with embodied difference. The games are built around popular music and dance styles that function as signs of gender, sexuality, race, ethnicity, and class; their screen dancers also bear marks of embodied identity categories, which may or may not match those of the musical and choreographic repertoires that they perform. I argue that dance games follow in the footsteps of minstrelsy and drag traditions by staging song-and-dance variety shows that center on racialized and gendered performances. Like minstrelsy and drag, the games afford performative possibilities for both reinforcing and destabilizing essentialist identity categories. In the second part of the chapter I show how constructivist gender theory directly informed the development process for the *Dance Central* series, and I explore what happens when designers enlist players in putting theory into practice. By design, *Dance Central* stages visceral encounters with gendered choreography, generating both embodied gender work in the course of gameplay and reflective gender discourse in social media contexts. In analyzing how these processes play out I attend to the intersectional quality of gendered experience—that is, how gender is intertwined with other social identity categories, including race, sexuality, class, age, and ability, in dance game design, gameplay, and reception of players' circulating dance performances.

Readers most interested in popular music and sound studies will find a sustained treatment of those subjects in Chapters 3 and 4, which show that dance games are fundamentally music games: They rely on popular music and associated listening practices for both their pedagogical efficacy in teaching choreography and their commercial success as media products. Chapter 3 addresses multisensory musicality in dance games, situating gameplay as a form of embodied popular music reception that intersects with other kinds of musical experience and social media practice. I show how game design, gameplay, and associated player discourse all deploy technologies of transduction, converting sound into forms accessible to other senses (Sterne and Akiyama 2012). Game choreographers translate song into dance, creating kinesthetic transcriptions of licensed popular music tracks; players learn how to feel out music with their bodies as choreographers do. I argue that interactive audio in dance games serves to cultivate a choreographic listening sensibility, bringing the listening ear and the moving body into intimate alignment.

Chapter 4 analyzes dance games as transmission systems. One of the most striking features of dance games is their capacity to notate, transmit, and archive embodied repertoires that are typically taught in face-to-face, body-to-body contexts. But exactly what kind of dance pedagogy do they offer? Dance games ask players to sight-read unfamiliar choreography in real time, mirroring the screen dancer as the routine unfolds. They imply that choreography can work like streaming audio or video—passing straight into a player's proprioceptive system—and challenge players to cultivate techniques of anticipation to minimize kinesthetic lag. I show how the games teach these techniques using hybrid notation systems, modular choreography closely tied to musical structure, and patterned repetition that integrates technical training into a repertoire of works. Through a close reading of an example drawn from each game franchise—*Dance Central*'s version of "Crank That" and *Just Dance*'s version of "Apache (Jump on It)"—I demonstrate how this technical pedagogy dovetails with the games' remediation of existing song-and-dance repertoires to reinforce racialized models of dance authenticity.

Chapter 5 focuses on choreographic labor. Drawing on interviews with game choreographers, I show how they function as cultural intermediaries between the game industry and particular dance cultures, and how their embodied and affective labor position them as representatives of "real dance." I discuss how the technical constraints imposed by motion-capture and animation processes impact the nature of creative labor in dance game production, and how choreographers have pushed against those constraints to assert their own creative agency and affirm particular dance values. This chapter also addresses issues of ownership—in terms of choreographic copyright, cultural heritage, and cultural appropriation—and shows how dance games reflect choreographers' experiences as teachers, students, competitors, and producers of creative content in an era of precarious labor.

The sixth and final chapter offers a series of object lessons demonstrating how dance games configure intimate relationships among humans, interfaces, musical and choreographic repertoires, and social media platforms. I present six portraits of collective body projects mobilized via social media, placing dance games in the context of a broader media ecology that includes user-generated content, advertising campaigns, commercial music videos, mobile apps, and viral videos. These six body projects—uploading, disciplining, infringing, autodancing, belonging, and circulating— show us players negotiating the dynamics of control and consent that drive so many interactive media experiences today.

Dance games encourage players to experience surveillance as intimate recognition and commodity consumption as a creative practice grounded in the cultivation of technique. It could be tempting to dismiss these experiences as false consciousness, an artifact of corporate manipulation. I will not shy away from critique in these pages, but I also believe we need to take these experiences seriously as lived realities: to imagine the possibility that feeling intimately recognized might change the way players recognize themselves, or that feeling engaged in a creative practice might reorient their relationships with other kinds of commodities. How do dance games persuade players to let their bodies be animated by someone else's intentions, and to take pleasure in that process? Answering this question could help us understand how other emergent interactive technologies are recruiting, training, and tracking users' bodies, in realms far removed from the dance floor.

CHAPTER 1

I See You, I See You!

"You got this on lock? A'ight, jump right in."

I'm learning a move called the Dodger. *Dance Central*'s voiceover dance teacher counts me in, chanting "5, 6, 7, 8 . . ." A flashcard icon reminds me that for this move I'll be stepping off with my right leg, but with a front cross, so I'll be moving to the left. I bend at the waist, raise my fists. Step/feint one way, then the other, make a mental note. Most moves head to the right first, so this is the kind of thing that could trip me up when I do the whole routine. (See Figure 1.1.)

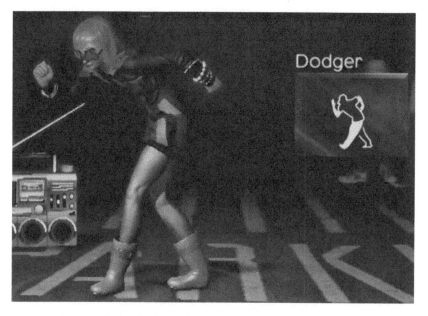

Figure 1.1: Learning the "Dodger." Detail from a player-produced gameplay video of the *Dance Central* routine for Lady Gaga's "Just Dance" (Calfin 2010). (Screenshot by the author.)

"You're tearin' it up! All right, check it. 5, 6, 7, 8 . . ."

I move through the Shuffle, the Prep & Spin. The short instrumental loop from Lady Gaga's "Just Dance" keeps cycling around; there won't be any lyrics to distract me until it's time to piece the moves together into a longer subroutine. Things are going well. The teacher voice eggs me on: "*Hell* yeah!" Next move: the Hit Me.

"Maybe you already got this. So go for it! 5, 6, 7, 8 . . ."

I try it, and the voice says "Perfect!" But the text at the screen dancer's feet only says "Nice!" Where's the "Flawless!!!" assessment I got on the other moves? What did I do wrong? I wave my hand to signal for a Retry. Maybe I was just a little behind the beat?

"All right, once more then. 5, 6, 7, 8 . . ." Punch one fist high, pound the other diagonally down across the body. Now I have to get the move right three times before I'm allowed to move on. "5, 6, 7, 8 . . ." Punch high, pound low. There's that Flawless. "5, 6, 7, 8 . . ." Green checkmarks signal my progress. On the third try, the screen dancer's hair-swishes catch my eye, and I manage to work in the head-turn, looking right and then left as I punch and pound. The Kinect didn't seem to notice that I missed it before, and turning my eyes away from the screen feels risky. But I've got it now—third green checkmark, Flawless.

"Yeah, I see you, I see you! Nice. Practice makes perfect." I realize I've been holding my breath. Shake it out, focus: on to the next move.

"I see you, I see you!" What does this game see, who is watching, and how do players experience being seen? Dance games offer private dance experiences driven by surveillance technologies. For many players, this embedded contradiction is at the heart of their appeal. Players can work through a dance curriculum and master a particular choreographic repertoire without ever submitting themselves to human evaluation. The games promise players that they can leave behind anxiety about their technical skills, body type, and whether their identity traits "match" the games' club moves, musical repertoire, or expressions of gender and sexuality (see Chapter 2). But these are also social games, designed for groups and popular at parties; they are engines of humor, shame, pride, and intimacy. Even those who only play at home alone or with family members and close friends may participate in a broader community of practice via social media. For instance, a player commented on *Dance Central*'s Facebook page that the routine for Carly Rae Jepsen's pop confection "Call Me Maybe" is "dope," but followed up with, "I mean I'm a dude so I wont be dancing to this song in public" (posted December 3, 2012, to Dance Central 2016). For this player, public sharing of his private enjoyment of performing un-dude-like choreography felt less risky than putting his moving body on display.

This chapter focuses on privacy, surveillance, spectatorship, and intimacy in digital dance gameplay. I explore how dance games' shifting dynamics of seeing and being seen engender feelings of vulnerability, courage, shame, pride, suspicion, and trust as players move across a spectrum of private and public gameplay situations. How do these games use surveillance technologies to frame safe spaces for dance? How is having one's dancing assessed by a machine different from having it assessed by a human? An array of human and non-human performers, audiences, and translating intermediaries participate in any given episode of gameplay. This chapter investigates how they learn their roles, negotiate status and agency, evaluate each other's performances, and develop intimate relationships. I also begin to address a theme that will run through subsequent chapters: reworking existing theories of spectatorship in order to account for media technologies that look back at their users.

The intimate relationship at the core of digital dance gameplay is the relationship between the player and the on-screen dancer, which upends conventional player-avatar relations. In most video games, an avatar serves as the player's representative in the game world; the player manipulates the avatar like a puppet, using a controller interface.[1] Dance games break this control chain. Players pair themselves with screen dancers who might be expected to function like traditional avatars, but in fact the screen dancer does not represent the player, and players don't direct the screen dancers' movements. Instead, players receive feedback on how well they are matching the screen dancer's performance. Thus even in solo play, there are at least two dancing performers in every game session: a human player and an animated character, who dance in a face-to-face mirroring relationship. This pairing raises questions about the implied dance context: Is the on-screen dancer a partner, as in couples dancing? If so, is one partner leading and the other following? Or is the screen dancer supposed to be a teacher, or a member of a larger dance crew, or an idealized mirror image? Each game offers different cues as to the nature of this relationship. Players' interpretations of these cues are colored by their prior gaming and dance experiences, as well as whether they are playing alone or with others.

There are also at least two lines of observation in every game session: The dancing player watches and imitates the screen dancer, while the game apparatus tracks and evaluates the player's moving body. The screen dancer is designed to be an accomplished and compelling performer who will dance on command; in this sense the screen dancer performs at the player's pleasure. But by modeling the choreography, the screen dancer also dictates the terms of the player's performance for a non-human connoisseur: the motion-tracking sensor. Playing by the rules of the game means calibrating one's movements to suit the perceptual constraints of this machinic audience. Since players generally do not know exactly what or how the machine can "see," they must find out through trial and error: They experiment with gestural inputs and then must interpret the feedback each game provides through visual and audio channels.

Like the players and industry reviewers I will be quoting in this chapter, I often rely on visual terminology in addressing the perceptual work that drives digital dance gameplay—terms like surveillance, spectatorship, observation, watching, looking, seeing and being seen. Lest I risk reinforcing the "hegemony of ocular-centrism" in game studies (Behrenshausen 2007:335), I should emphasize that

I proceed from the assumption that human visual perception cannot be disentangled from multisensory experience, and that we all learn and practice multiple forms of vision. For example, someone who is watching a moving body while trying to mirror those movements must cultivate a distinctive visual technique alongside her kinesthetic technique. The images of moving bodies presented by dance games might be considered "haptic images," Laura Marks's term for images that "do not invite identification with the figure so much as they encourage a bodily relationship between the viewer and image"; players therefore could be said to practice "haptic visuality," in which "our self rushes up to the surface to interact with another surface. . . . We become amoebalike, lacking a center, changing as the surface to which we cling changes" (Marks 2002:xvi; see also Gibbs 2010:202). Marks was primarily writing about the sensuous qualities of certain representational strategies in digital video; she was not discussing situations where a viewer literally moves her body to match the moving form of the screen image. But her discussion of the "dynamic subjectivity between looker and image" (2) captures something important about how players watch the screen dancers in dance games and how motion-sensing technologies perceive and model the data points presented by a human player.

Marks developed her concept of "haptic vision" from theories of haptic perception, "the combination of tactile, kinesthetic, and proprioceptive functions, the way we experience touch both on the surface of and inside our bodies" (2). But her emphasis on touch, tactility, and texture is a better match for the extreme-close-up digital video works she discusses than it is for dance games, which often depict bodies as high-contrast silhouettes, always frame a complete moving body rather than zooming in on individual parts, and won't function unless the player stays well back from the screen and sensor. In this context, then, I suggest that players draw on all their senses as they practice "kinesthetic vision," while each gaming system's sensor apparatus draws on multiple technologies to engage in "virtual proprioception." These are two distinct forms of dynamic mimetic vision. Human and machine each perceive something in motion, map it, and respond to it in real time, aided by the predictive powers of prior cumulative knowledge. The human player watches in order to map visual information onto her own body schema, while the machine watches in order to map the player's relative body positions and check them against a codified standard for correct performance. Meanwhile, players also deploy musical listening techniques in the service of aligning these visual and kinesthetic channels; locking into the beat of a song and listening ahead for predictable structural elements reduces the sense of "kinesthetic lag" that comes along with mirroring an unfamiliar dance in real time (see Chapters 3 and 4).

Thus human and machine square off face to face, senses mutually attuned, like partners on the dance floor. But wait! Don't let this appealing metaphor leave a crucial third party on the sidelines: The player's gaze is not trained on the sensor but rather on the screen dancer. This screen body might seem to be the more obvious dance partner in this scenario; it certainly looks the part, being a digital archive of another moving human. Yet the screen dancer's partnering capacities are radically restricted by her sense-blindness: The screen dancer cannot perceive the player and does not respond to her movements. Indeed, though they all seem to be looking at each other, not one of these three parties can meet the gaze of any of the others. Perhaps this partly explains how dance gameplay can feel "private."

Game systems perform, too, although they don't dance. Game console producers compete for sales by touting the performance capabilities of their hardware, and novel technologies like motion-sensing systems face a special burden of persuasive performance: They must convince the player of the accuracy of their own observations (Auslander 2005, cf. Bogost 2007). Is that thing working? Can it really tell dancing from flailing? Can it be trusted—and can it be fooled? What if it is fooling the player into making a fool of herself? "I see you, I see you!" Like a parent at the edge of the playground, the game offers reassurance: You have an attentive audience. But players are skeptical. They put each technical system through its paces, testing its limits. They check each game's perceptual capacities and evaluative judgments against human standards, beginning with their own.

DARE TO FLAIL

From the earliest published reviews of *Just Dance*, game industry media coverage of motion-sensing dance games emphasized their capacity for generating shame, humor, and visceral awkwardness. Full-body choreography might be daunting for anyone without much dance experience, but it presents an especially stark contrast to the gestural economy and rapid-fire fine-motor coordination of using a traditional controller or keyboard. Just standing up and holding one's arms out to the sides is a radical shift from a gamer's customary bodily comportment.[2] Experienced gamers have their own "techniques of the body," Marcel Mauss's influential term for the kinesthetic practices that distinguish particular "societies, educations, proprieties and fashions, types of prestige" (1992 [1934]:458). Gamers' acquired techniques exemplify what Mauss calls "education in composure," the bodily training that allows for "coordinated response of coordinated movements setting off in the direction of a chosen goal" (474). That education is indexed by "isolated, precise actions governed by a clear consciousness," actions that display a "resistance to emotional seizure" (475). These qualities were considered hallmarks of civilization when Mauss was writing in the 1930s, and retain those associations in many cultural contexts today. Gamers practice the art of disciplined anticipation, and score-oriented players often celebrate bodily efficiency as a mark of accomplishment (Miller 2009, cf. Taylor 2006:73–74, Bench 2016). Uncoordinated, disorderly, reactive, and excessive movements indicate betrayals of this "education in composure." As T. L. Taylor observes in her work on competitive e-sports, "Language like 'flailing' or 'button mashing'—where the link between what you see and want to act on runs up against the actual ability to act—highlights how central control of one's body is for computer gaming" (2014:38). In industry reviews of dance games, accounts of "flailing" routinely include references to physical, mental, and/or social disability, usually framed in humorous terms. Reviewers dwell on the out-of-control motions of inexpert players, including themselves; they often poke fun at their own ineptitude as dancers. The typical reviewer persona is that of "a woefully uncoordinated dude who doesn't know what rhythm feels like" (Dyer 2012).

Sam Bishop's early review of *Just Dance* for the prominent industry website IGN.com summed up the main game directive this way: "Memorize the handful of moves and flail around." A distaste for disorderly motion also surfaced in his account of why the game failed to meet his standards for authentic gameplay: "There are no buttons to be pressed, no unlockables, no tiers of songs, no progression of any kind. You fire up the game, spaz out, and your motions are 'graded' and you're given points." Bishop rated *Just Dance* a 2 out of 10, declaring that "unsuspecting, uneducated consumers" who purchase it have "paid to act like an idiot" (Bishop 2009). Martin Gaston opened a review for Eurogamer.com with a similar warning: "*Just Dance 2* will make you look like a tit. Especially if you're drunk, though this is exactly what most people will need to be in order to even contemplate having a go" (Gaston 2010). A year later, Eurogamer reviewer Jamin Smith wrote that playing the newly released *Dance Central* is "entirely comparable to that moment you first try Guitar Hero on hard [an advanced difficulty level], and all those notes come whizzing down the screen and your brain turns to mush. The only difference is instead of staring dumbfounded at the neck of a plastic guitar, you'll be flailing around in front of the TV like somebody in the process of turning to jelly" (Smith 2010). Tom Hoggins, the videogames editor for the London *Telegraph*, described the risks of playing *Dance Central* with a human audience: "From her lofty perch [my wife] passes judgment on my own curious jiggling, describing it as 'comedy gold', 'like an embarrassing grandad at a wedding' and 'as if someone was having a seizure to music'" (Hoggins 2010).

It's worth noting that "flail" is a kissing cousin to "fail"—a keyword in gamer culture since the late 1990s that later circulated as a social media meme (Beam 2008). But remember, too, that in digital gameplay failing is both routine and temporary: Even after an epic fail, players dust themselves off, press restart, and try again based on what they have learned (Gee 2006). For gamers, then, the journey from flailing/failing to coordinated, controlled mastery follows a well-trodden path. But it's impossible to follow that path without the infrastructure provided by game design, mechanics, and a trustworthy evaluation system; otherwise you'll just be "dancing in your living room like a loon" (Gaston 2010). This is a risky business on at least two fronts: Dancing is a potentially humiliating activity, and if the game doesn't work properly, then you've also proven yourself to be a gullible consumer.

What makes dancing embarrassing? What drives its social riskiness? Can dancing alone be embarrassing? Is it less risky to dance along with someone else? Does it matter whether that person is a friend, a stranger, physically present, or an animated character? Imagine the nightmare scenario of dance humiliation: the laughing crowd. What are they laughing at? Perhaps the dancer doesn't look the part—too old or young, the wrong race or gender for the moves, a body shape out of line with stereotypical ideals (see Desmond 1997, Muñoz 2001, Fisher and Shay 2009). Or maybe it's more about the execution: jerky moves that should be smooth, feet behind the beat, sweaty exertion, over-reliance on a signature move, the squint of concentration, the lip-bite that betrays unease and inauthenticity (sometimes called the "white man's overbite"). The 2007 film *Knocked Up* offers telling examples: In an early scene at a club, the schlubby lead character dances with a hot girl who is way out of his league, fueled by liquid courage. He shakes a clenched fist high and low, and a wingman worries from the sidelines: "Dude, I think he's doing the dice thing too much." "That's really all he's got," another friend replies. Later in the film, that same hot girl is turned away from the dance club by a bouncer because she is now visibly pregnant and her sister is "too old" (Apatow 2007).

Consider the laughing observer again. That laugh might be cutting: Who do you think you are? Who do you think you're fooling? It might be affectionate and patronizing, as when small children dance with unselfconscious abandon: How charming that you don't yet know who you are! It might be incredulous and tinged with admiration: You must have "balls of steel," fat guy tearing it up to "Single Ladies" (Bench 2013:147). It might have a bitter note of dispossession: That's my dance, what makes you think you have the right to do it? It might be uneasy: That dance is too sexy for a 9-year-old. It might come with the pinched wince and whimper of empathy: I'd look funny doing that dance, too. The laugh might be anxious: What if my hips moved that way? Could my body betray me like that? Am I who I think I am? Dancing along with someone else, the laugh might ring with exhilaration and relief: We *both* look ridiculous—thank God it's not just me! It might have the intimate warmth of social reciprocity: We're in this together.

The development teams for *Just Dance* and *Dance Central* were well aware of the precarious vulnerability of social dance situations. For one thing, they could relate on a personal level. Matt Boch, the series project director and lead designer for *Dance Central*, told a game industry convention audience, "We were making a game that was a little outside the comfort zone of a lot of people who were working on it, in terms of their dance skills. We had dance classes and really tried to jump into the whole thing. . . . The videos are amazing but I'm not allowed to show them" (Boch 2012). Ubisoft producer Florian Granger told a Eurogamer interviewer, "Everyone remembers going to a nightclub or school disco where it takes a couple of hours before anyone has the bottle to get up and dance. Most guys do the fix-placed-beer-bottle dance or neck-shake to the beat. Everything in Just Dance is designed to sidestep those natural inhibitions" (Parkin 2010). Of course, there is nothing natural about those inhibitions; they are deeply enculturated, and sidestepping them requires culturally specific tactics. Granger suggests that the first step is redirecting the player's attention: "That's achieved partly by having the focal point of the screen for people to focus on, so they don't feel like they're being watched, but also in giving players a constant stream of new moves to learn, we're building up a vocabulary for people, and by having a dancer on screen to follow, giving them permission to try out that language in a safe context" (Parkin 2010).

Granger is counting on the established social norms of screen spectatorship: When people are looking at a screen, "they don't feel like they're being watched"—even when they are facing a motion-tracking system and may be surrounded by human observers. The dancing player keeps his or her eyes locked on the screen, attending to a flood of multisensory cues; caught up in this task, it's easy (and reassuring) to assume that others in the room are similarly absorbed by the digital spectacle. But for the game to work, it has to be watching the player. After Granger riffed on how dancing together cultivates positive social bonding, his interviewer turned the conversation back to the player-machine relationship: "In the light of this impassioned defense, I ask Granger how much is really going on in Just Dance's code. Does the game really track player movements? Or is the scoring all smoke and mirrors, designed to give the player the illusion that the game is monitoring more than it really is able to?" (Parkin 2010). In other words, can the player game the system, or is Ubisoft gaming the player?

SMOKE AND MIRRORS, TRUST AND CONTROL

As players get acquainted with new games, they engage in an experimental process by which they learn rules, test constraints, and discover exploitable loopholes (Gee 2004, Salen and Zimmerman 2004). When a new game also involves a new interface, this exploratory process becomes more complex. Players can't confidently assess how the game works if they lack a clear channel for communication with the system. When the screen says "Push A to continue," you can hit the A button on a traditional controller or keyboard and be reasonably confident that you are sending a specific signal through a clear channel. Tactile feedback suggests that you pushed the button properly, and audiovisual feedback swiftly confirms that the signal was received. But what if you aren't even sure you can identify the A button, let alone push it properly?

Dance games involve not one but two new interfaces: a motion-tracking system and the player's defamiliarized body, each of which can be unpredictable and unreliable in its own way. For motion games, Parkin's "smoke and mirrors" question is crucial, because knowing whether the game "really tracks player movements" is the first step to knowing which interface is more trustworthy. Is it the body or the tracking technology that needs to be recalibrated? Do you trust the game's feedback, or trust yourself? These are the deeper, more intimate questions that run below players' surface-level anxiety that a corporation has conned them into "paying to act like an idiot." This is about trust and control, working out the rules of engagement and the terms of a social contract with a new technology.

The Nintendo Wii and the Xbox Kinect employ very different motion-tracking systems, and their differences are instructive not only for comparing the *Just Dance* and *Dance Central* games but for understanding the enculturation of these hybrid surveillance/controller interfaces. The Wii console tracks the movement of a handheld Wii Remote, which contains accelerometers that sense tilt, rotation, and directional acceleration. The remote also includes an optical sensor that picks up points of infrared light from LEDs arrayed along the Wii Sensor Bar, a slim, inconspicuous device placed above or below the television screen. (The Sensor Bar's name is misleading, since in fact its main purpose is to emit light signals that are "sensed" by the handheld remote.) The remote sends accelerometer and optical sensor data back to the Wii console over a Bluetooth connection, allowing for triangulation of the distance between the remote and the Sensor Bar. In some sense, the player's body is incidental to this three-piece system; the Wii Remote could hang from a string on the ceiling in a drafty room and still engage in dynamic communication with the Sensor Bar and game console. The Wii Remote and the complementary Nunchuk controller also incorporate a minimalist array of conventional button, joystick, and trigger input options. In the *Just Dance* games, players only use these buttons for basic menu navigation; playing through a song relies exclusively on gestural input.

The Xbox Kinect system takes the handheld controller out of the equation. The Kinect is a sensor that plugs into the Xbox console; like the Wii Sensor Bar, it is placed above or below the player's television screen. It includes an RGB camera, a depth sensor that relies on an infrared laser projector interacting with a video sensor, and a microphone for voice commands. The laser projector emits patterned infrared light that reflects off objects in the room, allowing for the creation of a depth map; the Kinect system infers the player's body position from the depth map and maps this data onto 20 points of articulated joint motion on a virtual human skeleton (MacCormick 2011, Beleboni 2014). Simply put, the Kinect is designed to look for a human body in the room and break it down into individually trackable moving parts. Updated versions of the Kinect firmware and hardware have also incorporated increasingly sophisticated face-recognition and voice-recognition capabilities.

Two fundamental distinctions between the Wii and Kinect systems have major implications for dance game design and production processes, choreographic repertoire, and player experiences: (1) the number and nature of tracked points, and (2) a controller paradigm versus a camera paradigm. I will explore these implications over the course of the book; in this chapter I focus on how they relate to the "smoke and mirrors" question, concomitant issues of trust and control, and the themes of privacy, surveillance, and spectatorship.

The Nintendo Wii was released in November 2006, three years before the first *Just Dance* game. While the possibilities of the Wii platform had not been exhausted by 2009, a first wave of popular games had established some basic expectations for mimetic gaming and the typical uses of the Wii Remote (Juul 2010, Jones and Thiruvathukal 2012). Other peripherals were also available, including the Nunchuk (a second remote that allows for two-handed play and more accurate motion tracking) and the Balance Board (a pressure-sensitive platform that tracks the player's weight shifts). Games that relied on a single handheld Wii Remote typically treated it as a stand-in for another object and/or emphasized a distinctive one-arm motion, such as swinging a tennis racket, throwing a punch, or rolling a bowling ball. In the early days of Wii gameplay, players often let go of the remote along with a virtual thrown object, resulting in cracked TV screens, the hasty distribution of wrist straps, and new warning documentation. This phenomenon generated a publicity windfall for Nintendo; videos of comical Wii mishaps circulated online and on the news, presenting evidence of the technological novelty and deeply engaging physicality of Wii gameplay.

One might have expected a full-body dance game to employ multiple Wii peripherals, for the sake of more detailed and accurate tracking of players' performances. *Just Dance*'s immediate precursor, a mini-game built into the *Raving Rabbids* series (see Introduction), used both the Wii Remote and Nunchuk. The Balance Board was a key peripheral for many contemporary fitness games; as Brad Millington observes, the "tactile vision" afforded by "the conjoining of flesh and technology at the site of the balance board . . . permits not only control over activity, but also an awareness and control over patterns of inactivity; the gaze of the Wii identifies disruptions in the body-machine continuum" (2009:631). But in developing a standalone version of *Just Dance*, creative director Gregoire Spillman wanted to employ less hardware and encourage a different approach to dance. He told Eurogamer interviewer Simon Parkin,

> The term "dancing game" is usually a misnomer. More often than not you're not being asked to dance so much as push buttons—either on a dance mat, plastic peripheral or controller—in time with the music. Our concept was to inspire people to overcome their inhibitions and encourage them to actually dance. . . . In order to encourage players to be free we had to reduce the amount of hardware the game required them to use to a bare minimum. We forced ourselves to achieve a meaningful level of rhythm and movement detection using the Wii Remote alone. We wanted complete freedom of arms and legs, so the idea of using nunchuks, elastic bands, leg straps or balance boards was thrown out at an early stage. (Parkin 2010)

Note how Spillman's invocations of uninhibited freedom and authentic "actual dancing" rely on a direct contrast to conventional button-pushing gameplay, and on an invidious comparison with previous music/rhythm games like *Dance Dance Revolution* and *Guitar Hero*. Dance mats, plastic guitar controllers, leg straps, and balance boards are lumped into the same category: shackles that inhibit players' freedom. Of course, economic drivers also come into play here; a game that does not require an additional peripheral will be cheaper to produce and distribute, meaning it can sell at a lower price point. It may also come across as relatively simple and accessible—key selling points for the Wii's casual-gaming target market, and neatly telegraphed in the title *Just Dance*.

As virtually every published review of *Just Dance* noted, evaluating full-body gameplay by tracking the motion of the player's right hand opens up a gargantuan loophole for gaming the system and raises concerns for players who sincerely desire accurate performance feedback. In consumer reviews and comment threads, countless players boasted about their abilities to achieve high scores just by moving one hand. When Parkin asked Ubisoft producer Florian Granger "whether the machine can be duped by flailing arms and raw energy," Granger asserted that "a better dancer will always beat a poorer player," and urged players to try to "keep the rhythm with both your lower and upper body" (Parkin 2010). A commenter on this article described an alternative approach, recounting the evasive maneuvers that helped him win a minor victory in the gender wars:

> I am banned from playing this game at a friends house. She made me play it. So I sat on the couch and shook the wii remote for however long the song lasted, drinking a glass of wine and gabbing to someone else. I won from my frantic moves. I am never allowed to play again, I am the envy of my other male friends. (TeaFiend, comment posted on Parkin 2010)

For this player, it seems that "freedom" resides not in uninhibited living-room dancing but in asserting control over the game technology, his social situation, and his own body: He refused to be coerced into dancing and found a way to deceive the technology designed to dictate and evaluate his every move. TeaFiend's strategy recalls the "microresistances to managerial control" practiced by workers subjected to closed-circuit television (CCTV) surveillance and other forms of monitoring at their places of employment (Brown 2015:6, in a discussion of Frantz Fanon's 1950s lectures on surveillance). He playfully contests routinized surveillance by flouting the game rules.

Other consumer reviews take a different tack, highlighting the upside of *Just Dance*'s technical limitations for those who are playing by choice:

> I am not a dancer and can't figure out my right foot from my left. Thankfully, I didn't have to worry about my feet; all I had to concentrate on were my arms and having a good time. The game doesn't fail you, so again, you can leave worry behind and just have a good time.

> I'm overweight and scared of dance pads (would I break one?) . . . I hate stepping on the balance board to be weighed. . . . [T]his game doesn't have any of that. . . . I always liked to dance but I've got a foot injury that restricts me. You really DO NOT have to move your feet all that much to do this if you don't want to, or can't. You get out of it what you are able to put into it. That's nice. :) (reviews posted 2009–2010 to Amazon.com 2014)

In different ways, TeaFiend and these Amazon customers seem to find comfort in the Wii's surveillance limitations. In the era of the "quantified self," GPS-equipped phones, and ubiquitous user-facing cameras, players might well experience nostalgia "for a time when organisms didn't need to produce quantitative data about themselves … when one didn't need to report back" (Galloway and Thacker 2007:124; see also Staples 2014:48 on "participatory monitoring"). Note also the telling ambiguity of the phrase "The game doesn't fail you." In gamer parlance this means that it isn't possible to "fail out" of a gameplay session, dancing so badly that the game cuts off your performance. In a review focusing on dance-related anxiety, observing that "the game doesn't fail you" also conveys a note of appreciative trust: You can count on the game to offer the support required to allow you to "leave worry behind." The second reviewer likewise identifies a reassuring, supportive mutuality built into *Just Dance*: "You can get out of it what you are able to put into it." Unlike TeaFiend and most industry reviewers, these Amazon reviewers present the absence of full-body tracking and detailed technical evaluation as praiseworthy design features. *Just Dance* only provides positive feedback, and it is relatively vague; points and stars accumulate as players proceed through a routine, but the game does not highlight the particular moves players are getting wrong, nor provide any way to workshop them.

But what about the players eager for feedback on their developing dance skills and faithful performance of choreography? Moreover, as a matter of principle, if the game system can't provide that kind of feedback, then why not stick with a broadcast medium instead? If you want to dance to pop songs in private while following specific choreography, there are other options available; you can just dance in front of the TV, like the generation of children who grew up learning Michael Jackson routines from music videos.

The *Dance Central* series was designed to address this line of questions. *Dance Central* was released in 2010, a year after *Just Dance*, as one of the launch titles for the Xbox Kinect (see Introduction). Harmonix designed the game around the still-developing affordances of the new device so that hardware and software could go to market at the same time. The Kinect was a new peripheral for the Xbox 360 console, an established platform with more than 1,000 games already available. Thus *Dance Central* and the other Kinect launch titles had to do the work of persuading Xbox owners to purchase a pricy new device, or of recruiting current/potential Wii owners to do their motion gaming on the more expensive Xbox platform instead. (The Kinect cost $150 at launch; the Xbox 360 console retailed for about $300 in 2010, making for a combined cost of $450, as compared to about $200 for the Wii system.) This attempt at a "platform wars" coup built on the Wii's own marketing tropes. Microsoft marketed the Kinect with the slogan "You are the controller," promising players enhanced and seemingly unmediated agency: This motion-sensing camera peripheral could offer even more "freedom" than the Wii, since it required no body-encumbering hardware at all. Instead of waving a Wii Remote in space or pressing buttons on a traditional controller, players could achieve the magical extension-of-powers experience of digital gameplay by moving their own bodies, with prosthetics cast aside. The Kinect was positioned as the next step in a lineage of interfaces "driven by a dream of individual control" (Chun 2011:62).

Industry reviews of *Dance Central* made direct comparisons to *Just Dance* and approvingly noted the ways in which *Dance Central* adhered to traditional gaming standards for interactivity, feedback, and challenge/mastery cycles. Reviewers assured players that *Dance Central* would hold them accountable: "Random flailing gets you nowhere; the game marks errant limbs in a castigating red glow, docking you points for faking the funk" (GameTrailers.com 2010). *Dance Central* provided quick-play possibilities along the same lines as *Just Dance*—pick a favorite song and dance along with the animated character—but it also included a choice of three different difficulty levels for each routine, a skill-and-drill rehearsal mode for perfecting individual moves, and a much more elaborate scoring system. Its evaluative feedback in the course of gameplay conjured a body broken down into its constituent moving parts: If the player had trouble with the left-leg motion for a particular move, the screen dancer's mirror-image leg would glow red. However, the screen dancer continued to perform the move correctly, leaving the player to work out how to bring the "errant limb" into line. A dance game offered the perfect proving ground for the Kinect, verifying that the sensor could really see the player's whole body while also teaching the player how to communicate with the game system using a standardized gestural vocabulary.

The Kinect's perceptual scope and analytical specificity offered a line of defense against "smoke and mirrors" skepticism. But these features also emphasized the Kinect's surveillance powers in a way that potentially undercut Microsoft's "You are the controller" promise. The Kinect looks and acts like a camera; starting with the initial set-up process, players have to place themselves within the Kinect's optimal field of view and make sure they stay in-frame while interacting with the sensor. *Dance Central's* full-body choreography requires players to stand about eight feet away from the sensor to create enough frame space for head-to-toe tracking and lateral movement. Players also have to maintain a frontal orientation to the camera for accurate evaluation of most moves. Many begin each play session by rearranging their furniture to make space for this virtual proscenium. *Dance Central* also includes some on-screen representation of the player's body, which is completely absent from *Just Dance*. A small inset box displays a silhouette of the player's moving body during gameplay, confirming that the Kinect has locked onto the body and providing guidance for keeping all of one's limbs in-frame (see Figure 1.2). During the brief "freestyle" interlude in each *Dance Central* song, an abstracted version of this moving silhouette fills the screen, and camera-click sound effects signal a series of snapshots. At these moments the game takes photo booth–style pictures that are presented as souvenirs at the end of each song—a series of entertainingly unflattering freeze-frames of players dancing in their living rooms.

All these features serve up continual reminders that players are performing in front of a camera rather than "just dancing" with uninhibited abandon. Moreover, players are not controlling the screen dancer; their direct manipulative agency is limited to menu navigation. Many players find this limitation surprising. Without

Figure 1.2: The player's silhouette, positioned between the game score and a flashcard, offering feedback on what the Kinect can see. Detail from a player-produced gameplay video (AverageAsian Dude 2012). (Screenshot by the author.)

background knowledge about the nature of motion-capture systems and game animation, it is easy to assume that if the Kinect can track 20 points on a player's moving body with a high degree of precision, then the game should be able to map those movements onto a screen dancer. But in fact the motion-capture process for the animated dance performances is a world away from what happens during gameplay, with technical requirements far exceeding the Kinect's capabilities. Recording routines for *Dance Central* involves 24 cameras placed in a 360-degree array around a studio. These cameras collect data from 40 LED emitters on a dancer's bodysuit (Pitts 2012, Figure 1.3; see Chapter 5). The Kinect collects comparatively limited data about the player's performance—far too little data to support high-quality animation. Game writer Russ Pitts laid out some of the technical issues in a *Polygon* feature on *Dance Central*'s development processes:

> Harmonix uses some of the most advanced and expensive equipment in the world to capture highly detailed nuances of highly choreographed dance routines which you, the player, will then interact with using an astronomically less expensive piece of equipment in your living room. . . .

Figure 1.3: The Harmonix motion capture studio (Pitts 2012). Screenshot by the author.

I ask: If the trick is in figuring out how to translate the dances captured in their studio to dances you can perform in front of Kinect, then why don't they simply capture the dances with Kinect in the first place? [Harmonix QA Tester] Colin Sandel practically chokes.

"We're using 3D models of the characters," he says. "While the Kinect builds a depth map of your body, the way that it actually tells where your limbs are is through the firmware. It estimates a skeleton, which is basically a stick figure, of you. Let's just say that if we tried to do it that way, our characters . . . they would occupy a lower part of the Uncanny Valley, so to speak." . . . Kinect, in short, makes a lot of "guesses" to compensate for the fact that its two cameras are essentially in one place, giving it a limited, almost 2D perspective. . . . The trick, then, is to make it possible for Kinect to tell if you're doing what the dancer is doing, using less data. (Pitts 2012)

While this is a key restriction on the Kinect's surveillance capacity, it is not immediately evident as such to most players. Instead, experienced gamers tend to perceive it as a design choice that disempowers players, eliminating their customary control over a lead character. As two commenters responded to the GameTrailers. com review of *Dance Central,*

SikeOsoshull: without a controller can we still call ourselves gamers?
Tilian: So you're not controlling anything then? Just trying to mimic an avatar?
  Lame. (GameTrailers.com 2010)

When they realize that the on-screen dancer is a model, not a mirror or a puppet, and that the gaming challenge involves transferring this screen body's choreographed repertoire into their own bodies, players must reconsider the implications of the game interface. Who is the controller? Is the player's body functioning as an input device, or is it an output device?

Nevertheless, fans of both *Just Dance* and *Dance Central* have praised the games specifically in terms of empowerment and privacy. These assessments hinge on comparisons not with other game experiences but with other dance or exercise experiences. One of the great comforts and selling points of both games is that no *humans* can see you unless you want them to. Indeed, for the most part, you can't even see yourself. In contrast to typical dance classes, there is no mirror in these games. *Dance Central's* abstracted silhouettes are a far cry from realistic video of one's dancing; in my gameplay/interview sessions, beginning players were so intent on following the screen dancer that they typically did not even notice their own silhouettes in the inset black box. Beginning with *Dance Central 2*, players could also turn off the souvenir snapshot feature—an option introduced in response to player feedback on the first edition of the game.

In an Amazon.com review of *Dance Central 3*, a player who identified herself as "a 32 year old woman who presently weighs 270 pounds" explained that the opportunity to learn the dances in private first had helped her get over her self-consciousness about moving her body in public:

> The best part is that you can turn the "pictures" mode OFF. I'm so grateful that I don't have to be photographed when I'm working out!! . . . I have always been that one that "won't work out around anyone" because I feel fat, slow, and incapable. But I play this game so often, that I now host Dance Central parties and join in with my friends. . . . The bottom line- don't be intimidated by this game. . . . Close the window blinds, turn off the photograph option in the game, crank up the volume, and rock it out! (Liraella 2012)

This reviewer implicitly splits the Kinect's gazing powers in two: The souvenir photograph option makes her feel like she is being watched, but the skeletal tracking system apparently does not. Or rather, unlike many contemporary interfaces, the motion sensor doesn't seem to be watching her as a "cybertyped" body, "always tagged with a certain set of affective identity markers" (Galloway 2012:137, building on Nakamura 2002). It doesn't know or care that she is a 32-year-old woman who weighs 270 pounds, and it can't tell how heavily she is breathing, how much she is sweating, or what she is wearing. Her body could be any body equipped with the requisite 20 trackable points: When she plays *Dance Central*, her body feels normal and anonymous. These affordances were already beginning to seem quaintly outmoded by 2012. Since then, interactive fitness technologies have increasingly focused on collecting and processing highly individuated data, defining the terms of our "quantified selves" and our personal potential for change. The "electronic leash" devices worn by paroled convicts have evolved into wearable fitness trackers employed for self-surveillance (Marx 1988:214). More generally, as Minh-Ha Pham observes, self-surveillance technologies "have expanded away from the masculine spaces of discipline and punishment" and are "increasingly central to the feminine spaces of self-expression, social interactivity, and consumerism" (2015:185–86).

Notably, Liraella's sense of anonymity hinges on her body's conformity with the Kinect's normative standards for what constitutes a complete, fully operational, and properly proportioned human. A player who can't move her right leg or left arm will never earn a five-star rating on a *Dance Central* routine, and many players with Afros or other "big hair" silhouettes observed that the first-generation Kinect could not lock onto their bodies at all. As one man explained, "The Kinect picked up my 'fro as my head, therefore making my head disproportionate to my body and giving the Kinect trouble recognizing me! I tie down my hair when I play now and it works flawlessly" (JWMidnight, email interview, August 18, 2011; see Chapter 2 and Chapter 6). As Simone Brown writes in her work on "racializing surveillance," "understanding how biometric information technologies are rationalized through industry specification and popular entertainment provides a means to falsify the idea that certain surveillance technologies and their applications are always neutral regarding race, gender, disability, and other categories of determination and their intersections" (2015:128).

THIS GAME IS LYING!

My opening gameplay notes for this chapter are from *Dance Central*'s rehearsal mode, which allows players to work through a routine one move at a time, repeating difficult sections as needed. (This mode was called "Break It Down" in the first two editions of the game.) Rehearsal mode shows players how closely the Kinect is scrutinizing their dancing. Through trial and error, they become aware of the subtle distinctions that can generate three different accuracy ratings for a given move: Almost, Nice, or Flawless. As in the game's performance mode, a screen dancer demonstrates the moves. In the rehearsal mode a voiceover dance teacher also offers verbal instruction and encouragement. This dance teacher has no human body; he is represented on-screen by a stylized boombox (Figure 1.4). All the teacher's technical and emotional feedback is conveyed through the voice, which is conventionally masculine and further marked by accent and vocabulary as African American, urban, and young-but-authoritative. The boombox is an emblem of old school hip-hop street culture, and it speaks in hip-hop vernacular.

The boombox has a voice, but no eyes. Indeed, the artist's choice of speaker configuration seems to deliberately avoid giving any impression of eyes. Yet one of the teacher's distinctive encouraging catchphrases is "I see you, I see you." Here *Dance Central* stages surveillance as recognition. "I see you" is an expression of praise from the dance teacher, and it draws a parallel to expressions like "I hear you" and "I feel you," which convey empathy and respect. "I see you" says your performance is so good, so convincing, that it has broken the fourth wall. You have transcended the TV screen and the Kinect lens, merging virtual and actual performance spaces.

Figure 1.4: Miss Aubrey dances beside the *Dance Central* boombox, known to fans as "Boomy." Detail from a player-produced gameplay video (AverageAsianDude 2012). (Screenshot by the author.)

I previously glossed "I see you" as a contact-call from the edge of the playground or the side of the pool, a virtual tether from parent to child. Spoken by a teacher in an approving tone, it implies attention and conditional praise from a benevolent authority figure. Spoken in a racially marked voice, this phrase also calls attention to itself as an African American idiom (though not all players will recognize it as such). Expressions of mutual recognition hold special power in communities with long histories of marginalization and structural oppression; acknowledgments like "I hear you," "I feel you," and "I see you" can also serve as bridges of affinity across diverse populations who have been rendered invisible by race, gender, sexuality, class, and/or disability. This is how game design decisions enculturate surveil-lance: A recorded voice declaring "I see you" accomplishes crucial affective labor, converting being watched by a machine into a virtual relationship with a black male dance teacher whose approval might authenticate your dancing. The nature of that relationship will vary depending on each player's own identifications and history.

But exactly who has seen you? Every so often, when you're struggling to get full credit for a move, the teacher voice consoles you by exclaiming, "This game is lying!" The teacher voice is not the voice of the Kinect or the game code. He is someone/something different, your ally and guide, a specter who "can 'see but not be seen' thanks to our embodied knowledge of how to attend to appearances" (Schneider 2011:110). He is the genie inside the boombox—an index of both hip-hop authenticity and technological nostalgia. In the first two *Dance Central* games, the voice was recorded by Arthur Inasi, a senior sound designer at Harmonix; he was not a named character. In *Dance Central 3*, the R&B artist Usher took over this voice role as part of an endorsement partnership. His celebrity status substantially shifted the terms of the teacher's implied relationship with players, who could now imagine being "seen" by Usher. But spoken by either voice, "This game is lying!" is a reminder that the seemingly impartial tracking technology is also both imperfect and inhuman. Rushed to market when it was barely out of beta, the Kinect *might* accurately assess whether your elbow is out of alignment, but it definitely *can't* know whether you're really a great dancer.

This seed of doubt can take root and spread. Should players trust the Kinect, trust the boombox teacher, or rely on the evidence provided by their own senses? GamePro.com reviewer AJ Glasser explored this issue at length, putting it front and center in her launch-day review of the first *Dance Central* release:

> Dance Central asks a lot of you as a player. Not only do you have to get up off your couch, somehow create six to eight feet of space in your living room for Kinect to register your coordinated flailing as "dance moves," and *gulp* actually dance, you also have to have faith in yourself. That last bit is something no video game ever asked of me before and I'm not sure if I delivered.
>
> Here's what I liked about Dance Central: It lied to me. For the most part, the only feedback I had from the game came in the form of a glowing circle that widens or shrinks to tell me how much I'm scoring on a move, an occasional red glow on a character's body part to tell me my corresponding body part wasn't matching up, or an aggressively positive street-talking boom box making excuses for my failures in tutorial mode ("Aw, this game is lying!" etc). . . .
>
> This is what's actually wrong with Dance Central—it doesn't trust me to push myself to do better. It's almost like Harmonix knows gamers have trouble with coordination and rhythm outside of finger movements and the occasional arm-swing and is doing its best to trick gamers into thinking that dancing is not that hard. . . . I don't feel like I really danced the song, I just feel like I stumbled through it. And I feel worse for having the game patronize me with a four-star rating and a happy hip hop dancer yelling "Yo, yo, yo, that was off the hook!" (Glasser 2010)

Glasser's review includes a photograph of herself playing *Dance Central*. It is taken from the Kinect's perspective, like the in-game souvenir snapshots. Caught in an off-kilter speed-skating posture, she looks flushed and disheveled; a long strand of hair has escaped her ponytail and bisects her face. She is dancing in front of an office desk cluttered with papers, coffee cups, tangles of cable, and action figures. Her brow is furrowed, her mouth tight. Point taken: This photograph depicts a radically unhip performance, with no markers of "off the hook" virtuosity. Tom Hoggins, the

London *Telegraph* reviewer, also made much of the gap between the game's evaluation and that of a human observer: "After a few songs I was getting some respectable scores, with *Dance Central*'s hip DJ telling me, in all seriousness, that I was 'on fire'. Tempered slightly by the love of my life collapsing into a fit of giggles at my uncoordinated attempts at heel flicks" (Hoggins 2010). But both reviewers ultimately awarded the game high marks. Hoggins praised *Dance Central* for "breaking down the introverts, simply by making the player feel good about themselves." Glasser gave a more expansive account of the game's social affordances and persuasive power: "It can bring my friends and coworkers together for thirty minutes while we try to figure out what a 'real' Cabbage Patch is. It can tempt non-gamers into giving it a go because unlike you maybe they actually can dance. And even if it can't wave a wand and make me a good dancer, it can inspire me to at least try" (Glasser 2010).

IN PRAISE OF SHAME

Dance Central makes a virtue of the Kinect's gazing powers, staging surveillance as recognition and binding that recognition to the core game theme of authenticity. Only a highly observant and sophisticated machine could give you the objective feedback required to help you cultivate genuine dance skills and gain the confidence to risk exposing yourself to human audiences. The marketing apparatus for *Just Dance* presents the public/private paradoxes of dance gameplay differently, toggling between emphasizing the private, guilty-pleasure affordances of the game and celebrating the social intimacy that can result from getting caught indulging in such pleasures. That is, *Just Dance* acknowledges shame and celebrates shamelessness. Like many talk therapists and life coaches in our current anxious era, it asks, "What's the worst that could happen?" As Sara Ahmed observes, "Shame as an emotion requires a witness," whether actually present or imagined (2004:105). This distinctive quality is what makes shame such a useful exemplar for Ahmed's theory of affect as an effect of the circulation of value among various objects and signs (45). Shame is generated by the social dynamics of witnessing and of trying to escape the judgment of witnesses: "Shame feels like an exposure—another sees what I have done that is bad and hence shameful—but it also involves an attempt to hide. . . . To be witnessed in one's failure is to be ashamed: To have one's shame witnessed is even more shaming. The bind of shame is that it is intensified by being seen by others *as* shame" (103). *Just Dance* capitalizes on these principles and celebrates the restorative potential waiting on the other side of shame. In Ahmed's terms, "Shame binds us to others in how we are affected by our failure to 'live up to' those others, a failure that must be witnessed, as well as be seen as temporary, in order to allow us to re-enter the family or community" (107).

Just Dance has no virtual dance teacher and offers very little evaluative feedback, so here the gaze of other humans is the primary driver for shame. In typical gameplay settings observers can only watch the player from behind or from the side, since they cannot come between the player and the screen/sensor apparatus. This configuration resonates with Ahmed's discussion of how shame involves "the de-forming and re-forming of bodily and social spaces, as bodies 'turn away' from the others who witness the shame" (103). *Just Dance* players are automatically turned away from onlookers, facing a different surveillance system—but one with reas-suringly limited capacities. Every 3 minutes, it is someone else's turn for exposure. When the song ends, dancers and witnesses exchange places.

In a series of making-of videos posted to YouTube to promote *Just Dance 3*, cre-ative director Grégoire Spillman said that the series was developed for

> 30-year-olds who don't have time to go out clubbing, people who like dancing but lack courage, people who need a bit of inspiration. . . . It's a swimming pool, you can go there to be sporty or just sit on the side and watch. You can take part in a competition. And one of the most fun things is to push someone in who doesn't necessarily want to put their toe in the water. That's what Just Dance does really well. When someone's not quite sure and gets pushed into the pool of Just Dance, something special happens. (Ubisoft 2011)

The theme of watching from the margins and then being enticed or pushed into the swimming pool was already present in the marketing materials for *Rayman Raving Rabbids* (Ubisoft 2006), the Wii game that first established the core elements of *Just Dance* gameplay. In a promotional trailer video, two kids enthusiastically explore some of the *Raving Rabbids* mini-games while their disaffected grandfather sits next to them on the couch reading a newspaper (IGN 2011). The kids seem to be a brother and sister rather than two friends, based on their age difference and contrast in personal styles. The presence of a live-in grandparent and the sleekly modern liv-ing room furniture hint at a European cultural context (a reminder that Ubisoft is a French game company), but there is no spoken dialogue in the trailer, allowing the ad to present a pan-Euro/American portrait of white middle-class domestic leisure. The girl, on the cusp of adolescence, is a black-clad goth with spectacular spiky hair; at the beginning of the trailer she sits on the couch looking bored as her more conventional-looking younger brother enters the room and picks up the Wii controllers. He quickly becomes immersed in high-intensity play, wielding the Wii Remote and Nunchuck in both hands. The girl is soon sucked into the action as well; she grabs the controllers from her brother, delights in the game's character and costume options, and swings her hips in a circle as she lassos the remote over her head to knock out advancing enemies in the gameworld.

Here we have a stereotypically gendered division of appealing features in a game that promises fun for the whole family. But viewers don't learn anything about the dancing mini-game until the stinger section, a surprise ending tacked on after the "Rayman Coming Soon" title screen has signaled the apparent conclusion of the trailer. The grandfather sneaks into the living room under cover of night; as he enters, we hear him shush a fussy baby on the verge of waking, emphasizing the riskiness of this clandestine mission. He picks up the Wii controller, selects a female game character with a gray beehive hairdo and hot-pink granny glasses, and begins dancing around the dark room to a disco beat. The ad's viewers now play the role of the children, who have surely been awakened by the music and must be spying from the edge of the room. What do they think of Grandpa's dance skills and unbridled enthusiasm for a Nintendo game? The trailer doesn't tell us, but if *Rayman Rabbids* could bring together this sister and brother we can only expect that it might also foster intergenerational family bonding in the light of day, once Grandpa's guilty pleasure has been revealed. Meanwhile, in a bit of humorous hyperbole, the dancing grandpa also stands in for the target demographic of "30-year-olds who don't have time to go out clubbing"—adults with increasing work and family responsibilities, more likely to be up all night with the baby than out on the town, just starting to feel "old" for the first time.

Like *Rayman Rabbids* and most other Wii and Kinect games, *Just Dance* and *Dance Central* were designed and marketed with social play contexts in mind—not only formal multiplayer options but also individual gameplay that would engage the attention of onlookers, structured by short play episodes that allow for frequent turn-taking. Drawing on their own experience trying out these games at home or in the office, industry reviewers were immediately attuned to how dance games could convert humiliation into social intimacy. This process hinges on courage and trust: As an IGN reviewer wrote, "It takes a special kind of bravery to get up in front of a group of friends and dance around like a crazy person" (Clements 2010). That bravery then results in a special kind of bond; those who participate in the gameplay session have both made themselves vulnerable and acquired the power to shame each other. A reviewer for 1up.com testified to this risk: "As a true testament to the level of hilarity the game provides, 'Do not post these photos on Facebook,' echoed throughout the duration of game play" (Troup 2010). I heard similar accounts from many players; in an interview, one player described the special satisfaction he derived from "the camaraderie where you can look kind of stupid in front of somebody. . . . Because you laugh at yourself and you look stupid, but because you're with people who you can look stupid in front of, the looking stupid doesn't take away from the experience" (post-gameplay interview, July 31, 2013).

Ubisoft producer Florian Granger suggested that *Just Dance* was simply building on an inherent quality of social dance: "Dancing with someone has this weird effect: It's like you know him or her in an intimate way or share a secret together somehow" (Parkin 2010). But reviewers and players have highlighted the more specific experience of dancing *badly* together: barely stumbling through a routine, transgressing the norms for what your particular body is supposed to do, and generally embracing the flamboyant silliness that characterizes the *Just Dance* aesthetic. As a reviewer for Videogamer.com wrote of *Just Dance 2*, "One reason it works so well is because the moves are absolutely ridiculous. There is simply no way for two fat men to look cool when trying to pirouette around each other in Vampire Weekend's A-Punk, for instance, but seeing as it's so outlandish you don't have to worry about looking like a pleb" (Gaston 2010). Meanwhile, the screen dancers move with silky fluidity but do their part to maintain the absurdity quotient by cavorting with brightly colored mermaids, crocodiles, astronauts, and other fantastical characters in surreal cartoon settings.

With its focus on authenticity and mastery, *Dance Central* seems to take dance more seriously and cultivates a cooler aesthetic, affiliating itself with contemporary global hip-hop dance culture (DeFrantz 2014). Partisans of the series often express their distaste for *Just Dance* along these lines. For instance, in a thread on the *Dance Central* player forums, a frequent poster named Lauson1ex suggested that comparing the two series is like "comparing an artificial, decorative apple with a real, edible apple." He went on to post links to several *Just Dance* videos on YouTube, explaining, "Just Dance is just silly and plain embarrassing. . . . I couldn't feel comfortable doing *any* of these, not even in the privacy of my own residence while alone, let alone in public with friends. It seems as though they craft these dances/costumes on purpose, to humiliate and embarrass you in front of your friends at parties. . . . This is just shameful" (DanceCentral.com 2012c). But *Dance Central* also invokes celebrations of shamelessness and social risk-taking, by requiring players to turn their bodies over to the game choreographers as they channel unfamiliar movement styles and work to master complicated routines. Even players with substantial prior dance experience often look like badly manipulated marionettes during a first attempt at a new song. Again, reviewers highlight the social potential of such "flailing." As *Telegraph* reviewer Tom Hoggins writes of his gameplay session with his wife, "But however much it looked like I was in the middle of a nervous breakdown during Push It by Salt-n-Pepa, the point is that I was dancing, and *Dance Central* had us in giggles the entire time" (Hoggins 2010).

Others draw attention to a transformative progression, as they come to "own" their dancing: "At this point, Dance Central isn't even a guilty pleasure anymore. I played it so much and loved it so hard that the series is no longer that shameful secret I had to keep from my family and friends" (Dyer 2012). For some, this achieved "shamelessness" is a reclamation of childhood freedoms:

> As a hyperactive third grader with a penchant for hamming it up, I had no shame publicly recreating the carefully choreographed moves of the Fly Girls. I relentlessly rewound Bell Biv DeVoe's cassette single "Poison" until the tape was reduced to a tangled mess (symbolic of my dance moves, I'm sure) in an attempt to learn the way of the Fly Girl. I was the tender age of eight, the world (or shall I say, the dance floor) was my oyster.
>
> So naturally, I couldn't pass up the opportunity to try Dance Central; self-awareness had tamed my ability to dance carefree, but a wild energy longed to pop, lock, and drop it without reservation. In reviewing this game, dancing became my new job, and there was no reason to hide from the exhilaration and hilarity of unrefined coordination. (Troup 2010)

For this reviewer, it was an official work assignment that provided the cover required to experiment with that long-lost "wild energy" despite the risk of looking ridiculous. (I can relate, having attended numerous Zumba classes at my local gym in the name of research.) For many other players, the gaming context itself provides sufficient cover; rules, point-scoring mechanisms, competition, and progressive challenges frame a safe space for performing under the watchful, evaluating eyes of both machines and humans. But one can also abandon cover and celebrate shameless dancing for its own sake—particularly if it might be regarded as shamefully *bad* dancing in one way or another. This anti-mastery doctrine calls on players to take one for the team, sacrificing their dignity for the sake of turning a public stage into a shared intimate sphere, leveraging risk to generate trust.

Dance Central promises that it can teach you to dance well; *Just Dance* instead promises that it can teach you that it's okay to dance badly. Indeed, *Just Dance* goes further, implying that dancing badly might be more fun, satisfying, and praiseworthy than dancing well. Daring to "flail" becomes a mark of personal courage and a generous contribution to the collective stockpile of fuel for the game's engine of social intimacy. This valorization of shame resonates with the contemporary phenomenon of the "epic fail," which Harmony Bench characterizes as "a failure that is so complete and so miserable as to have been previously unimaginable," with the potential to "become a 'win' in its own right . . . [and] rival skillful execution" (2013:139). Bench draws attention to how the spectacular epic failures in viral dance videos circulating on YouTube often hinge on "gender fails" and homophobic or queer performances; the dance repertoires featured in *Just Dance* and *Dance Central* also afford ample opportunities for "race fails" (see Chapter 2). When dancing feels shameful, that shame can be temporary in part because it can be converted into humor at another's expense, reconfirming one's own sense of self and affiliations. I will return to these implications of the celebration of courageous shame in the coming chapters.

HIDING IN PLAIN SIGHT

In the summer of 2011, I contacted and interviewed seven *Dance Central* players who were particularly active and popular in the YouTube-based player community. I was surprised to encounter players who had attracted tens of thousands of views for their YouTube channels but who told me that their local friends and family weren't aware of their *Dance Central* videos. Several interviewees also described themselves as too shy to dance in public. Riffraff, a Canadian player who uploaded over 130 dance gameplay videos between 2010 and 2013, described his initial process of "testing the waters" by posting a single video to YouTube. He told me, "The first 12 hours were probably the most tense for me when I put that video up because I was like, 'If I get a negative review, I'm out. I am shutting this down. I don't want to be this kind of public persona. I don't want to be that guy that gets sent over to thousands of other people . . . ridiculing the inanity of my performance or the gall that I would have to put this stuff online" (phone interview, August 24, 2011). By

Figure 1.5: Riffraff's gameplay video of the *Dance Central 3* routine for Carly Rae Jepsen's "Call Me Maybe" (riffraff67 2012). (Screenshot by the author.)

2016, his YouTube channel had attracted over 19,600 subscribers and accumulated nearly 7 million views. (See Figure 1.5.)

Even after Riffraff received a positive response to his early videos, put some effort into tags for search-engine optimization, and built up a group of loyal viewers, he also noted that no one on YouTube knew his real name, and he said he felt too old to go to hip-hop dance classes anymore. As he put it, "It is a weird thing, right? I mean like I'm fine with being on stage in front of 50,000 people, but if I'm in a room with five other people, then all of a sudden, I'm awkward." Another player, DRAGNARON, an accounting student in Mexico, told me that he "can't dance at clubs with friends or family," has never taken dance classes, and is "really, really shy." (See Figure 1.6.) DRAGNARON started posting *Dance Central* gameplay videos at the urging of other players online, after he "got nice scores on the game Leaderboards." He described the motivating force of online comments: "The response has been amazing, with many positive comments that keep me going, that's why I go all out every time. I'm also glad that my videos help people to get some of the moves right and improve their skills!" (survey response, Miller 2013a).

Dance games offer these players a curiously public privacy, the ability to hide in plain view from the potential humiliations of dance (cf. Lange 2008 on other "publicly private" YouTube practices). Their camouflage is complex and multidimensional: It includes the dance repertoire, the gaming context, the multiple pseudonyms used across various online platforms, and the reassuringly vast sea of YouTube content. By submitting their bodies to someone else's choreography, players can disavow creative responsibility for their moves. By pursuing this activity in the context of a game, they can say they are only dancing in this way to these songs for the sake of high scores, reaching the next level, or achieving fitness goals.

Figure 1.6: DRAGNARON's gameplay video of the *Dance Central 3* routine for LMFAO's "Sexy and I Know It" (DRAGNARON 2012). He includes the note "The first time I danced to this routine I was laughing so hard I couldn't complete it!" (Screenshot by the author.)

By cultivating an audience of fellow players online, they can take refuge in a community of practice where other players fill their comment threads with positive feedback and technical discourse about the repertoire. (However, the nature of that feedback may vary depending on a player's perceived gender, race, and/or sexual orientation; see Chapter 2.)

Many aspects of this hiding-in-plain-view also structure face-to-face social gaming situations. Players dance with friends in front of the Wii or Kinect in ways that they would otherwise never dance in front of each other. On YouTube and in living rooms, these public/private dynamics can generate unexpected intimacy. Kirk Hamilton, a writer for the gaming website Kotaku, vividly described such a scenario in a piece called "On Playing Dance Central 2 While Male":

"You know, I've got Dance Central 2 here, let's play that!" I said, pointing to the shiny, colorful box of Harmonix's Kinect-only dancing game.

"Sure," Dan said, though in retrospect he was doubtless entirely unsure what he was getting himself into. And so we played Dance Central 2, two dorky bros in the mid-afternoon, standing in front of the TV and swinging our hips to "Toxic" and "Bad Romance." It was funny, it was dumb; it was uniquely uncomfortable.... [Dance Central] requires an entirely different sort of physical interaction than most other video games. It was as though Dan and I had been sitting around pondering what to do and one of us had said, "You know what? Let's go dancing together, just you and me at the club!" Suffice to say, that is not something either of us would likely ever suggest....

Dance Central 2 is a bit uncomfortable . . . but it's also funny, and fun. In fact, the discomfort of the situation is what makes it fun. (Hamilton 2012)

This account brings us back to how dance games frame performance and orient multiple screen bodies and human bodies in the play space (cf. Landay 2012). *Dance Central* privileges a frontal orientation to both the Kinect sensor and the TV screen; these two dorky bros were swinging their hips to "Toxic" side by side but would never have turned to face each other unless they chose to do so during the freestyle section. In the course of typical gameplay, each could observe and evaluate the other's performance only by looking at his partner's tiny inset silhouette on the opposite edge of the screen or by glancing at his accumulating numerical score. Meanwhile, they would be aware that they were each performing the same hip-swinging choreography; as long as they both kept dancing, they would be holding up their end of a social bargain, a mutual promise to get through this awkward and transgressive experience together in the name of fun. In my gameplay/interview sessions, I observed that even in two-player situations, players' eyes often don't stray from their own on-screen character until they have played a particular song several times, which means they have demonstrated a certain investment in the material. This kind of side-by-side play has a virtual variant in the form of YouTube split-screen collaborations; Riffraff and DRAGNARON produced such a video, bringing together their separate gameplay sessions in Canada and Mexico. (See Figure 1.7.)

At first glance, this account might seem to suggest that hiding-in-plain-view performances rely on taking creativity out of the equation: Players can mirror the on-screen dancers like automata and find safety in conformity. But the situation is far more complicated. Performing choreography always involves elements of creative

Figure 1.7: A transnational collaboration video of the *Dance Central 3* routine for Panjabi MC's "Beware of the Boys" (RiffraffDC 2012). (Screenshot by the author.)

interpretation, and when players post or seek out YouTube videos of *Dance Central* gameplay, they are attuned to the differences in individual performances. In addition to virtual collaborations, many players create split-screen videos that juxtapose their own dancing with that of the on-screen character, a clear invitation to comparative analysis. YouTube further encourages a comparative orientation by offering up lists of related videos. Moreover, as Kirk Hamilton observed, dance games ask players to move in ways that may feel unfamiliar, viscerally uncomfortable, or precariously nonconforming. As I will discuss in Chapter 2, the *Dance Central* games were designed to encourage experimental performance and interpretive reflection with respect to players' embodied experience of gender, sexuality, and race. Other dance games might not share this agenda at the design stage, but they nevertheless stage visceral encounters with gendered and racialized choreographic repertoires, inviting players to imagine how it might feel to dance in someone else's body.

The examples in this chapter begin to outline a range of dance gameplay practices, including the diverse pleasures and perils of private, public, side-by-side, and hiding-in-plain-view performance and spectatorship. Dance gameplay cultivates particular techniques of looking and binds them to techniques of moving. Practicing this kinesthetic vision also leads players to reflect on their proprioception, becoming conscious of the quality of their own bodily motion. Engaging in repetitive trial-and-error as they work their way through patterned choreography, they learn to carry out analytical self-assessments that are shaped by each game's available feedback mechanisms. As I will discuss in the coming chapters, these processes also rely on and re-channel other modes of sensory experience, particularly musical listening. At heart, dance games are games of synesthesia. They engage us in the playful work of "transform[ing] the effects of one sensory mode into those of another," thereby generating "virtual synesthetic perspectives" (Massumi 2002:35)—new realms of potential experience, both sensory and social.

The distinctive technical affordances of the Wii and Kinect make a big difference in how this process unfolds, through their formative influence on basic game design as well as how their perceived surveillance capacities intersect with players' feelings about dancing in front of an audience. Both systems have evoked anxieties about the trustworthiness of motion-sensing technologies, with respect to personal privacy and technical accuracy—two sides of the same player-agency coin, the currency of control. Each system assuages those anxieties differently. The Wii's relatively limited surveillance capabilities offer reassurance in terms of privacy, freeing players to "just dance," while the Kinect's promise to "see you" and analyze your entire moving body offers comfort to those anxious about their dance skills. Meanwhile, both *Just Dance* and *Dance Central* seem to extend some version of the "You are the controller" promise, with a twist: Players can't fully control each game's technical apparatus or the performances of the screen dancers, but they can learn to control their own bodies and self-regard. And both games also present a maxim about giving up some control: If you want feedback—whether it be for the sake of social relations or technical mastery—you have to make yourself vulnerable.

Dance games are intimacy machines. They run on the push and pull of recognition and misrecognition, control and consent, self-examination and efforts to comprehend others' embodied experience. They encourage players to explore the risks and rewards of self-exposure. Like streaming music, video, and online dating services, dance games promise an endless supply of new opportunities for intimacy. All of these services say: Let us recognize you. The better you let us get to know you, the more satisfying the experiences we will be able to offer. They stage data collection as recognition: "I see you, I see you!" They invite users to develop new relationships with their own sensing bodies, other humans, and interactive technologies, to explore each relationship's potential for transient pleasure and/or long-term commitment—and to pay for the privilege, piecemeal or by subscription.

⊕ ⊕ ⊕

"Three times now. You got this? 5, 6, 7, 8. . . . You killed that!" But I know I didn't, because I wasn't even moving. I hit pause and scroll the video back, studying the tiny white silhouette of the player who posted this video to YouTube. She's good, gets most of the moves right on the first try—though who knows how much she practiced before making a video of her practice session for public consumption. Her silhouette is only an inch tall on my computer screen, but sometimes it feels easier to follow her than the game's animated dancer. I also get to soak up all the praise she's earning from the teacher voice. I ripped this video from YouTube in 2011 so I could practice the routine in my office.

The Lady Gaga loop begins again. "5, 6, 7, 8. . . . Aw yeah, lookin' fly!" The player has a little trouble with the Hip Swing & Grab. The voice gets more specific: "Swing, grab, swing, grab. Pull, open, twist, down!" I'm lost. The player signals to the Kinect to slow it down. The voice says, "All right, goin' into slo-mo. Let's chop it and screw it." This game is so hipper-than-thou, I think, but it's an interesting connection—slowed-down choreography tied to the production conventions of "chopped and screwed" hip-hop remixes. "5, 6, 7, 8. . . . Swing-grab-left, swing-grab-right! Step, right, left, together!" My faceless fellow player is getting the hang of the move and brings it back to full speed. Suddenly a black screen with white text flashes up: "Sadly, my hard drive filled up at this point and the video stopped recording. Just in time to hit YouTube's 15 minute cap! More to come soon".

In 2014, I go back to the original YouTube video to check my reference data. The player, formerly known as mDaWg0, has apparently complied with Google's persistent requests to display the same name (often one's legal name) across its various services. His name now shows as Mike Calfin, and this video has collected about 53,000 views since 2010 (Calfin 2010). Glancing through his 206 uploads, I can see that what I took for a skirt in the player silhouette was probably knee-length baggy shorts. In the "About" text, he notes, "I'm still not able to put the whole song together, but these moves as individuals are INSANELY fun to perform. I could play through break it down mode several times and not get tired of it."

CHAPTER 2
Dancing Difference/Gaming Gender

The Kinect sensor bows its motorized head, scanning me up and down, assessing my body's dimensions and position in relation to my game space. My silhouette appears in a small frame in the corner of the screen, a miniature shadowbox theater. "Wave for Kinect," the screen text suggests. I comply, and a cartoon hand appears, moving frenetically over the screen. I calibrate my motion until the cartoon hand hovers over the *Dance Central 2* icon, and the game loads. Presented with a song list ranked in order of difficulty, I choose "Reach," by Atlantic Connection and Armanni Reign (2011). The default game character for this song is Bodie, a white surfer/bro type with shaggy blond hair, an athletic build, and a friendly grin. As the song begins, Bodie appears at a sunset beach party, surrounded by friends.

Bodie starts to dance, and I try to mirror his movements. His body is loose-limbed, his gestures expansive. A series of flashcards scrolls down one side of the screen, providing an icon and a name for each upcoming move. As moves begin to repeat, I can use the cards to anticipate the choreography rather than always trailing Bodie by microseconds. The first move is called the Frat Step, and the name reorients my body: My shoulders broaden, my chest puffs up, my knees and elbows open out wide. I think of the guys who spread their knees out on the subway, unapologetically claiming space. The next move is the Select, a hand wave that seems to say "Bring me bottle service over here!" Bodie is relaxed and confident; I channel his easygoing entitlement.

A brief freestyle section arrives, and Bodie's animated body gives way to my abstracted silhouette. I keep doing the Frat Step while I try to code-switch to dance-floor creativity. Camera-shutter sound effects alert me to virtual paparazzi, and a few still images of my performance flash across the screen—souvenirs that I can revisit or share later. Bodie returns and we finish the song together. He grins, and speaks to me for the first time: "Hey, watch out everybody, there's a new contender in town!" The scoring screen comes up, displaying a star rating, a numerical score, and a photograph of me striking the final pose. In the photo, my brow is furrowed in concentration. My shabby around-the-house clothes and cluttered basement TV room seem hilariously distant from any beach party.

I move to the next song in the list, "Real Love" (Mary J. Blige, 1992). Now the default screen dancer is Miss Aubrey, a tall, white, curvaceous redhead whose ice-queen bearing is only slightly undermined by her close-fitting sailor-suit romper. Her routine starts with the Old Bop: legs together, alternating knee bends with cocked hips, arm motions constrained in front of the body. Then there's the wide-stepping Boardwalk move, followed closely by the Bunny Hill: legs together again, a hop-swivel-crouch that presents her (and my) rear end in profile, as though posing for a ski-resort fashion shoot. This routine involves more hip action, asymmetrical postures, and diagonal motion. Bodie's blocky power stances have been replaced with flirtatious freeze-frame poses. As I come to the end, I wonder what Miss Aubrey might say to me, but she remains silent. It could be a programming bug, or did I score so poorly that she won't acknowledge me?

I decide to try "Real Love" again, but this time I change the on-screen dancer to Mo, a wiry black man in hip urban streetwear. We do the dance again. It is exactly the same, the same motion-capture data mapped to a different animated skeleton and skin. But the femme hip swivels seem to change their character on Mo's b-boy body, and the Shoulder Pep now invokes an old-school hip-hop move. The No Worries—crossed hands fanning downward in front of the chest—projects a dismissive non-chalance infused with cool masculinity. Mo and I are making it look easy, casually fending off an ineffectual challenger. I score better this time. Mo approves: "That technique? Oh, it is just too sweet." (Gameplay notes, June 2012.)

In the last chapter I discussed some of the perceptual techniques that players bring to bear in digital dance gameplay, with an emphasis on kinesthetic vision: watching a body in motion while trying to simultaneously mirror its actions, aided by the coordinating auditory timeline provided by the music. This home-fieldwork vignette introduces another layer of perception, whereby players attend to the visible, audible, and kinesthetic identity markers of the screen dancer, draw meaningful connections from the confluence of music, movement style, and model dancing body, and make comparisons based on their experience of their own moving/marked bodies.

Popular dance genres transmit and reinforce established norms for moving one's body in ways considered appropriate to one's identity. Dance practices often articulate a bodily habitus that "matches" an individual's intersectional profile of gender, sexuality, race, age, class, and ability, while dance-floor interactions model possible social relations. (See, e.g., Desmond 1997, Desmond 2001, Simonett 2001, Bosse 2007.) At the same time, dance may harbor the capacity to denaturalize these identity categories, by highlighting the learned, stylized, citational, and presentational qualities of bodily practice. As Susan Foster observes, "Dancing dramatizes the separation between the anatomical identity of the dancer and its possible ways of moving" (1998:7). This separation is at the heart of what Jonathan Bollen calls "queer kinesthesia," a concept that describes how the regulation of gender and sexuality "may be negotiated through movement, through a marshaling of kinesthetic resources that disarticulate ways of moving from the demand for consistently gendered performance" (2001:309). Writing about social relations on queer dance floors, Bollen raises a critical question for dance games and motion-sensing interfaces: "What would it take to register what matters about a body in terms of the body's experience of moving, its capacity for action, its choreographic repertoire?" (301).

The transmission of dance practices relies on imitative repetition—the acquisition of kinesthetic resources—but also presents opportunities for repetition with a difference, whether it be through deliberate experimentation, fortuitous discovery, or frustrating failure. As Carrie Noland puts it, "The kinesthetic knowledge gained through gestural performance both permits the acquisition of these durable norms and introduces the possibility of realizing a potential beyond them" (2009:15, cf. Gibbs 2010). Standards for what counts as success/failure or sameness/difference may be linked to the kind of body that undertakes the movement; for instance, if a dance move has a gendered or racialized association, then a kinesthetically faithful repetition by a differently gendered or racialized body might not be considered "the same" at all. Meanwhile, subtle changes also accrue through circulation: Imagine the gradual blurring of a series of low-fidelity copies-of-copies, the audible artifacts introduced by sound reproduction technologies, or the signs of wear on objects that pass from hand to hand.

Such processes play a role in the transmission of any embodied repertoire, but special circumstances apply when dancing bodies circulate through mass-mediated representations (Blanco Borelli 2014). Screen bodies present themselves as models for private imitation in a sphere set apart from the norms of public social dance practices. Thus they lend themselves to experimental forms of repetition in which practitioners engage *with* difference, trying on unfamiliar kinesthetic styles— feeling where they fit like a second skin and where they flap awkwardly away from the accustomed body, where they flatter and where they create unsightly bulges, where they bind and where they allow unexpected freedom of movement. These techniques of somatic prospecting have been integrated into contemporary dance pedagogy in a range of styles; teachers engage students in "exploring the body's possibilities" and "questioning through our body" by "dancing like someone else . . . replicat[ing] movement in order to challenge their usual way of moving" (Buck et al. 2012:243, 246–47). Dance games present similar challenges, and players voluntarily take them on—but not necessarily in the service of cultivating dance technique.

This chapter proceeds in two parts. I will first offer an overview of the domains of difference that dance games present as zones for playful performance, with an emphasis on race and gender. I will then move on to an analysis of how the *Dance Central* series choreographs gender. *Dance Central* offers an illuminating example of what happens when game developers attempt a political intervention within the strictures of designing a mainstream commercial product. Matt Boch, the lead designer of the first *Dance Central* game and later the project director for the franchise, has been an outspoken advocate on issues of diversity and inclusion in the game industry. He and his colleagues at Harmonix Music Systems brought this perspective to their work on a series that revolves around embodied engagement with difference. As Boch noted, "What's interesting about dance is that it's incredibly performative, and it implicates the body in a way a lot of other video game-type interactions don't. . . . We implicate the players' identity in their body in a novel way, in an unfamiliar way" (Alexander 2012). While all games that incorporate contemporary popular music and dance styles necessarily traffic in signs of gender, race, and other social identity categories, *Dance Central* offers a case study of special interest because its developers deliberately advanced a particular theory of gender through their design choices. I explore the consequences of those choices: What happens when designers enlist players in putting theory into practice?

I. DANCING DIFFERENCE

Dance games present idiosyncratic archives of choreographic styles, including elements drawn from hip-hop, Latin dance, aerobics, cheerleading, music videos, club dances, YouTube dance crazes, and social dances of past decades. Foster offers a useful basic principle for considering such an archive: "Any notion of choreography contains, embodied within it, a kinesthesis, a designated way of experiencing physicality and movement that, in turn, summons other bodies into a specific way of feeling towards it" (2011:2). That is, dance games archive not only motion-capture data but also ideas about how certain kinds of bodies are supposed to move— sometimes with direct reference to cultural/historical sources, and sometimes obscuring those sources by lifting a gestural repertoire out of context. By compiling collections of gestures and sounds that already circulate in popular culture as signs of gender, race, and sexuality, dance games give players the tools to stage domestic song-and-dance variety shows with strong family resemblances to two other venerable popular performance traditions: blackface minstrelsy and drag shows.

Dance games follow in a long tradition of popular media that bring the performing bodies of people of color into domestic spaces as models for private imitation. From their earliest days, popular music recordings, radio, television, and web-based streaming video have all played vital roles in producing and transmitting racially marked performance, including blackface, black-voice, and black-body repertoires and their "Latin" and Orientalist counterparts. Representations of racially marked musicians and dancers entered domestic spaces through mass distribution channels even before the advent of commercial sound recording, through the sheet music industry that supplied amateur parlor musicians with the latest hits from "coon shouters," Orientalist vaudeville shows, and touring minstrel troupes in the late 19th and early 20th centuries. In his book *Segregating Sound*, Karl Hagstrom Miller traces the emergence of a "musical color line" in American popular music in the decades around the turn of the 20th century, moving from a period when both black and white performers "regularly employed racialized sounds" without being expected to embody them to one when musical performance became linked to the newly dominant paradigm of biological racial difference—a connection reinforced by race-based market segmentation in the music industry (Miller 2010:4–5). Susan Manning traces a similar trajectory in American theater dance, from a "dominant convention" of "metaphorical minstrelsy" in the 1930s, "whereby white dancers' bodies made reference to nonwhite subjects," to "an emergent convention of black self-representation" after 1940, with African American dancers creating works "premised on black bodies representing black subjects" (Manning 2004:9–10). Today, racialized sounds and gestures still circulate as signs of musicians' and dancers' racial authenticity yet also function as detachable elements that can be employed for racial masquerade.

Minstrelsy remains a charged subject. It is a regular topic in my American music courses, and year after year I bear witness to the anxiety, shame, and anger that surfaces around the seminar table as students struggle to come to grips with the enduring legacy of a thriving entertainment industry based on pernicious racial stereotypes. In popular and scholarly writing about digital games, invoking blackface typically signals a devastating critique; for instance, elsewhere I have addressed the charge that *Grand Theft Auto: San Andreas* is "nothing more than [a] pixilated minstrel show" (Marriott 2004, discussed in Miller 2008b; see also Leonard 2005 on sports games). My aim here is different: By placing dance gameplay in this performance lineage, I do not mean to advance an incendiary takedown of dance games or their players but simply to acknowledge the history of the repertoires they circulate. Forms of racial masquerade have played a significant role in mainstream American music and dance entertainments since at least the 1820s, when Thomas Rice's "Jump Jim Crow" became a hit across the nation through both live blackface performance and mass-produced sheet music. Minstrel troupes and their repertoires also circulated transnationally, as emblems of both American popular culture and the emerging racialized category of "black music." Minstrelsy inspired numerous blackface performance practices in other parts of the world, and it influenced the global circulation and local adoption of subsequent American popular music exports, including jazz and hip-hop.[1] This history inevitably structures the sonic, visual, and gestural materials of dance games, as well as influencing players' engagements with these materials.

While dance games draw from a huge range of popular culture sources, music and dance moves with strong historical connections to African American, Latin Caribbean, and/or queer club cultures tend to dominate the mix. Key genres include disco, house, hip-hop, ballroom/vogue, and contemporary electronic dance music genres that incorporate salsa, merengue, cumbia, and dancehall rhythms. The screen dancers are the vehicles for these repertoires. Their virtual bodies come accessorized with their own collections of identity signs—including their voices, in the case of *Dance Central*—interpretable using a tool kit that includes conventional gender norms, systems of "racial sight" (Guterl 2013), and close listening to vocal accent, timbre, and speech rhythms, among other learned classification techniques. The available musical tracks also come loaded with connotations, both as individual songs and as curated playlists that players assess when considering whether a game's offerings line up with their own musical tastes. These evaluations of musical material and dance routines rely on the kinds of distinctions that have long delineated markets for popular music by race, gender, and generational cohort. For instance, when game industry and consumer reviewers repeatedly differentiate *Dance Central* and *Just Dance* by suggesting one franchise's dance-music playlist is weighted toward hip-hop and the other toward pop, they retread the musical color line established by the production and marketing of "race records" (Miller 2010). That same hip-hop/pop divide can also serve to invoke gender distinctions ("hard" vs. "girly," masculine authenticity vs. feminine artificiality), subcultural capital (underground vs. mainstream; see Thornton 1996), and generation gaps (contemporary club hits vs. disco favorites of an older generation). These links between musical styles, movement styles, and embodied identity categories are continually remade through practice and become "perceptual constructs . . . for reading bodies in motion" (Manning 2004:xv). We might ask, then, how dance game design and player experiences reconfirm or disrupt them.

Meet Your Screen Dancers

Most digital games that incorporate identity play give players considerable latitude in shaping the appearance of their avatars. Players typically select a male or female gender for their avatars and often choose from a menu of available "races," each with their own special capacities (Taylor 2006, Nardi 2010; see also Fine 1983 on earlier role-playing games). Additional character-customization features are common, including slider controls for changing facial features or body type; players engage extensively with "menu-driven identities" (Nakamura 2002) even before they embark on gameplay missions, much like actors getting into costume and character backstage before a show. As discussed in previous chapters, dance games present an entirely different model of avatar relations: Players do not direct the actions of the screen dancers and have little control over their embodied identity traits. Neither *Dance Central* nor *Just Dance* offers any identity menus or explicit gender-designated content, such as options for selecting masculine or feminine dance routines—despite the fact that players regularly requested such features, as I discuss below.[2] There is no character customization in *Just Dance*; in *Dance Central*, customization is limited to clothing options. However, like traditional avatars, the screen dancers bear signs of gendered and racialized identity, through their appearances, voices, and the movement repertoires they enact.

In *Just Dance*, players have no choice of screen dancer. Part of the fun of playing a new song is seeing what kind of dancer and scenario have been devised for it. The dancers include both humans and cartoonish animals; they appear as brightly costumed silhouettes with near-blank faces. All exposed human skin is colored white, with an important exception: In *Just Dance 2* and all subsequent games, each screen dancer has one brightly colored hand, corresponding to the player's hand holding the Wii remote. Despite the obscured facial features, whited-out skin, and absence of speaking voices, ample signs of gender and race remain, including costuming, body shapes, hairstyles, and hair movement patterns. Game choreography includes heteronormative dance-partner interactions for two-player songs, such as bows and curtsies matched to gender-conforming male and female costumes and body types. The eye-catching single glove and whitewashed facial features of the screen dancers also conjure the spirit of Michael Jackson, who might be considered the patron saint of dance games. As I learned through interviews and surveys, many players grew up watching and imitating Jackson's music video dance routines; in 2010 Ubisoft released a stand-alone dance game called *Michael Jackson: The Experience*, packaging a sequined glove with the launch edition (see Fritsch 2016).

The *Just Dance* screen dancers are vehicles for a kind of anonymous identification. The game was designed to encourage players to occupy these silhouettes, donning the costumes and acquiring the embodied skills of the screen dancers all at once. Alkis Argyriadis, the creative director for *Just Dance* as of 2014, told an industry interviewer that this effect was a matter of cognitive science: "It's what we call the power of perception, the fact that you can feel like it's you in the TV. The dancer on the screen is moving beautifully, but the basic movement [that you're doing] is the same. You can feel that you're doing it just like the dancer, because of the mirror effect. . . . That's one of the advantages of using real people, rather than animations" (MacDonald 2014). Argyriadis is invoking the theory of "mirror neurons," "a class of neuron that modulate[s] their activity both when an individual executes a specific motor act and when they observe the same or similar act performed by another individual" (Kilner and Lemon 2013:R1057). Whether or not *Just Dance* gameplay can indeed make players "feel that they're doing it just like the dancer," the design intentions are clear. The blank faces of the screen dancers are like the empty faceholes of a painted tableau made to stage tourist photos. Players are invited to imagine that they are peering out through these faces, their own bodies safely hidden, obscured by generic types painted in the broadest of strokes.

In the first song offered up by the original *Just Dance* game, a white woman in a hot-pink dress dances to Cyndi Lauper's "Girls Just Want to Have Fun" (1983), tossing a Lauper-esque mop of curls. Next, a black woman dances to Anita Ward's "Ring My Bell" (1979); her silhouetted Afro hairstyle "confirms the outlines of the racial body" (Guterl 2013:59), though the skin of her exposed arms and legs is whited-out like her face. Later a man sporting a '70s mustache and bellbottoms does disco moves, and a green alligator in a dapper naval uniform takes on Wilson Pickett's "Land of 1000 Dances" (1966). Players cannot go back and try "Ring My

Bell" with the mustache-man or the alligator. Couples songs or ensemble songs do offer one element of character choice: These songs always have two or four dancers on screen, even if only one person is playing the game, and each player must choose to be paired with one of the available screen bodies. But players cannot mix and match characters across songs and routines. Like a music video, each *Just Dance* song presents a unique, unchangeable performance by one or more specific screen dancers in a scenario devised for that song. This presentation reflects the production process for *Just Dance*: The dancing silhouettes are derived from videos of costumed human dancers in whiteface makeup who perform in front of a green screen. These video performances can then be digitally edited and transposed into fantastical graphic settings.

Dance Central was created using a different production process: Its screen dancers are animated characters whose movements are driven by motion-capture data derived from human performances. This means that the motion-capture data from a single human performer can be mapped onto a potentially infinite array of characters with distinctive body types, voices (recorded by voice actors), and multiple costume options. Producing animation based on 3-D motion-capture data is likely to be more time-consuming, labor-intensive, and expensive than digitally editing a video recording of a dance performance, but it also affords user options that might increase players' sense of agency and interactive engagement. *Dance Central* players can choose from a selection of characters, which might lead players to develop a relationship with one or more favorites, enriching their experience and increasing their emotional investment in this franchise. Character choice might also increase the repeat-play potential of each individual song by offering multiple versions of every screen-dance performance. The animation approach also supports the production of *Dance Central*'s interactive rehearsal mode, where individual routines are broken down move-by-move and recombined into longer subroutines at various difficulty levels (see Chapters 4 and 5).

Using motion-capture animation techniques immediately raises a fundamental design question for game developers: What kinds of motion will be mapped onto what kinds of bodies? If the visual appearance of a character, its ways of moving, and the sound of its voice are all independent elements, derived from different sources, then game designers are in the position of deciding how these identity traits should be combined and what range of combinations should be made available to players. *Dance Central*'s game characters were designed "to represent a wide range of archetypes and dance genres," as lead character artist Matt Perlot explained in a making-of blog post (Harmonix Music Systems 2011c). Mo, for example, the first character created for *Dance Central*, is marked as a black male archetype and representative of hip-hop not only by his brown skin tone, conventionally masculine body shape, and African American vocal accent, but by a hoodie that obscures his eyes. Perlot noted this decision was "controversial at first," but asserted that the hoodie "gave him a quirkiness that made him feel real." The blog post describes Mo's style as "influenced by West Coast B-boy aesthetics" and lists his imagined hobbies as "B-ball, battles, hopping turnstiles, chillin' with the boys." Additional characters vary slightly across game editions, but the core group is presented in five "crews" in *Dance Central 2*:

Riptide: white male Bodie, white/ethnically ambiguous female Emilia

Hi-Def: African American male Mo, Asian American male "child prodigy" Glitch

Flash4wrd: African American "big sister" Taye and "little sister" Lil' T

Lu$h: white female Miss Aubrey, Latino male Angel

The Glitterati: white gender-ambiguous identical twins Jaryn and Kerith

This collection of characters constitutes a Benetton-style utopian racial array that "awakens the senses to difference" (Guterl 2013:83). *Dance Central's* screen dancers are young, slim, conventionally attractive bodies whose racial/ethnic diversity is indexed by skin tone, hair texture/style, facial features, and vocal accent/idiom. The racial and ethnic composition of this group is extremely unusual for a mainstream commercial digital game. The 10 core characters include three African Americans, placed in "crews" that highlight key transmission contexts for hip-hop culture: a biological family crew and a multiracial "chosen family" b-boy crew. (Glitch represents the figure of the West Coast Filipino b-boy virtuoso, a key type in contemporary dance competition TV shows such as *America's Best Dance Crew*.) In a striking inversion of the tokenism that often constitutes "diversity" in game character line-ups, there is only one gender-conforming white male character. A promotional video draws parallels between the diversity of Harmonix staff and that of the characters: Chanel Thompson, an African American game choreographer, asserts, "If I can see someone that acts like me, talks like me, dances like me, I'm more likely to be more comfortable in who I am self-esteem-wise" (Harmonix Music Systems 2011a). Note that Thompson is referring to a relationship of recognition, not of role-playing; the video implies that this game might offer something special for players of color (see Chapter 5).

In general, the relationship between player and screen dancer in *Dance Central* is not meant to be one of identification. These animated characters are considerably more detailed and individually distinctive than the "real people" whose silhouetted bodies appear in *Just Dance*. While they represent archetypes, they also have personal quirks; their configuration into "crews" and some narrative elements imply personal relationships among the characters. In his public statements, lead designer Matt Boch often stressed that *Dance Central's* screen dancers are not traditional playable characters: "We wanted to make that very explicit, very clear: that they are them, you are you, the playspace is as big as your whole living room. . . . You're not being *represented by* that person—you're dancing *with* them" (Harmonix Music Systems 2011d, cf. Shaw 2012). Nevertheless, the established conventions of digital game design, the games' real-time multisensory feedback, and the embodied experience of mirroring the screen dancer all encourage players to approach *Dance*

Central's characters as avatars. These mixed cues have led players to imagine the screen dancer as an idealized mirror image, a teacher, a star musician dancing in a music video, a representation of the choreographer, or sometimes just another person on the dance floor at a club—a potential friend, rival, or romantic partner. This multivalent relationship between player and screen dancer is profoundly important when we consider what might happen when people perform choreography that indexes gender, sexuality, race, ethnicity, class, and musical taste—among other identity traits that implicate our embodied experience and the way we perform who we are in everyday life.

Race and Gender Discourse in Player Reviews

Although dance games present stylized representations of racial bodies and feature racialized musical and kinesthetic styles, direct references to race and ethnicity are few and far between in my archive of industry and consumer reviews, player forum discussions, and YouTube comment threads. Much of this material has passed through some form of moderation filter that might have resulted in the deletion of derogatory racial language, but even so, race-related discourse is conspicuously absent. For instance, I read roughly 900 Amazon.com consumer reviews of *Dance Central* (534 reviews) and *Dance Central 2* (363 reviews)—the complete set of reviews posted from November 2010 to July 2013—and encountered only a handful of references to race (Amazon.com 2013a, 2013b). There were no uses of the terms "black" or "African American." A single review referenced a black character by name (Mo) and also mentioned a "Latina boxing girl" character (Emilia); there were no other references to Latino/a or Hispanic ethnicity in any of the reviews, except via a few mentions of salsa moves or "Latin" songs. One reviewer mentioned trying out screen dancers of "both sexes and all races." Another objected to the game's "strongly sexual subject matter," citing songs about "pushing it or pumping it," and coupled these concerns with an assertion that "the graphics look like they were inspired by blaxploitation films and Fat Albert." Two reviewers used "ghetto" as a racial code word: One wrote that "some of the characters are too 'trashy' and some are too 'ghetto' "—a telling class/race distinction—while the other cautioned, "The instructor's ghetto talk is amusing, but not necessarily something I'd want kids picking up." Given *Dance Central's* exceptionally diverse character lineup, I was surprised to find that only about one-half of 1 percent of the reviews mentioned the race or ethnicity of the game characters.

A similarly small number of Amazon reviewers included references to their own race. All of them self-identified as white, and all of them linked their whiteness to poor dance skills. "An obese white-chick" wrote that she likes to think she has "rhythm, a little soul, a little shake to my groove thing" but then confessed flatly "I don't. Really." A review titled "Makes a white girl dance" begins, "I am not a dancer. Oh I wish I could be!" This reviewer recounted her initial reluctance to play in front of her friends "or even attempt the booty shaking songs." White men also made their lack of dancing prowess known: These reviewers included "a short little white guy with virtually zero dancing ability," an "old, uncoordinated Caucasian," a "happy, dancin' redneck" who stipulated that "no one and I mean no one besides the o'lady is gonna see the action as it takes place," and a reviewer who neatly summed up the essentialist logic at play here: "Being a big white guy, I'm not much of a dancer." In addition to these six white-identified reviewers, about a dozen others invoked the often-racialized trope of "having rhythm," but without direct reference to race. Most described themselves or a family member as *not* having rhythm, and they expressed varying opinions as to whether *Dance Central* could help them acquire it. A single reviewer mentioned racialized embodiment when describing "issues with the Kinect sensor," noting that the Kinect "doesn't always see my right side," possibly due to the room lighting, and that "it can't see my husband at all unless he ties his hair (massive afro) back. So that's a little weird. But if you have a normally shaped house, and non-extraordinary hair, you should be fine."

We could speculate about exactly why these 900 reviewers engage in or refrain from racial discourse, but it would be hard to draw persuasive conclusions without knowing more about them. I don't have statistics on their racial and ethnic self-identifications, nor do I know whether this subset of Amazon customers constitutes a representative sample of the several million people who purchased these two games through all retail channels. And this is only one aspect of the methodological challenge here; regardless of whether one is conducting interviews face-to-face or making a close reading of anonymous online reviews, it's a tricky business to build interpretive arguments based on the absence of discourse. Not a single Amazon reviewer refers to particular dance moves as "black" or "white," and no one explicitly raises the possibility that the games might teach a player to dance like a black person. Traces of these ideas do circulate in the reviews, but they are folded into references to racially coded musical genres, as when reviewers observe that *Dance Central* "is more hip hop than Just Dance but still very mainstream," or suggest that "[Dance Central] will let you live out your fantasy of being a hip hopper in the privacy of your own home."

I will put forward my own critical arguments about how dance games remediate racialized performance in Chapters 4 and 5. Meanwhile, however, the meager inventory of race-talk in these reviews offers a useful point of comparison when we consider how the same players discuss gender and sexuality. Here reviewers are far less circumspect; they routinely refer to dance moves as feminine or masculine, and many lodge gender-related complaints about the choreography. For example:

> The majority of the songs on the game are girly which is ok for me since most of the people who come to visit my house are women. But its not good because I just paid 50 bucks for a game that I can only dance to maybe 3 or 4 songs on. One thing I noticed is that even on the more masculine songs its one move only fairies would feel comfortable doing. [review titled "Not Very Gender Friendly"]

not geared towards men to much a lot of girly dances alot a whole lot. milk shake and dont cha stuff like that.it was kinda a turn off for me but the wife loves it. and i love watching her do those sexy dances . . . . . . nice ;)

[Dance Central 2] isn't as male friendly as the first game. Too many songs with too many girly moves that even I ["Pam in Boston"] feel ridiculous doing.

Most of the dances in the game are gender oriented. If you're a guy like me, you're gonna feel like a fool dancing to "Rude Boy" for example because of how feminine the moves are. I wish there were both male and female versions of dances for each song instead of just one.

most if not all of the dance moves are quite feminine, even if it's a male character. Felt pretty awkward trying these feminine moves in front of the wife.

I'm a bit disappointed by the look of some of the routines. They should make them more gender neutral. It's just disappointing to see so many of the harder songs have such feminine looking routines. I'm not trying to discredit the difficulty of the feminine looking dance moves, but I would appreciate learning a dance move that wouldn't make me look like a fool trying in a club seeing as this is probably my only formal lesson of dancing I would ever attempt. HAHA!

In addition to pointing out the perceived gender attributes of the game choreography, reviewers frequently refer to the gender of the dance-game players in their households, often in the context of describing family relationships (wife, husband, daughter, etc.); they also describe gendered social dynamics during gameplay, or report gendered motivations for buying a game. For example, several men write that they bought *Dance Central* so that their wives or girlfriends would look more kindly upon the Xbox in the household: "My wife almost hate[s] videogames . . . and I love my . . . xbox 360 (and my wife too LOL) . . . so I got this game to invite her to play. . . . NOW she enjoys dancing and having fun with this (looking so sexy)" [ellipses original]. Several other reviewers also note this voyeuristic fringe benefit: "nothing better than a beautiful woman dancing in your living room!!!" Meanwhile, some parents dwell on the question of whether the songs or the moves are too sexually suggestive for children. (The games are rated "T for Teen" due to references to sexuality and violence in the song lyrics; the ESRB rating summary does not assess the choreographic content [Entertainment Software Rating Board 2016].) This kind of gender discourse turned up regularly in all my research channels, including player forums, YouTube comment threads, interviews, and survey responses. In one way or another, players surmise that dance games are "about" gender, and they talk about it openly.

As the Amazon reviewers reflect on their gameplay experience and write impressionistic evaluations meant to help others decide whether to make a purchase, they seem to prioritize descriptions of how it feels to play and what kinds of people are having those feelings—identifying those people by gender, age, and family/friend relationship categories. There are likely many reasons that reviewers mention gender more than race, including their ideas about the relative sensitivity of these topics. But without making too many speculative generalizations, we can note that this disparity dovetails with another: These players discuss *what the choreography feels like* more than *what the screen dancers look like*. This is an important cue for a researcher interested in investigating gameplay as a dynamic multisensory experience rather than making a close reading of a game as though it were a cinematic text. It raises the question of when and how the embodied identity of the screen dancers matters to players.

My research with beginning players and my own gameplay experience strongly suggested that when players are still learning to practice kinesthetic vision, the surface details of the screen body's appearance often escape conscious attention. Instead, players focus on tracking gestures and mapping them to body parts: the right hand looping here, the left knee lifting there, the anticipation that this pattern may repeat in the opposite direction or perhaps change with the next phrase of music. When I conducted post-gameplay interview sessions with inexperienced players, or introduced friends to the games at home, I asked them what they had noticed or could remember about the screen dancers; in many cases they remembered virtually nothing. Some mentioned a piece of apparel that had helped or hindered them in following the choreography, such as a screen dancer's brightly colored shoes or trailing sleeves. New players also often completely missed the scrolling flashcards in *Dance Central* (which stream up one side of the screen, displaying icons and names for the upcoming moves), and they were unaware of their accumulating numerical scores and star ratings until the end of each song. Their eyes were riveted to the moving body at the center of the screen, as they learned how to watch it in the same way each game's sensor apparatus was watching them: with the aim of extracting data about the relative position of moving body parts.

This is not say that players don't register the race or gender of the screen dancers at some level; rather, these identity attributes become noteworthy mainly when they generate cognitive/kinesthetic dissonance, defying players' expectations or posing challenges to their own embodied identities. Across all my research channels, players remarked on gendered choreography that felt unfamiliar in their own bodies; in these circumstances, they seemed to pay more attention to the gender of the screen dancer, asking themselves whether these moves were a better match for that body than for their own. But relatively few players seemed to experience such dissonance or discomfort with respect to racial masquerade—perhaps because it is so normalized in contemporary global popular culture, which still routinely trades on the appropriation, commodification, and "mainstreaming" of African American popular culture and artistic practice (see DeFrantz 2012, Salkind 2016).

Players' perceptual strategies shift over time. I observed that as players grew more experienced, or as they watched from the sidelines while someone else took a turn, they began to notice and comment on more of the available visual information, including "mismatches" between certain dance moves and the screen dancer's embodied identity. The appearance of the screen dancers is also a crucial element of game advertising and player-circulated gameplay videos. Some players have their first significant encounters with dance games through these media; game graphics likely play a stronger role in shaping their early impressions. Still, as I move on to unpack players' engagements with "girly" choreography in detail, it is worth emphasizing that when it comes to engaging with difference, the bodily sensations that players experience as they dance are at least as important as what they see on screen. As someone else's choreography passes through players' bodies, it calls attention to existing structures of embodied experience: The moves can feel easy or challenging, natural or alien, permissive or compulsory.

II. GAMING GENDER IN *DANCE CENTRAL*

While numerous intersecting cultural connotations render *Dance Central*'s screen bodies and dance styles legible to players and their audiences, gender distinctions play a starring and explicit role. As we have seen, players routinely refer to particular moves as "masculine" or "feminine." An interview with an experienced 23-year-old male player offers some clues as to what drives these distinctions:

KM: Were there any particular kinds of moves that felt less comfortable in your body, compared to others?

PLAYER: [*laughter*] There were definitely times where it was a woman singing the song and they were doing moves that would be interpreted as sexually attractive for a woman to do, but probably not for a man to do. But for all my self-consciousness about dancing, I don't really care about that kind of stuff. I'm comfortable enough with my gender identity where—I was kind of laughing to myself when I was doing those. I wasn't embarrassed or anything.

KM: What would characterize the feminine moves?

PLAYER: Oh, the ones where they're like drawing their fingers down their body, or on "Bulletproof" [by La Roux, 2009], when she was doing the gun one across her face, kind of like a James Bond girl or Charlie's Angels girl. And then there's also the fact that most of the time I was actually a girl [screen dancer] dancing to those moves. [*laughter*] That probably augmented that sense of things. Can I think of any others? Oh, yeah, then the ones for Katy Perry where there's the hip movements and stuff like that.

KM: So as those passed through, you registered them as being gendered moves?

PLAYER: Yeah, every once in awhile. Only in that I kind of giggled to myself.(post-gameplay interview, July 31, 2013)

As this example shows, gender ascriptions for game choreography are rooted in existing gender ideologies and intensified through a confluence of signs across linguistic, gestural, aural, and visual domains (see Chapter 3). *Dance Central*'s move names often allude to gender: Consider the Frat Step, Diva, Eyeliner, Bromance,

Muscle Man, Booty Pop, and Pretty Face. Regardless of their names, moves invoke gendered movement styles from other contexts: a hip shimmy versus a pelvic pop, a football throw versus a pom pom shake, a flexed chest with open arms versus a "heartbreak" clutch at one's sternum as the chest collapses. These moves tend to reflect or reinforce gender connotations in the musical material, including lyrics, the singer's gender, and more subtle aspects of production that have coalesced into gendered genre norms for pop, rock, hip-hop, and electronic dance music; for instance, "Bulletproof" is a British synthpop track. The particular symbolic baggage of a given song may further inflect gendered moves with respect to race, sexuality, or class. As demonstrated in this interview and my gameplay notes at the start of this chapter, the player's choice of on-screen character may also reinforce or destabilize the associations of some moves. The range of available characters lets players treat race and gender as separable variables, encouraging experiments with recombinant intersectionality: How does a Frat Step or Booty Pop look on a Latino adult man's body versus an African American young girl's body? How do these moves feel in one's own body when dancing along with different screen bodies?

The perceived qualities of the choreography, the screen body, and the music can compete for dominant influence over this interpretive process. For instance, rolling hips might trump the apparent gender of the screen body: Players might see a male dancer engaged in cross-gender performance. But that same male screen body might infuse a sweeping arm gesture with masculinity—for a hard-edged hip-hop track. If it's girl-power pop, all bets are off. These readings of how moves fit various screen bodies also affect how players feel the choreography in their own bodies: Can I channel the coy white feminine artifice presented by Miss Aubrey, or the cool black masculine authenticity presented by Mo? Which comes more easily or feels more awkward—and what if I feel unable to make a convincing performance of either archetypal standard? These are the kinds of questions that come up when the same choreography circulates through categorically different bodies, including one's own.

In considering questions of representation and engagement with difference in dance games, it is important to bear in mind that these games were developed and achieved chart-topping commercial success during a period when issues of diversity and inclusion were roiling the game industry and many player communities. Women, people of color, and queer people were increasingly speaking out about pervasive cultures of discrimination and harassment within the industry and in online multiplayer gameworlds; many met with a stream of retaliatory social shaming and threats of violence. A series of incidents of this kind constituted the "Gamergate" debacle of 2014, characterized by a *Washington Post* reporter as a "freewheeling catastrophe/social movement/misdirected lynch-mob" (Dewey 2014). In this context, dance games stand out for being expressly marketed to women and people of color. They have made that appeal in large part through their reliance on gendered and racialized repertoires that were already circulating in popular culture.

One might easily imagine dance games as a disciplining apparatus, reinforcing established norms through repetition in the guise of play. Indeed, all dance repertoires discipline bodies, and "choreography presents a structuring of deep and enduring cultural values that replicates similar sets of values elaborated in other cultural practices" (Foster 2011:5). The same could be said of video games. As Matt Boch, the series project director and lead designer for *Dance Central*, observed, "You're always modeling aspects of the norms of *your world* in these games. . . . I think a lot of times we forget that that's one thing we're doing as designers and developers" (Boch 2013). Boch is a queer-identified man who has urged the game industry to advance "a social progressivism that matches our technological progressivism" (Alexander 2012). In a video interview for the Critical Path Project, he described how these principles informed his approach to *Dance Central*:

> We had done some initial mocap [motion-capture] of one of our choreographers, I think it was to Salt-N-Pepa's "Push It." You know, she is an awesome dancer, and she did this somewhat feminine take. . . . And we had our male avatar, I think the first one that we built, or male character, sorry, the first one we built, and he was going to dance "Push It." And a bunch of people walked in and saw this happening, and were like, "That doesn't look like Mo dancing." . . . And we started to go down this path and have these conversations: Will we mocap everything and have a man dance it, and have a woman dance it, will we say what gender a particular dance belongs to, will there be dances that are neutral? And to me, this is just a horrible path to go down. What I want to do is let the player decide what's valid in *their* context. And so we made a lot of really careful decisions to make that possible. . . . I think as we went down those paths it was just a lot of open, honest conversations about what kind of future we were building. (Boch 2013)

In his public statements, Boch pursues multiple rhetorical strategies to make the case that game developers should intervene in the perpetuation of some social norms. He appeals to progressive principles ("what kind of future we are building") while also issuing a subtle challenge to other designers by invoking the sacred industry values of creativity and innovation. As he said in the Critical Path interview,

> We're trying to create new and exciting imaginative spaces—it's curious to me that we can imagine elves and orcs and whatever else, but men and women behave in a very particular way still. Like Skyrim [a role-playing gameworld] has all sorts of crazy races we never even heard of or thought of, and two genders. . . . It's a rich source of potential new gameplay and new types of imaginary spaces you can create. (Boch 2013)

Boch also makes pragmatic arguments that link themes of diversity and inclusion to sales potential: Game developers can make money by appealing to the broadest possible consumer base and offering novel experiences. The business model for dance games relies on persuading people to keep buying new repertoire, some of which will stretch the boundaries of their usual musical and choreographic tastes.

As Boch told me, "We want people to play all sorts of different songs, and I think it's exciting and compelling to break out of your assumed gender norms and try something different" (Boch 2012). These principles guided Boch's work on *Dance Central*, a game series that aims to denaturalize gender binaries by inviting players to experiment with gendered movement.

In interviews and public presentations, Boch often spoke about gender as performance, the familiar shorthand distillation of the constructivist gender theory typically associated with Judith Butler. As he told me, "I think in playing with gender you become aware of the fact that it is a performance. I think that's one of the most powerful things" (Boch 2012). But the gender work in dance games seems to model a somewhat different theory: gender as choreography. Susan Foster has written extensively about the difference between performance and choreography as frameworks for understanding the construction and transmission of gender norms. As she observes, Butler's focus on reiteration "stresses the repetition of acts more than the relationality among them. How are these 'acts' organized so as mutually to reinforce and/or expand on one another? How do acts not only reiterate social norms but also vary them so as to establish resonances among distinct categories of normative behavior?" (1998:5). Foster makes a case that choreography better accounts for these structural relationships among repeated acts, while also expanding the scope of Butler's "performatives" from speech acts to bodily practice. This is not to say that Foster throws out the concept of performance; rather, she suggests that choreography and performance are complementary. Choreography is "a slowly changing constellation of representational conventions" (17) and performances are the individual iterations of those conventions through which that slow change might transpire. Gender-as-choreography emphasizes that the constellation of conventions that constitutes "masculine" and "feminine" kinesthetic styles in any given situation is culturally and historically specific; in later work, Foster describes how particular gendered choreographies are being "uploaded into a globally circulating set of codes [that] can be tapped for multiple purposes" (2009:62). Dance games now form part of the infrastructure for this global circulation.

Foster's "choreographed body" is not an automaton, a marionette, or a metaphor, but a living, breathing, moving, and changing human body shaped by training in a particular style. She suggests that gender, like dance, is a form of creative expression that "relies on the inculcated capabilities, impulses, and preferences that years of practice produce, but . . . also leaves open the possibility for the unprecedented" (1998:30). Carrie Noland likewise suggests that paying attention to the moving body might help theorists "find a way beyond the impasse of constructivist theory" to account for the possibility of change effected through individual experience and agency (2009:7, cf. Massumi 2002). She locates this possibility in moments of interpretive reflection, "when the situated subject must make propositional sense (meaning) of what she feels" (10). Such an argument relies on the idea that "performing gestures can generate sensations that are not-yet-marked, not-yet-meaningful" (17). Returning to Foster's terms, it is the performer's engagement with choreographic codes that structures this meaning-making process and that ultimately makes new choreographies possible.

Dance game design and episodes of gameplay closely parallel Foster's distinction between choreography and performance: "Dance making theorizes physicality, whereas dancing presents that theory of physicality" (1998:10). But such a distinction does not entail the separation of theory and practice, nor a "consumption" model of active/creative production followed by passive/imitative performance or gameplay. In both game development and choreographic work, these processes are inextricably intertwined as they drive iterative cycles. Game developers continually playtest games-in-progress and draw on player feedback in designing sequels, just as choreographers continually test their theories on dancers' bodies (often including their own), and fold their findings back into their choreographic process. This was certainly the case for the teams of game developers and choreographers who created the dance repertoire for the *Dance Central* games (see Chapter 5). As I will show, it also characterizes some players' efforts to re-choreograph their own kinesthetic experience of performing that repertoire.

For the remainder of this chapter I will focus on the gendered pleasures and perils built into *Dance Central*'s "theory of physicality" and realized through players' dancing, in counterpoint with their own gender identities and ideologies. How do players negotiate their participation in a game that stages gender as choreography? In exploring the nature and consequences of gender-related game design choices, I build on the growing literature on "girl games" and the experiences of adult female gamers, while also giving sustained attention to male players' engagement with gender play and performance.[3] I follow other game scholars in focusing on "technologies of the gendered self," "integrating Foucault's 'technologies of the self' into the feminist model of 'technologies of gender'" (Royse et al. 2007:560, citing Foucault 1988 and Balsamo 1996). This approach acknowledges players' agency in their individual negotiations, while still "attending to the multiplicity of forces" that organize the gaming situation and interpellate players (Behrenshausen 2013:11). For example, players who encounter a "feminine" *Dance Central* move—say, a hip swivel in "Call Me Maybe"—might construe it as an accurate and straightforward choreographic translation of a "girly" song; as reinforcing or conflicting with their own embodied gender identity; as an opportunity for camp or drag performance (Meyer 1994) or "queer kinesthesia" (Bollen 2001); as hazardous to players' conventional masculinity and/or their feminist ideals; as too sexy or too gender-nonconforming for one's children to perform, and so on.

Scholars of games and gender have called for increased attention to how games may "help [players] to define their gendered selves ... through integration, negotiation, or rejection," rather than simply through identification or disidentification with stereotypically "masculine" or "feminine" games (Royse et al. 2007:561). *Dance Central* presents some unusual affordances in this regard. Like most videogames, the series offers opportunities for voluntary identity play; it is distinctive in that its developers also deliberately posed discomfiting identity challenges for some players.

Thus, while much could be said about pleasurable "identity tourism" in *Dance Central* (Nakamura 2002), I will dwell more on the experiences of players who are reluctant or ambivalent about the kinds of gender performance this game requires.

Dancing Like a Lady, Dancing Like a ****

Shortly after midnight on May 27, 2012, a *Dance Central* player from Atlanta, Georgia, posted a cry for help to the player forums, starting a new thread called "Dancing Like a Lady."

> Even tho some of the Dance Central soundtrack is awesome! But lately i feel like some songs got my feeling like I have to close my shades or wait till everyone is sleep to dance to some of those songs. Well, what I'm saying is lots of songs are for the ladies not guys. Can you have male, female same song DLC [downloadable content]? My hips are getting sore . . . and for some reason going shoe shopping. (blaksonatl, posted to DanceCentral.com 2012a)

This player is describing a visceral encounter with gendered choreography. "Dancing like a lady" feels wrong in his body, so wrong that it would be shameful for anyone else to witness. He testifies to the lingering physical effects of unaccustomed movements—it's no exaggeration to say that *Dance Central* gameplay can make one's hips sore—and he closes with a half-joking allusion to deeper transformative consequences: Perhaps dancing like a lady might even reprogram a man to think, act, and consume like a woman.

Another player contributed to a forum thread on "Requests, Suggestions, & Features Feedback" with a similar account of gender trouble: "I suggest that every song should have a male routine and a female routine. Shaking my ass like a **** is not really my type lol" (xXShadowFrostXx, posted to DanceCentral.com 2011b). After the moderator called attention to the implied use of profanity and requested more "constructive" feedback, xXShadowFrostXx clarified:

> I'm sorry for that I just auto-censured myself lol. What I meant is that every songs should have a male and a female routine because as a guy, I do like [for] example: doing Just Dance routine because [the song is] one of my favorite but some moves are a little bit too girly to perform. I think it would be a good idea if both male and female routine could be similar but more suitable for our own gender, you know what I mean? [NB: In this post "Just Dance" refers to the Lady Gaga song, not the game franchise.]

Both blaksonatl and xXShadowFrostXx make a case that *Dance Central* should accommodate gender-normative performance for every song by offering separate male and female performance options. This is a common request, one that the Harmonix developers encountered regularly during pre-release playtesting. Boch described "a strong push from a bunch of people to record [i.e., motion-capture] every song with a guy and record every song with a girl. And not have the routines necessarily be different, but have the *performances* of those moves be masculine or feminine" (Boch and Miller 2012). Boch rejected this gender binary out of hand, asserting his own belief in a gender continuum. He told me it would be "heart-breaking" and "disenfranchising" if a gender-queer or transgender player were required to "make some binary assertion" at the beginning of gameplay. Instead, players can select from an array of characters with conventionally male or female body types and names, but the choreography and motion-capture data don't change when players switch characters. Even if players only use male characters, they still have to perform "girly" choreography (and vice versa); one can't play for long without encountering stereotypically "masculine" or "feminine" moves, sometimes juxtaposed within a single song. By design, *Dance Central* regularly prompts players to engage in "corporeal drag," "a process of queer play in which performers try on and refashion movement as sensory-kinesthetic material for experiencing and presenting the body anew" (Bragin 2014:62). Boch framed this requirement as an opportunity: "That's part of the nature of dance. . . . We want to offer people that fluidity." But for some players, it presents a problem—most notably for men who are uncomfortable with feminized movement.

Dance Central players developed a variety of strategies for performing or avoiding corporeal drag. Responding to blaksonatl's discomfort, one female-identified player offered a list of " 'guy' or gender neutral songs," along with the names of the game choreographers who tended to produce more masculine routines—though she also ended her post with "Lose your inhibitions or you'll never have any fun" (LadyHaHa2It, posted to DanceCentral.com 2012a). A male-identified player seconded this suggestion and added:

> Doing "girly" dances on a video game isn't the same as going out and busting some moves to "It's Raining Men" in a club or at a school dance or something. . . . To me, dancing to a "girly" song just shows confidence and / or the ability to disregard what other people think, and not dancing to them is just like a waste of $15- $20 or however much the songs would add up to. (Seanyboy99, posted to DanceCentral.com 2012a)

This response rationalizes corporeal drag in the context of digital gameplay—partly on the grounds that gameplay needn't represent or reflect one's real-life gender identity, but also drawing on the gaming imperative to complete all available missions, and the neoliberal imperative not to squander one's investment in this media product and its associated competences. The player's allusion to wasting money also invokes the underlying business model for the *Dance Central, Rock Band,* and *Guitar Hero* games (all developed by Harmonix), which resurrects the sheet-music industry of earlier centuries. Once players purchase particular hardware, become fluent in a notation system, and gain competence in its associated performance techniques, they will continue to pay for additional repertoire (Miller 2012:112).

Ignoring some of the songs included with each game edition or refraining from purchasing new downloadable content (DLC) constitutes a "waste" of one's investment and a restriction on one's full participation in a community of practice (cf. Galloway 2012:29 on the "ludic economy"). From this perspective, taking on the games' gender-play missions becomes an act of responsible consumption.

Other forum respondents asserted that it was possible to maintain a robust heteronormative sexuality even while indulging in cross-gender performance. One male player suggested that it might help to play "girly" songs with a female character: "Try dancing with Emilia to those routines; they have become some of my favourites LOL" (Derek555, posted to DanceCentral.com 2011b). This player's other posts about Emilia, which dwell on her sex appeal, clarify his advice: He recommends selecting a female character not in order to role-play as a female performer but rather to admire the sexy spectacle of the character's performance. Indulging in the pleasures of heterosexual voyeurism could offer an antidote to "girly" choreography, even as the player simultaneously performs those same moves. The player's ambiguous relationship to the screen dancer generates an unstable power dynamic. The screen dancer is an authority figure, empowered to animate the player's body, but the player can turn the tables by making the screen dancer perform on command, converting a virtual dance teacher into the object of an erotic gaze.

A player called Kat Rina offers a variant of this approach by making her game character dance for a wider audience in her YouTube gameplay videos. Many of her videos don't show her own dancing body at all but instead the performances of Angel, a character whose voice and name mark him as Latino (Kat Rina 2011; see Figure 2.1).

Figure 2.1: Kat Rina's video of Angel's performance of "Lapdance" (Kat Rina 2011). (Screenshot by the author.)

In the comment thread for her video of "Lapdance" (N.E.R.D, 2011), Kat Rina and her viewers engage in playful sexual banter about Angel's performance:

125AcDc: Did it just get steamy in here? LMFAO
darkria4: Whenever Angel makes direct contact with "you" his eyes are so sparkly. I can sense attitude and ego in those eyes . . . mmf *swoon*
Kat Rina: @darkria4 *gasps* me too, but i find it's his smile and grin that really gets me, hahaha! . . . . . oh my

To produce this video, Kat Rina had to perform stereotypical feminine "stripper" moves, which then allowed her to watch and record a male game character performing them *against* his gender type. There is a peculiar deferral of agency here: The dancing player submits her own body to the will of the game choreographers so that she can in turn fetishize the dancing character. Kat Rina told me that she received some viewer complaints about "having Angel doing feminine moves in girl-only songs" (email interview, 2011). Some viewers suggested that forcing Angel to engage in drag performance was deviant or exploitative—"just not right," though sometimes also funny.

Butching Up or Crossing Over?

Another strategy for approaching the gender politics of *Dance Central* involves butching up one's approach to feminine moves. In an interview for a player's video blog, Harmonix choreographer Ricardo Foster Jr. offered some tips:

FOSTER: "Rude Boy," we all know, yeah, it feels like more of a female song. But: you can make every one of those movements masculine. . . . Focus more on the arms. Like in "Rude Boy," you definitely see this going on. [*gyrates hips*]
MIGHTYMECREATIVE (INTERVIEWER): You can't hide from that.
FOSTER: Exactly! . . . Guys, just really move more back and use your arms more. That takes away all of the things that may be uncomfortable for you, but being able to really whip it down [*demonstrates with arms*]: the Kinect still sees that you're doing the movement and still reads you as a "Flawless" score. You just gotta make sure that everything is clear and precise. So you can focus more on the arms, and be more of a—bam!—masculine, dominant effect, rather than being real roll-y [*gyrates hips*]. . . . We made sure that it was for y'all too, so y'all could feel like men after you do it! (MightyMeCreative 2011a)

While some players take Foster's advice, finding ways to perform all moves in a way that lets them "feel like men," others embrace the opportunity to engage in cross-gender performance. Many enjoy playing with their gender identity or exploring the possibilities of a fluid gender continuum, in line with Matt Boch's intentions.

Figure 2.2: rosroskof's performance of "Lapdance" on YouTube (rosroskof 2011). (Screenshot by the author.)

However, some virtuosic cross-gender performers have unassailable confidence in a fixed gender identity—indeed, it is that very conviction that leads them to recognize a satisfying technical and artistic challenge in the task of embodying another gender through dance. For instance, one player posted a YouTube video of his performance of the "Lapdance" routine, which juxtaposes strongly marked masculine and feminine segments (rosroskof 2011; see Figure 2.2). He told me, "I have received a few comments referring to my moves being too feminine, or the choreo was too feminine for a straight guy to perform, but I don't mind them at all. I considered them as compliments. Comments along those lines confirms that I performed the moves correctly" (email interview, 2011). Meanwhile, information in his YouTube profile and comment threads shores up his heterosexuality and normative masculinity: Viewers learn that he has a wife and small child, and that he serves in the US Navy.

Another player, Riffraff, told me that in the case of "Lapdance" he thought the *Dance Central* choreographers had deliberately included both "male" and "female" moves as a sly joke on players:

> It's funny just how quickly the mood changes from really rough guy moves to really girly, girly moves. . . . I thought they were kind of drag-esque, almost. It was a little *too* exaggerated. . . . When I was first trying out the song, I was like, "What is this?" and I just started laughing because I found it really funny how they snuck that in there. . . . You already bought the track, so what are you going to do? (recorded phone interview, 2011)

Like many experienced players, Riffraff positions himself as a "hospitable host" for *Dance Central*'s choreography, allowing alternative gender performances to pass through his body without ceding his own "possession of the premises" (Sobchack 1992:271–72). He interprets "Lapdance" as a deliberate rejoinder to players who believe in fixed gender identities: In the course of performing this song, their own bodies will betray them, revealing flexible capacities that testify to the radical contingency of gender performance. However, *Dance Central* also leaves room for players to reinforce established gender and sexuality norms through ironic engagement with deviance, "a strategy of un-queer appropriation of queer praxis" (Meyer 1994:5). Matt Boch expressed pride in the possibility that "people who may not feel very comfortable in their current gender, or are discovering exactly where they fit on a gender continuum" might find a greater range of expressive possibilities in *Dance Central*. But he also acknowledged, "There are plenty of times when you have people who are cisgender male, like alpha kind of dudes. And you get them up and they're playing some type of feminine song and they're totally into it—but it's funny to them, and it's funny to everyone else around them" (Boch and Miller 2012). These players are engaging in generic, stylized gender performances that may pose little risk or challenge to their own identities. As Lauren Berlant observes,

> Even the prospects of failure that haunt the performance of identity and genre are conventional: The power of a generic performance always involves moments of potential collapse that threaten the contract that genre makes with the viewer to fulfill experiential expectations. But those blockages or surprises are usually *part* of the convention and not a transgression of it, or anything radical. They make its conventionality interesting and rich, even. (2008:4)

Accommodating these generic performances is part of Boch's ethos of inclusive game design, which dictates that designers should "reveal to the player what the type of experience could be, and then allow the player to make their own choice" (Alexander 2012). It also resonates with a choreographic orientation that situates corporeal drag as just another dance technique to be practiced and ultimately mastered in the course of one's training (see Chapter 5). As *Dance Central* choreographer Marcos Aguirre told me,

> You can always make something feminine or make something masculine or make it look like another gender or make it no gender. . . . It's just all about learning and experiencing something new, learning what your body can do. Growing up I always did hip-hop, and when I went to school I didn't want to do ballet, I didn't want to do modern, but as soon as I started taking those classes I realized, hey, I can move my body like this now, so now I can make my choreography even better. (Aguirre and Miller 2015)

This approach does not necessarily undo gender binaries, but it denaturalizes them. In Aguirre's account, masculine and feminine kinesthetic styles are "real," but their material reality derives from artificial codes that can be taught and learned. Gender can be a matter of choice and of skillful art. Here the technical challenge of dance training converges with the game challenge that motivates players: Gender performance is figured as an arbitrary yet amazingly satisfying achievement. Finding ways to perform a feminine move in a masculine manner is like finding ways of squeezing out extra points from a scoring algorithm: a matter of discovering exploits in the system. Taking a broader view, Aguirre's and Boch's accounts show how theories of gender-as-choreography can dovetail with gender-as-technology (Balsamo 1996). *Dance Central*'s gender codes are not dictatorial programming with straightforward outcomes, but tools, interactive by nature and mobilized through bodily techniques (cf. Chun 2009).

Going Public: Gender and Sexuality Discourse on YouTube

The filmic perspective in *Just Dance* and *Dance Central* eschews the close-up shots, rapid edits, and camera motion that chacterize other popular screen genres, where filmmakers often "rechoreograph bodies through a reworking of time, space, and energy," break the laws of physics, or create "superbodies" that exceed human abilities (Dodds 2014:447). The games maintain a full-body frontal perspective that aids players in mirroring the screen dancer and framing themselves for the sensor apparatus, and they promise players choreography that real humans can perform in real time. Players who post dance gameplay videos to YouTube adhere to these same conventions: They generally keep their entire bodies in-frame and refrain from any cuts or other edits that could raise questions about the veracity of their skills and scores. Those with the technical resources often create splitscreen videos, turning the face-to-face player/character relationship into a side-by-side performance.

Such marks of "liveness" are familiar from other gameplay videos circulated on social media, but the evaluative terms are different here. Virtuosic players of first-person shooter games must demonstrate that they are really playing the game, not that they are really firing a gun; there is no expectation that FPS gamers will physically resemble their avatars or be able to perform the avatar's corporeal repertoires. Dance game players are often held to both standards: Their audiences assess them as dancers and as gamers. The full-body framing and one-take editing conventions of dance gameplay videos create opportunities for visual juxtaposition and point-by-point comparative analysis of filmed player bodies and game character bodies, raising the question, "Who performs better?" (Burrill and Blanco Borelli 2014:437). Thus when players post their gameplay online, the unstable power dynamic between screen dancer and player/spectator takes another turn. In video performances, the player reprises the role of the game character: She or he may be perceived as a respected authority and role model—an expert gamer/dancer—or as the object of an erotic gaze, available for instant replay on demand. Viewer comments on these videos offer telling examples of "the process whereby new technologies are articulated with traditional and ideological narratives about gender" (Balsamo 1996:60).

When male players take their gender-bending *Dance Central* performances public on YouTube, they generate predictable derogatory comments about their sexuality—an established trolling tactic. However, a community of players often rallies around the dancer, sometimes voicing support of more flexible gender and sexuality norms (cf. Sutton-Smith 1997:105). For example, a YouTube user uploaded a "Call Me Maybe" gameplay video, using a female game character and never showing his own body on screen (AverageAsianDude 2012b). When I was reading the comments, I encountered a post that had been hidden from view after receiving too many "thumbs-down" from other users. Upon clicking through to see it, I found a typical misogynist/homophobic insult: "If guys dance this song, they're considered bitches" (posted by Disbanded2012). Other commenters responded:

> Beato Carlos del Toro: if you don't have your masculinity well marked and you doubt about it just for dance a song that's your problem
>
> AverageAsianDude [video uploader]: the only bitch in here is you [226 "thumbs-up"]
>
> Tu Nguyen: Out of all 47,783+ viewers, you are the only 1 bitch. Congrats bitch.
>
> VIDGamefrk9: FYI I have DC2 and I can do better on most songs by females, with means I am a total feminist! I love how people diss guys for having feministic viewpoints. I wonder what would happen if I were to make a feministic comment on a CoD [*Call of Duty*] gameplay. (comments posted to AverageAsianDude 2012b)

This discussion shows how "a media text becomes material that drives active community discussion and debate at the intersection between popular culture and civic discourse—conversations that might lead to community activism or social change" (Jenkins et al. 2013:168). While one might wish that these respondents had not been so quick to redeploy the derogatory feminine epithet "bitch," this is still an intriguing example of gender and sexuality discourse in a public online forum where participants bring a variety of ideologies to the table.

Female players who post to YouTube are working with a different set of gender and sexuality norms. I have yet to encounter a woman who expresses discomfort with performing "masculine" *Dance Central* moves, or a YouTube comment that criticizes a woman for cross-gender peformance. By recursive definition, "masculine" moves convey physical strength, technical prowess, and/or sexual dominance; female players often descibe them as empowering (cf. Taylor 2006). Yet there is little risk that a woman's "masculine" performance will be perceived as threatening, because these power moves have no direct object. Even in the two-player mode, *Dance Central* players perform the same routine side by side, rather than engaging in the gendered power dynamics of partner dancing. Certain moves do conjure an invisible partner, but there is no direct representation of dominant/submissive dance-floor relations. A woman cannot perform a "masculine" routine that complements another player's simultaneous "feminine" routine.

While female players seem untroubled by cross-gender performance, they sometimes express discomfort with moves that invoke sexuality, especially feminized, racialized, or "low-class" sexuality. As one woman told me, citing some of the moves in "Lapdance": "For example, the moves called 'dirty dog,' 'caress up,' 'caress down' & 'caress front.' I just don't feel comfortable to make those moves in public" (Lola, email interview, 2011). These anxieties are exacerbated for women who post gameplay videos online, a "public" context very different from a club dance floor; performances may circulate indefinitely, and comment functions invite direct evaluative feedback from anonymous strangers whose own bodies are safely invisible. Women who post dance gameplay videos routinely contend with sexual objectification, including comments on their bodies, comparisons to the bodies of the game characters, speculation about their relationship status, and explicit sexual harrassment. For women of color, these comments often include a racial valence.

For example, consider a video uploaded by Latty2cute, a Canadian woman of Afro-Caribbean heritage, featuring her performance of Kelis's 2003 hit "Milkshake" (Latty2cute 2012). In this video, Latty2cute wears high heels and an outfit that nods to the style of the on-screen dancer, Miss Aubrey (see Figure 2.3).

Numerous commenters complimented Latty2cute on the technical tour de force of doing a challenging routine in high heels. Many also addressed her as an eroticized spectacle:

Robert Taylor: is it the shoes!!!! u rocked it . . . when this song play in the club i bet u be doing this whole dance lol. . . .

yan Leonardo: Dang girl, you sure got style! In your clothes and dancing. Good job on dancing with heels! Are you african american or hispanic?

Figure 2.3: Latty2cute's performance of "Milkshake" on YouTube (Latty2cute 2012). Note that her stiletto heels one-up the screen dancer, who is wearing flats. (Screenshot by the author.)

deanna bull: i am a boy on my sis acownt. me the boy: you are so hot and sexy. o btw my name is darrell and i am 11 and sexy

In one thread that played out over several months, a commenter informed Latty2cute that he was treating her video as pornography. As she worked through the process of decoding his slang, other commenters offer wincing condolences-in-advance:

stareco copeland: fap mode -activated-

Latty2cute: yaaay! i think? wats fap?

JessicaCIH: omg . . . you dont want to know

Shining Armor: You're kidding right?

kayiscool12: i love u girl . . . . . but u reallllllllllyyyy dont want to know. . . . . .

SmashJohn: FAP is the sound you make when you masturbate so . . . . yes . . . [i.e. "yes" to the "yaaay! I think?" that implied a perceived compliment]

Latty2cute: OMG thats sick!

stareco copeland: lmao!! now you know

Latty2cute: i found out from a friend on Twitter. . . . . NOT COOL. . . . . lol

(comments on Latty2cute 2012)

Ending with a "lol" [laughing out loud] that undercuts the serious reprimand "NOT COOL," Latty2cute seems to be trying to restore this episode to "only a game" status—corralling her performance back inside a "magic circle" of gameplay whose borders are always breaking down (Salen and Zimmerman 2004, Jones 2008, Miller 2008b). This example illustrates the uncontrollable "collision and disruption of frames" (Fischer-Lichte 2008:47) that characterize YouTube reception. Viewers are free to approach such performances as virtuosic gameplay, ironic femme drag, or soft-core porn, and to comment accordingly. However, performers can and do talk back, influencing the formation of competing interpretive communities.

CONCLUSION: PLAYABLE BODIES AND EMBODIED DIFFERENCE

By design, *Dance Central* makes an argument about gender. Through its own procedural rhetoric, "the practice of using processes persuasively" (Bogost 2007:3), the games present gender in terms of technique, repertoire, and voluntary creative practice. Some players resist or reject the terms of this argument, because it conflicts with their own gender ideologies; even if they engage in cross-gender performance, they might be reinscribing essentialist gender binaries through parody (Butler 1990:139). Nevertheless, *Dance Central* asserts not only that everyone can dance but that everyone can dance as a virtually gendered body; that gender feels viscerally real in practice but is a quality cultivated through performative repetition;

and that players can choose which repertoires to repeat. By producing "intense kinesthetic and affective experiences of dissonance," *Dance Central* demonstrates that "the moving, trained, and trainable body is always a potential source of resistance to the meanings it is required to bear" (Noland 2009:175). It promises anxious players that "you can still feel like men after you do it," while putting other options on the table.

Dance Central can persuade players to engage in gender work because it conjoins a dancer's orientation to a performance repertoire with a player's orientation to a game challenge. Like theatrical performances, games invite participants to "play with the frames of the mundane" (Sutton-Smith 1997:148) in a context where "the consequences of the activity are negotiable" (Juul 2005:36). In a game where, as Matt Boch put it, "You might be giving [players] instructions or content that is unfamiliar to them, or uncomfortable for them, or somehow inconsistent with their own notion of their identities" (Alexander 2012), players can claim that they're only doing these moves for the sake of high scores, getting to the next level, or completion. As we saw in Chapter 1, players also engage in the pleasurable process of analyzing the Kinect's potential, including how to game the interface: Exactly what range of physical performances will lead to full credit for a move? Adopting a gaming sensibility leads *Dance Central* players to try out kinesthetic styles and repertoires that they might otherwise reject, especially in a public setting. Some will never perform those moves again, some find ways to rechoreograph them to feel less transgressive, and some gradually open themselves to unknown possibilities:

> First of all, I am a guy, and I am not a dancer. I got this game because I saw it was the highest rated game for the Kinect and I wanted to see how it worked. At first I felt totally gay playing it and almost had to stop. But I got addicted to the challenge and liked the exercise, especially as the routines got more difficult and there were some moves I just couldn't seem to nail. I am no longer so self conscious watching myself dance. I still wouldn't let anyone else watch me, but who knows, maybe eventually I will get enough confidence to change my mind on that. (player review, Amazon.com 2013b)

Dance Central shows how the technical affordances and limitations of a motion-sensing interface can be marshaled in the service of experiential education—in this case, teaching theories of performativity through embodied practice (cf. Gee 2004). Players must engage in an extensive trial-and-error process to render their bodies legible to the Kinect. Successful play requires attending to the smallest details of the on-screen dancer's gestures and bodily comportment, working out what counts for credit and where there is more latitude. Is it the angle of the torso, the rhythm of the pelvic popping, the coordination of hands and feet, or the precision of finger snaps that will push the score from "Nice" to "Flawless" on this move? This trial-and-error citational process is at the heart of performativity (Bollen 2001:290, following Butler 1993). It requires heightened attention informed by phenomenological reflection: Players become conscious of themselves and the game as mutually implicated perceiving subjects and objects of perception (Sobchack 1992).

Consider a thought experiment: Suppose Harmonix had set out to create a game that made a similar argument about race. What would such a game look and feel like? *Dance Central*'s argument about gender relies on the deployment of strongly marked and closely juxtaposed "masculine" and "feminine" material—an exaggerated contrast. Attempting a similar project by juxtaposing over-the-top racial caricatures would be a much riskier proposition, regardless of the developers' intent. While both racial masquerade and gender masquerade might have the potential to undermine biological essentialism and advance ironic critiques of conventional norms, minstrelsy has different stakes because of its long-standing association with racial hierarchies and institutional racism. (Recall that the "Jim Crow" system of legislated racial segregation in the United States took its nickname from a blackface stage character.) But there would also be another problem: What kind of dance moves could be coded "white"? Perhaps they could come from ballet, though this would also introduce an art dance/popular dance binary and a distracting mismatch with the music. Or the choreography could incorporate square-dance and hoedown references (occasionally deployed as musical signs of whiteness in hip-hop tracks). In fact, *Just Dance* does use some moves from this repertoire, but their incongruity with *Dance Central*'s guiding aesthetic could significantly undermine the franchise's claim to authenticity.

Think back to the Amazon reviews of *Dance Central*. They suggested that what really defines "whiteness" in popular dance contexts is a failed approximation of black or Latin dance (cf. Bosse 2007). In some households, then, both Harmonix and Ubisoft are indeed staging visceral experiences of racial difference—but the players are supplying the broad caricatures of "white dance," so the games don't have to. And in other households, there are players who embrace *Dance Central* and *Just Dance* as games choreographed by and for people of color and/or queer people. They recognize characters who "look like me, talk like me, dance like me," as game choreographer Chanel Thompson put it, and feel recognized in turn.

When do signs of race, gender, and sexuality in game content function as inclusive representation or critical interventions, and when do they perpetuate long-standing cycles of appropriation and exploitation? As players explore the repertoire in dance games, some find themselves reflecting on the kinds of motions that are "supposed" to feel familiar or natural for them. For example, one player told me, "Hip shaking for me is always awkward, but I'm Latina so I have to get over that even if I feel awkward." Others begin to consider how signs of race, gender, and sexuality intersect on the dance floor; a self-described "uptight white guy" observed, "I feel [hip motions] as blacker moves. I mean, when I see black guys dancing. When white guys do those moves, they look really gay, which is to say feminized" (post-gameplay interview sessions, 2013). Such accounts show how kinesthetic experience interacts with a "system of racial sight" (Guterl 2013:45) and how "gestural performatives" (Noland 2009:17) might simultaneously destabilize norms in one domain of essentialized difference and reconfirm them in another. In Chapters 4 and 5 I will return to the thorny questions raised by entertainment products that rely on collecting data from the dancing bodies of people of color and repackaging it as an invitation to mimetic performance.

Dance games ask players to forfeit traditional puppet-master control over an avatar and instead investigate the performative affordances of their own bodies. These investigations hinge on embodied difference; as players feel out each routine, they rely on and construct ideas about the difference between their own and others' kinesthetic experiences. Visceral engagement with difference is part of learning any codified performance practice: Every ballet rehearsal, b-boy cypher, rock guitar lesson, or aerobics class offers stark evidence of the variable capacities and acquired competences of human bodies. Dance games intensify this process by encouraging players to adopt movement styles that don't match their own sense of self. When players submit their dancing for public evaluation, they experience the cultural consequences of "mismatched" performances; these experiences may generate both personal reflection and public discourse, extending the games' procedural arguments about performativity. But we should also attend to the consequences of "matching" performances—as when YouTube viewers treat a player's over-the-top, role-playing performance of femme dance moves as an opportunity to reconfirm her sexual objectification as a woman of color, and she responds with an ambivalent "NOT COOL. . . . . lol." There is another key lesson about difference and performativity here. When players accept dance games' invitation to explore theories of embodied identity through their own moving bodies, they may learn that the consequences of this kind of play are not equally negotiable for all participants.

CHAPTER 3
Listening Like a Dancer

Have you ever had a song stuck in your head? The chorus cycles around, repeating indefinitely, and might fade out only when you substitute something with an even catchier hook. Now consider what it might be like to have a song stuck in your body. As one *Dance Central* player put it, "Every time I hear the song—or I download the song for myself to listen to it because I like the track so much—then I can't help but think of the moves. When I'm listening to the track on my way to work, or if I'm at home: It runs through my head, and I can't help myself. It's become basically attached" (Riffraff, recorded phone interview, August 24, 2011). Riffraff is describing a dancer's habitual aural/kinesthetic experience of music. He explained, "For me, music isn't about just listening to music. There's always been a movement attached to the music. I can't listen to great music and not want to dance."

Just Dance and *Dance Central* are music games as much as they are dance games. Indeed, from the standpoint of recruiting and retaining players, they might be considered music games first and foremost, because of the way they capitalize on players' prior relationships with particular songs, artists, and genres. These games don't teach people a repertoire of basic dance moves and then set those moves to music; instead, they offer carefully curated collections of licensed popular music tracks, with choreography tailor-made to match each song. Their dance routines are kinesthetic transcriptions of existing musical works. Game choreographers cultivate special listening techniques to create these routines, and players report that performing game choreography transforms their listening experience. In this chapter I focus on three aspects of interactive audio in dance games: how game developers turn song into dance, how players learn to listen like choreographers, and how gameplay offers experiential lessons in multisensory musicality.

As I outlined in the Introduction, in many respects *Just Dance* and *Dance Central* are the direct successors of the *Guitar Hero* and *Rock Band* games, which offered players a new kind of musical experience at the intersection of virtual and actual musicianship (Miller 2012). In terms of both design and marketing, all of these games are built around their musical playlists. They attract players by advertising value-added interactive versions of popular songs: immersive, performance-oriented, and designed to foster social connections through shared musical experience. Whether they involve playing rock instruments or dancing, all these games share the same core play mechanics: kinesthetic engagement with recorded sound, mediated by on-screen notation systems that guide players through songs as they unfold. *Guitar Hero, Rock Band,* and *Dance Central* (all developed by Harmonix Music Systems) also present their musical repertoires as graded curricula. Each individual song can be played at multiple difficulty levels, the games provide separate "practice" and "performance" modes, and their complete playlists are organized from easiest to hardest. These design choices encourage repeated engagements with individual songs, while also creating a traditional game-challenge trajectory that appeals to achievement-oriented players.

However, in terms of sound design, there is one crucial difference between dance games and their rock-performance-oriented cousins: In dance games, game-play does not affect musical playback. The *Guitar Hero* and *Rock Band* games forge a connection between players' physical performances and pre-recorded sounds by providing separate audio tracks for each instrumental part, interrupting play-back of those tracks when players make technical errors, and offering customizable sound effects and opportunities for improvised fills. These games provide textbook examples of interactive audio; as Karen Collins writes, "While [players] are still, in a sense, the receiver of the end sound signal, they are also partly the transmitter of that signal, playing an active role in the triggering and timing of these audio events" (2008:3). A *Guitar Hero* solo dissolves into twangs and clanks when an inept player picks up the game controller, creating a persuasive relationship between physical input and audio output. Elsewhere I have characterized this kind of musical game-play as "schizophonic performance," which links the gestures of live musical perfor-mance to pre-recorded sound (Miller 2009).

Dance games are different: Their songs don't react to good or bad dancing. Nor are there variable outcomes in the screen dancer's performance. As discussed in previous chapters, the screen dancer offers a model for the player's dancing rather than a mirror that reflects the player's movements. No matter what the player is doing, the screen dancer keeps performing the choreography perfectly, and the song plays on, just as it would at a club. Thus, it seems that dance games do not revolve around interactive audio, at least not as it has traditionally been conceived in music games. Player inputs do not change musical outputs. Moreover, as we saw in Chapter 1, given that the player's movements don't guide those of the on-screen dancer, some gamers have questioned whether these games are truly "interactive" in any way.

But this player-input/system-output model tends to obscure other possible forms of interactivity, particularly those that rely on the plasticity of the senses and "the modularity of sensory technologies" (Sterne and Akiyama 2012:545, 547).

Digital gaming is always multisensory; it is a truism of game design that compelling games integrate audio, visual, and kinesthetic elements in the service of immersive experience (Grodal 2003, Salen and Zimmerman 2004, Collins 2008b). Game sound design that adheres to the player-input/system-output model often incorporates both dynamic musical soundtracks and sound effects that respond to player actions, blurring the line between diegetic and non-diegetic sound (Whalen 2004). Dance games present a different approach: They transform sonic material into visual and kinesthetic material, using processes that require the participation of dancing bodies at multiple stages of game production as well as during gameplay. Scholars of social dance practices and club cultures have offered ample evidence that when people dance to popular music, they bring techniques of listening, moving, watching, and touching into powerful alignment, generating immersive multisensory experiences and intimate social connections (e.g., Hazzard-Gordon 1990, Thornton 1996, Bollen 2001, Garcia 2011, Salkind 2016). Dance games aim to recreate this kind of experience, building on a fundamental affinity of digital gameplay and club dancing; both practices rely on sensory feedback loops driven by "the interplay, perhaps even tension, between sensation and perception" (Grimshaw 2012:358). These games challenge us to expand the scope of what constitutes "interactive audio," moving beyond considerations of dynamic soundtrack music, spatializing sound effects, or musical performance simulators to address the role of sound in multisensory interactivity.

In game development studios and in home gameplay, dancers become part of a chain of transduction technologies, which "turn sound into something accessible to other senses" (Pinch and Bijsterveld 2012:4). Consider the series of sensorial/technological transformations involved in producing and playing *Dance Central*: Game developers select songs based on their perceived musical, choreographic, affective, and commercial affordances. Choreographers draw on their own gestural repertoires to translate these songs into dance routines, a process that includes inventing a name and graphic icon for each move. Human dancers (typically the same choreographers) perform the routines in a motion-capture studio. The resulting data archives of moving human bodies are virtually reincarnated as the game code that animates digital screen dancers. The Xbox converts code back into sound and graphics, reuniting music and choreography. Players process this multisensory data through their own techniques of listening, looking, and moving. The Kinect transforms their performances into another data set, grist for the game's scoring mechanisms, which generate audio and visual feedback that may reorient players' listening and dancing experiences. Some players extend the chain further by recording their performances, posting videos online, and engaging in vigorous debates about the choreography for each song and how well it suits the music.

Dance games rely on the principle that "networked bodies generate data, which can arbitrarily be translated from one kind of output to another" (Bench 2009:8). But when people experience those "outputs" through their own bodies, the terms of the translation do not feel arbitrary; they become viscerally meaningful in relation to prior sensory experience and as bridges to others' experience. Bench has shown how this process plays out in the circulation of "viral choreographies," such as the dance routine for Beyoncé's "Single Ladies," which spread primarily via YouTube. She suggests, "It is the choreographic component that renders 'Single Ladies' a shared object of embodiment—that is, an object subject to physical restaging and not just digital reproduction, an object embedded in muscle memory rather than a surface of projected affects." Bench notes that the song sometimes travels separately from the choreography and may "outpace" it; "listeners sing along with the song playing on the radio more frequently than dancers embody its moves" (2013:133). I would argue that both listening-while-silent and singing along are also forms of rendering a song as "a shared object of embodiment." This is not to say that singing along is *the same* as listening-while-silent, just as dancing along is not the same as watching-while-holding-still. But these various modes of experience may powerfully inform each other through "cross-modal enhancement," in which "stimuli from one sensory channel enhance or alter the perceptual interpretation of stimulation from another sensory channel" (Serafin 2014:235; cf. Foster 2011 on kinesthetic empathy).

Singing along and dancing along have much in common as forms of participatory, multisensory engagement with popular music and as practices that fall under the broader heading of "playing along" (Miller 2012). Game choreographer Chanel Thompson drew out some of these connections for me when she described *Dance Central* as being like a karaoke game, but for dance. Just like musical artists, she and her fellow choreographers carried out their creative work in a recording studio, and the game made those recorded performances "playable" by circulating them in a format that created a space for players to fill with their own dancing bodies (Thompson and Miller 2015). Like karaoke systems, dance games support the transmission of embodied repertoires that can also be detached from proprietary hardware and software and deployed in other contexts. You can't play *Guitar Hero* without a guitar controller, but you can learn a dance game routine at home in front of a game console and then take the moves to a club, or chair-dance in your car when a song comes on the radio. Each song in a dance game's playlist is a hard-to-pirate, easy-to-sell, value-added musical product tailor-made for specific hardware. But this song-and-dance repertoire can also circulate in alternative formats, with music, dance, graphics, game structure, and interactive feedback mechanisms sometimes traveling together and sometimes parting ways.

TURNING SONG INTO DANCE: PROPRIOCEPTIVE INTERACTION

In April 2012 I paid a visit to PAX East, the annual Penny Arcade Exposition game convention in Boston, Massachusetts. Thousands of gamers and game industry employees milled around the Boston Convention Center, trying out new games and attending panel talks by game designers. Harmonix had built a *Dance Central* stage in the middle of the exhibition floor, where game choreographers, designers, player-relations staff, and convention attendees danced in front of a huge and varied audience. I attended a developers' panel featuring Matt Boch, who became the lead designer for *Dance Central* after working as a hardware designer for *Rock Band*. He agreed to an hour-long recorded interview after the panel, and we spent some time discussing the relationship between music and choreography in the games.

KM: I was curious about how you think of Dance Central as being about interactive audio, or as being about music? As compared maybe to Guitar Hero and Rock Band?

MATT BOCH: What's interesting about dance to me is that it has all of these different facets. . . . The core of Dance Central 1 is really the dance class experience. It's very indebted to the process that you go through learning a dance in a dance class, and it's about mastery of choreography. Then there are these breaks, the freestyle times, where you're encouraged to do whatever. . . . [The game presents] these two oppositional states, or I guess I wouldn't call them polar opposites but pretty different facets of dance. Sort of like, "Do whatever you want that is you reacting to the music" versus "Do this thing that is someone else reacting to the music in the same way that they did it." . . . The audio reactive parts to me are really about the ways in which the choreographers distill complex music down to the things which speak most to them rhythmically. (Boch and Miller 2012)

In this off-the-cuff response, Boch drew attention to aspects of "interactive audio" that have been part of dance experiences since long before anyone dreamed of dynamic game sound or motion-sensitive camera peripherals. He identified at least three distinct modes of kinesthetic interaction with music: improvisational "freestyle" dancing, which entails embodied interpretation of music as it plays; crafting choreography that presents an interpretation of a particular piece; and mastering *someone else's* choreography, which entails channeling that person's musical analysis and embodied interpretation of that analysis through one's own body.

Boch went on to describe the parallels between the core audio design features of *Guitar Hero* and *Rock Band* and the music-dance relationship in *Dance Central*. As he noted,

If you take a look at the choreography . . . there are these moves that are very, very linked to a particular sonic element. And it can do this strange thing that I think Guitar Hero and Rock Band were great at, which is—I have a sandwich metaphor for it. It's like if you're eating some highly complex sandwich like an Italian sandwich and you're eating this thing and it tastes good, but it's made of a whole bunch of parts. And in playing Rock Band, I think that the musical education part of it that's strongest to me is the way in which it shows you what a given instrument does to make a rock song. What a given instrument's role is, what it's playing, by showing you its absence and then its presence.

And I think that Dance Central can do the same thing in a lot of cases for the complex musical production that underpins all these songs. When the choreographers listen to all this stuff, some of them are reacting very lyrically, and you'll see songs like "Drop It Like It's Hot," which have almost miming elements to them. Then you have songs like "Down" or "Like a G6," where people are latching on to rhythmic elements and you are, to an extent, beat-matching, but what your beat-match is, is actually a dance that is distinctly aimed at musical elements of the song. So you are reacting to audio, but you're *reacting to someone else's reaction to audio*, if that makes sense. . . . I think that dance, in its expressiveness, takes a song generally more holistically. So you have those outlooks of particular parts where you're calling out a particular rhythmic pattern or a particular melodic pattern, but then you have maybe the majority of the dance moves that are taking the song holistically and trying to be reactive to that.

These observations point to the distinctive forms of musical listening that inform both choreographic work in dance games and players' subsequent experiences. Creating a notation track for a particular instrument in *Rock Band* involves analytical transcription that highlights the specific musical role of that instrument (see Miller et al. 2014). Creating choreography might mean attending to lyrics, distinctive rhythmic, melodic, and timbral features, and phrase structure. As Boch explained further, focusing on rhythm,

If you watch choreographers build the dances for Dance Central, they're sitting there, they have their headphones on, they're trying out different things, they're pointing out different things, and they have a unique verbal language for the thing, where they're talking about "the booms and the cats." And what they're talking about is usually the kick and the snare, or the hand clap, or whatever is subbing in for the bass and the percussive hit. And they're feeling out those boom-cats, is what they would tell you, and building moves around those patterns in the ways in which they understand the music. And then the player has the experience of dancing to the song and feeling those moments in the same way that the choreographer did.

As game choreographers carry out this task of "feeling out" each song, they are working within particular aesthetic and practical parameters. The licensed popular music featured in dance game playlists is crucial to marketing the games and plays a significant role in driving competition among game franchises. Game choreographers need to create a unique routine for each song—something that will feel right to players who are already fans of the music and might make converts of those who aren't. If the song is already associated with a particular dance style, signature moves, or a full-length choreographed routine—for instance, from the official music video—then choreographers need to consider whether and how to reference that material in the game routines. Choreographic variety and novelty are huge factors in selling additional downloadable content and game editions, so choreographers must avoid recycling too many moves from routine to routine—but some repetition across songs will make the routines easier to learn. Together, these circumstances constitute a central creative imperative for game choreographers: Their goal is to identify and kinesthetically amplify the distinctive sonic features and lyrics of each track. In the case of *Dance Central*, these kinesthetic transcription projects also entail creating a complementary layer of linguistic reinforcement for sound/movement connections, since every move must have a name. In an interview, *Dance Central* choreographer Marcos Aguirre discussed this naming process, giving examples that show how his translation of distinctive musical features was informed by his knowledge of dance history and particular dance cultures:

KM: It seems like there's a lot of history that gets built into the game and that people read out of it.

MARCOS AGUIRRE: Exactly. And that was also tough too, especially with certain songs: like if it was a hip-hop song, it has to be raw hip-hop dancing. We had to really think about certain things. It wasn't just, like, make up a dance—you had to really think about it.

KM: You mean as far as trying to be true to the genre of the music?

MARCOS AGUIRRE: Exactly. Like if something's Latin-based, like some Pitbull, do a little bit of salsa, so you feel more authentic with it. Or certain eras, like Salt N Pepa, very '90s, throw in the '90s moves. . . .

KM: In some of the really early songs from the first game, I remember when I first saw the Latino and the Latina, those moves. Did you name those?

MARCOS AGUIRRE: Yeah, we did. I remember those, specifically. The Latina I believe was the one with the hips, and the arms are rising up to connect at the wrist. I remember me and Frenchy [Hernandez] just making up the moves and naming them. It just felt like when a Latina does ballroom, and she's about to present herself, I feel like that's something that she would do. It's sensual, with the hips, it's showing arm movement, like in flamenco and tango and stuff like that, so we were just, like, "Oh, it's very Latina."

KM: And what about the Latino, the little shoulder pop and lean to the side?

MARCOS AGUIRRE: It's from when you're dancing with a girl and the girl's doing the hip movement, it's something the guys do more with the shoulder. They kind of roll it the same way, but it's more masculine with the shoulder. The girl's moving with the hip and the guy's moving in the same direction. So they complement each other. (Aguirre and Miller 2015)

In dance games players are not just in a face-to-face relationship with screen dancers but also an ear-to-ear relationship with choreographers, cultivating intimate common knowledge as they learn to channel someone else's listening orientation (cf. Gibbs 2010 on multimodal affect contagion).

But where does interactivity come into play in this process, for choreographers or for players? In my conversation with Matt Boch, I noticed that he was consistently using the word "reactive" instead of "interactive" when referring to audio design in *Dance Central*. When I asked him whether these were two different concepts for him, his response situated "interactivity" in the players' shifting perception of the music:

> I would say it is interaction. I'd say the process of dancing to a song is interacting with it. It is not changing what the song is, but it is changing your perception of what the song is. And I think that is as valid. If you think about Rock Band doing the same thing, you hear the whole song and then, here's someone who has very little understanding of how rock music is made. You hear the whole song and now you're going to play a bass part to it and you keep messing up and now you hear the song without the bass part. All of a sudden, all these things peel away and you're interacting with the audio in this very different way as a result of gameplay decisions that you made. I think your proprioceptive interaction with the game is also proprioceptive interaction with the music. And in feeling out with your body a given rhythm, I think it pushes your audio system to find the same pattern and to figure out where that is. . . .
>
> KM: That's really interesting, because I've been trying to think through, what's the [dance game] analog to missing a note and not hearing that note? Which is that tiny but huge design move for Rock Band and Guitar Hero, which makes such a difference in your interactivity, perceived interactivity. So you're saying, it's like you miss the beat and you feel that you missed the beat?
>
> MATT BOCH: Yeah, or you hit the beat and you feel that that is a pattern in the song. You notice that there is a bass synth that is doing that rhythm. You understand that rhythm better. You hear that particular part of the song because that's the part of the song that the choreographer is hearing when they're making the move for it. So that very tight linkage between the song and the choreography for it explicates a fair amount of musical information to the player. . . . I mean, you can also point to—we do direct audio manipulation and filter sweeps with your hands during freestyle, which is much more direct audio manipulation. But I think the interaction really comes in what is revealed to you and what is highlighted for you through specific rhythmic motion that then unpacks the song a bit.

In digital game discourse, "interactivity" usually describes a feedback process driven by player agency; "the user/player is able to change the visual appearance of a computer screen (and/or sounds from speakers) by some motor action via an interface" (Grodal 2003:142). As audio producer Lani Minella explains in a game audio textbook, "When players have a direct effect on what they hear, it's like they're the developers in some small way. They control the environment and have an audible impact and effect on it" (Marks and Novak 2009:150). Game audio pedagogy and scholarship often focus on this special quality of "adaptive," "interactive," "dynamic," or "non-linear" audio; they note how it differentiates game audio design from cinematic scoring, and they analyze what happens when "the player can become a causal agent in the audio's playback" (Collins 2008b:168; see also Collins 2008a, Cheng 2014). As Mark Grimshaw puts it, "Where the intended soundscape of a film is fixed at the point of production, digital game soundscapes are created anew at the point of reproduction" (2012:350).

Matt Boch's notion of proprioceptive interaction with music offers a different approach to conceiving of an "active relationship" between player and sound, one that seems more closely aligned with values from the art worlds of experimental electronic music and digital performance art. In these contexts, digital media artists and theorists often frame human-machine collaborations as partnerships, or as cyborg fusions. For example, in interactive dance installations, the dancers' gestures might generate changes in music, lighting, or an accompanying video projection; the dancers might respond to this multisensory feedback with new kinds of gestures. Experimental systems like the Embodied Generative Music project "lead movers to reconsider their 'natural' ways of connecting a certain movement with a sound" (Parviainen 2012:79) and create "the 'feeling' of cybernetic connection to the digital media they activate" (Dixon 2007:147; see also Kozel 2012). While this model potentially distributes agency more equitably among humans and machines, it resembles the commercial game development model in that it tends to frame interactivity as a process that generates perceptible effects—perceptible to a third-party observer, such as an audience at a performance. These effects serve to verify interactivity, proving that meaningful exchange is taking place. As we saw in Chapter 1, these authentication processes have played an important role in dance game reception, particularly with respect to evaluations of each game's motion-sensing system. How might they play out with respect to interactive audio?

In our interview, Matt Boch implicitly invoked the "perceptible effects" test for interactive audio, but he shifted the terms of the conventional player-input/system-output model. Rather than casting about for evidence of players' agency—their perceived control over the game technology, verified by their influence on musical playback—he pointed to how gameplay changes *the players*. He acknowledged that *Dance Central's* freestyle sections offer brief interludes of "kinetic gestural interaction" with the music (Collins 2008b:127), but he did not regard this feature as the core "interactive" aspect of the game. (Moreover, Boch observed that many players disliked the freestyle sections; in later game editions, players can turn off this feature.) Rather, Boch described how players' musical experiences flow from their proprioceptive interaction. As he put it, "It is not changing what the song is, but it is changing your perception of what the song is." A player offered an example:

> After you've learned choreo for a song, you kinda put emphasis on certain parts of a song differently. It's hard to describe in words. When your body's been trained to hit or move upon hearing certain beats or sounds in the song, you notice them a lot more. "Brick House" might be a good example. The beginning of the chorus that goes "She's a brick . . . house" has a couple little beats or sounds or something in the pause. Most people usually just focus on the lyrics, but after learning the dance moves that correlate to this part of the

song (and therefore, the fact that you have to move specifically to hit on those sounds) makes you start to recognize these a lot more in not only that song, but others as well. . . . Learning a dance to a song you already know is interesting, it's almost like you're hearing it again for the first time. It's so weird, since you're associating more images and movements to the song than you had before. (JWMidnight, email interview, August 2011)

In this form of interactive audio, the perceptible effects play out through players' bodies. Players learn to "feel out" the music as the game choreographers did. Playing dance games generates dynamic effects in real time, but these effects transpire on the players' side of the screen and speakers: in the actual world, not the virtual world (Boellstorff 2008:19, Miller 2012:8). Interactive audio in dance games is true to Torben Grodal's perception-oriented account of interactivity as "the creation of experiences that appear to flow from one's own actions" (2003:143).

Proprioception can be roughly glossed as the sense that tells us about our own bodily position, balance, movement, and intensity of physical effort. Are we standing on one foot, floating in a pool, running on sand, or wrestling in jello? Biomedical investigations of proprioception explore the functioning of various kinds of mechanoreceptors and how they interact with motor neurons: for instance, how nerve endings signal limits on a joint's range of motion (Stillman 2002). My own childhood enculturation of sensory experience included learning to differentiate "the five senses" and associate them with discrete body parts—eye, ear, nose, tongue, skin. Proprioception eludes such tidy reduction; it is a complex system of disparate perceptual mechanisms spread throughout the body, from the balance apparatus of the inner ear to the muscle spindles that relay information on the contraction and relaxation of muscular tissue. The proprioceptive system offers vivid demonstrations of the interconnectedness of the senses. Try balancing on one foot with your eyes open or closed. What if your eyes are open and you look around the room, and then switch to focusing on a fixed point? What if you add the lightest possible tactile connection to another object, like a fingertip barely touching a wall? What about a tactile connection to another part of your own body, like pressing the sole of your lifted foot against your standing leg? These kinds of examples are often deployed to illustrate the intersection of visual, haptic, and proprioceptive sensory systems. But what about auditory perception? Dance games invite players to explore how listening can inform proprioception, and vice versa.

In his theoretical work on movement, affect, and sensation, Brian Massumi describes proprioception as a sensory mode that "translates the exertions and ease of the body's encounters with objects into a muscular memory of relationality . . . [and] draws out the subject's reactions to the qualities of the objects it perceives through all five senses, bringing them into the motor realm of externalizable response" (2002:58–59). In the case of dance games, the "objects" of proprioceptive encounter include music and choreography, and the main game challenge consists of enacting a motor response to those objects through proprioceptive interaction. Performing pre-choreographed material is a prescribed motor response, but it is certainly not automatic; choreographers and players alike must contend with the fact that we don't currently have a mechanism for streaming kinesthetic data into the human proprioceptive system in the same way that we stream audio and visual content. As I will discuss in the next chapter, proprioceptive interaction with game music plays an enormous role in reducing the kinesthetic lag that besets players who are attempting to dance along with unfamiliar choreography in real time.

Dance games engage players in multisensory interactive exercises that create powerful and enduring connections between sonic and kinesthetic objects of perception. They are also designed to make this process feel good. This affective dimension is crucial: Dance games don't simply bring together music and movement but construct a mutually reinforcing relationship between the pleasures of listening and the pleasures of movement. This relationship can come to feel necessary, irresistible, and immediate, a "second nature" response—as Riffraff put it, "I can't listen to great music and not want to dance." Massumi's arguments offer some insight into the relationship between affect, virtuality, and multisensory experience in dance games; he writes that "affect is synesthetic, implying a participation of the senses in each other: The measure of a living thing's potential interactions is its ability to transform the effects of one sensory mode into those of another." He describes affective experiences in terms of "virtual synesthetic perspectives," where the virtuality of affect is associated with its potential for circulation: "Affect is autonomous to the degree to which it escapes confinement in the particular body whose vitality, or potential for interaction, it is" (2002:35). Dance games offer concrete examples of the production and circulation of "virtual synesthetic perspectives," in the form of digitally encoded song-and-dance repertoires that are actualized through embodied human performance. They also evoke productive resonances between Massumi's theory of affect and Sara Ahmed's work on the sociality of emotions. Ahmed describes affect as a value that accrues to signs in the course of circulation and argues that signs "become sticky through repetition" (2004:45, 91). Harmony Bench applies Ahmed's theory to "viral choreographies" that circulate via social media, aiming to account for how these dance routines function as "shared objects of embodiment" (Bench 2013:133). Dance games draw our attention to forms of repetition that involve circulation not only across bodies but across sensory modes. In this process, music and choreography each become "sticky," a stickiness that binds them together and encourages the accumulation of new layers of affective value as they move—"gatherings that become a part of the object, and call into question its integrity as an object" (Ahmed 2004:91).[1]

LISTENING LIKE A CHOREOGRAPHER

As commercial products, dance games have a symbiotic relationship with the songs and artists featured on their playlists. Some people will buy a game edition or additional downloadable-content (DLC) tracks because they already know and love the music; others will buy songs for listening or will seek out artists' other recordings after encountering music in the games. (Harmonix gained experience developing these mutually beneficial licensing agreements while building the song catalogs for *Guitar Hero* and *Rock Band*.) But while an initial purchase might be driven primarily by name recognition—the promise of dancing to a familiar track by Lady Gaga—experienced players bring other criteria to their assessment of new repertoire. During my years tracking the Harmonix-sponsored *Dance Central* community forum, I observed that when upcoming DLC releases were announced, players immediately began considering each song's possible choreographic affordances. When a preview of the choreography was released, they discussed how the choreographer's choices lined up with their listening expectations. Finally, once players had purchased and played through the track (or watched gameplay videos posted to YouTube), they offered detailed evaluative reviews of the routine.

For example, in May 2012 the Harmonix forum manager started a new discussion thread entitled "DLC discussion—Low by Flo Rida." ("Low," originally released in 2007, was Flo Rida's multi-platinum-selling debut single.) She posted a link to a 30-second preview video for the song, which included the dance steps for the song's chorus: "She hit the floor/Next thing you know/ Shorty got low, low, low…" (Harmonix Music Systems 2012). By featuring this portion of "Low," the preview not only reminded players of the song's most recognizable musical hook but gave them an opportunity to assess the dance routine's signature moves; the chorus subroutine will repeat at regular intervals. In this case, since the lyrics of the chorus explicitly describe movements on the dance floor, the choreographer could be expected to draw on them. Players could speculate about possible physical enactments of "hitting the floor"—perhaps striding onto the dance floor, or literally striking it with a hand or foot? And what about the title move, "getting low"? Would it entail bent knees, dipped hips, a limbo backbend, or a gesture connoting "low" sexuality?

The Harmonix forum manager seeded the discussion of this new track with a direct invitation for feedback: "Check out the sample of the new routine and share your thoughts in this thread. Once the DLC drops tomorrow leave your reviews here!" Players immediately jumped into the fray:

> heyoRADIO: Going to be immediately honest and say I was really disappointed with the use of Step Pump for "low low low low low low low low" as I was hoping we'd have a fun new move that went along with the lyrics. Oh well. :/ Nearly everything in the preview is a move we've seen before, so you could say I was pretty let down with this. . . . Here's hoping things are better outside of this little preview? I gotta keep *some* of my optimism. haha

Lauson1ex: Saw it coming, therefore I'm not deceived. Just face it, people: the song has been advertised as being in the Moderate category. Not Tough, not Legit. Moderate. I'm surprised that you guys expected anything more than what you actually got!

WhiteMo: Honestly though, D.A.N.C.E., Pon de Replay, Rude Boy, Right Thurr, Oops (Oh My) and I Like It, these are also moderate level songs and they have amazing and mildly challenging choreographies. . . .

Thus, we have the right to have high expectations for LOWer level songs [smile icon] (see what I did there?) For the 'low low low low' part, I imagined something like the Topple move in Down [a song by Jay Sean that features the lyrics "Down, down, down, down"]. . . . All we can do is to wait until tomorrow [smile icon] I've almost never been disappointed with a Chanel routine . . . and the song is pretty cool without the dance anyway.

BossPlayer: This is the type of DLC I buy off the bat because I enjoy the song, not for the difficulty or choreography.

Lauson1Ex: I was expecting a Muscle Swish [link to YouTube video of gameplay featuring this move] at the 'low low low low' part *at the very least*, but now that you have mentioned it, the Topple move would have worked SO much better.

(DanceCentral.com 2012b)

This discussion demonstrates the expectations that experienced players bring to new DLC tracks, informed by their knowledge of the existing choreographic repertoire. In the course of the discussion, many players mentioned the choreographer, Chanel Thompson, by name; several echoed the declaration that "you can obviously tell Chanel choreoed this song. It is written all over it" (Appamn). Players also acknowledged the practical constraints that shape the work of Harmonix choreographers. As Lauson1ex noted, songs assigned to the "Moderate" difficulty level simply cannot have showstopper routines. Another player observed, "Putting the song at a 'Moderate' difficulty level (probably to make it accessible to all skill/fitness levels due to the song's popularity) probably limited Chanel's options a little bit. . . . It isn't her best work, but I am still a Chanel fan and look forward to future DLCs by her" (Seanyboy99). ZJ11197 chimed in, "Yeah you guys have to give Chanel some slack. . . . We cannot be selfish. . . . They had to tailor low to be a song everyone at any level could play." (See Chapter 5 for Chanel Thompson's perspective on these constraints.)

After posting these lukewarm reviews of the "Low" preview video, forum participants played through the whole routine and returned to contribute more detailed evaluations:

WhiteMo: The renewed Victorious move is really great, but so tiring that I'm actually glad we don't have to do it for a second time in a row. As for new moves, there aren't many – what we mainly get is a bunch of old moves freshened up a bit, and it isn't a bad thing at all, for they fit the song and don't repeat themselves unnecessarily.

As I mentioned before, this dance is very tiring, as it involves quick leg lifts, bending knees and waist and wide arm movements, but that's what we expect from a Chanel routine. The finishing move is interesting, but it's similar to Gonna Make You Sweat's finishing move.

Seanyboy99: The Barreto Clap + Whatever Move (Crab Walk here specifically) combo feels better for slower songs, rather than faster songs like this one. I also felt that the Coconut Crab move was a lot similar to the Bobblehead Step move. The Freq Whip (/Jump) move does fit with the song, but I personally think that the slot where it appears would have been an excellent opportunity to do a new move and or one with more flavor (I could totally think of a move that borrows from "Scenario." It would be called "The Slipper Slap" Tee Hee.)

Appamn: Whenever I heard low on the radio, mainly the first thing I would note for this song was its heavy bass. I'd turn up the radio in my car and just have fun listening. Second, I would notice its badassness that it has. However, DC . . . Sort of made it a feminent, girly song. Don't get me wrong, I have no problem doing girly moves in the game, but DC ruined the reputation that this song had.

This critical analysis of new repertoire illuminates another facet of interactive audio in *Dance Central*, one that complements and informs players' visceral experiences in the moment of gameplay. Here players are engaging in what Eric Zimmerman calls cognitive interactivity and meta-interactivity: "interpretive participation with a text" and "cultural participation with a text," respectively (2004:158). But while Zimmerman's analytical categories are meant to account for players' interactions with a game narrative (following in the footsteps of reader-response theory), *Dance Central* players are reflecting on their multisensory embodied experience as dancers and listeners.

Importantly, *Dance Central* offers players a basic vocabulary with which to discuss and critique choreography. Game discourse grows from a lexicon of move names, a list of choreographer credits, and a common experience of a shared repertoire, allowing players to compare routines and identify specific choreographic styles. Forum discussions also give players space to hash out conventions for discussing how routines *feel* in practice: "tiring," full of "flavor," "girly," "badass," a good fit/poor fit with the music. The online format also makes it easy for players to include links to illustrative video examples when words fall short. Discourse can play an important role in transforming a song into a "shared object of embodiment" (Bench 2013:133), and dance games offer a wealth of terms that help constitute the discursive infrastructure for dispersed communities of practice (Hamera 2007; see also Wenger 1998). Drawing on Massumi, we might also observe that game discourse contributes to the process of converting affect into emotional experience; in his terms, emotions "capture" affect by fixing it in the form of "qualified, situated perceptions and cognitions" that are "ownable," "recognizable," and "narrativizable" (2002:28, 35). Dance game makers and players have much to tell us, and each other, about the process of listening for affective potential and realizing it through kinesthetic practice—and the telling can be a key part of the process.

CONCLUSION: SENSING LIKE A DANCER

Shortly after the release of the first *Dance Central* game, a commenter posted this skeptical rejoinder to a positive game review:

> I played the original version of this game just now. A song came on the radio while I was getting something to eat and I was like "this is fun" and started dancing a bit. The graphics were much better than the 360 version and it had less loading times. It also cost £0. I'd recommend it instead of buying this, I think it's called "Dancing in Real Life". (Stegosaurus-Guy-II, comment posted November 4, 2010, on Smith 2010)

Such criticisms invite us to consider what *does* distinguish dance gameplay from "dancing in real life." It's a tricky question, since the split between virtual and actual performance functions very differently here than in most digital games. Again, the comparison to *Guitar Hero* may be useful: Where *Guitar Hero* players serve as middlemen for a pre-recorded musical track, dance game players are actually dancing. They are not controlling an avatar's movements; their gestures do not shape musical playback. Because the model of proprioceptive interactivity described by Matt Boch reverses the conventional human-input/machine-output scenario, it implies that we might consider any kind of broadcast or playback technology to be just as "interactive" as a dance game. In the case of dancing to the kitchen radio, a machine provides the input in the form of musical sound, and a human carries out the kinesthetic translation of this material to create a danced output, while also accruing cumulative sensory experiences that may change the way the person interacts with music and machines in future. Dance games offer attractive commercial packages, curated song lists, the allure of trying out a motion-sensing interface, and social connections to a community of practice, but are they really doing anything special when it comes to interactive audio?

I believe that the answer is yes, and that this distinctiveness hinges on how dance games use choreography to remediate listening experiences—how they make it possible for players to "react to someone else's reaction to audio," as Matt Boch put it. Dance game choreographers are charged with interpreting musical structures and performing the resulting kinesthetic transcriptions for motion-capture systems, which archive them as digital data that can be reencoded into "playable" formats. Players learn how to make their bodies function as the playback technologies for this archived material, a process that relies heavily on musical listening (discussed further in Chapter 4). As numerous dance ethnographers have demonstrated, dance transmission is typically a body-to-body affair (e.g., Hahn 2007, Davida 2012). Dance games accomplish the feat of transmitting a dance repertoire from body to body without having both bodies in the room at the same time, and they do so in part by engaging players in proprioceptive interaction with music. Dance games offer a new channel for the transmission of embodied knowledge and for indexing that knowledge through popular music—"feeling out" music with one's body, and imagining how it feels in someone else's body. As players gain expertise in game repertoires, their new knowledge tends to transform their experience of music and dance; even when they are listening or observing, they do so with a dancerly sensibility (cf. Foster 2011, Goodridge 2012:122).

This will not be news to the musicians and dancers among my readers, who already know that there is something qualitatively distinctive about listening to a piece of music that one knows how to play, or watching choreography built from moves that one has performed. Cognitive neuroscientists have been investigating this phenomenon using functional magnetic resonance imaging (fMRI) scans, finding that "action observation in humans involves an internal motor simulation of the observed movement" and that significant "expertise effects" come into play in this process; that is, "the brain's response to seeing an action is influenced by the acquired motor skills of the observer" (Calvo-Merino et al. 2005:1245–46). Thus, when groups of expert ballet dancers and capoeira practitioners watched videos of people performing in these styles, "the mirror areas of their brains responded quite differently according to whether they could do the actions or not" (1248).

Neuroscientists have also designed experiments that investigate neural links between listening and motor action, producing findings that "support the hypothesis of a 'hearing-doing' system that is highly dependent on the individual's motor repertoire" (Lahav et al. 2007:308). One such experiment "examined the effect of listening to a newly learned musical piece on subsequent motor retention of the piece. Thirty-six non-musicians were trained to play an unfamiliar melody on a piano keyboard. . . . Subjects who, during their listening sessions, listened to the same initial piece showed significant improvements in motor memory and retention of the piece despite the absence of physical practice" (Lahav et al. 2012:1). That is, once organized sound has been associated with organized movement, that association has enduring effects that can be accessed via multiple sensory channels. Dance ethnographers have documented similar effects in numerous dance cultures; for instance, Joseph Schloss describes the enculturated/embodied response that summons hip-hop dancers to the floor when they hear canonical b-boy tracks, observing that "from the moment this ability becomes a part of any given breaker's disposition, that individual carries a piece of hip-hop history in his or her physical being and recapitulates it every time he or she dances" (2006:421). As *Dance Central* player Riffraff put it, "The experience of the game has become attached to the song—so when I listen to the song, I experience the game again" (recorded phone interview, August 24, 2011).

Since dance games are built around playlists of licensed popular songs, players often encounter their musical repertoires in the course of everyday life. My online qualitative survey posed several questions about players' musical tastes and how their listening practices intersected with their gameplay experiences (Miller 2013a; see Introduction). Their responses strongly suggested that playing dance games has offered a musical experience that stretches the boundaries of many players' listening tastes, introduces them to new music, and/or changes their experience of familiar music. (Most of the respondents were recruited from the *Dance Central* player forums, and some questions referred specifically to this series; but it should be noted that 70 percent of the 56 respondents also had experience playing *Just Dance*.) In a "Check all that apply" question, 58 percent checked "I liked all the musical genres in *Dance Central* before I started to play"; 58 percent checked "There are songs I enjoy playing that I don't enjoy as a listener"; 80 percent checked "Playing *Dance Central* has increased my appreciation for certain songs/genres"; and 80 percent checked "I have added new music to my listening collection because of these games." The next question asked, "After you have learned the dance routine for a certain song, do you hear that song differently? Please explain." Here I provided a text-entry box rather than a binary yes/no option, in hopes of encouraging respondents to reflect on what it might mean to "hear differently." This question was completed by 34 respondents, with 29 responding affirmatively and 5 responding negatively or ambiguously. Most of the affirmative responses address kinesthetic experience. A representative selection:

Every time I hear these songs, I want to dance to them.

I feel sort of compelled to dance to it. For example, S and M by Rihanna. I just imagine the dance routine and I sort of "hear it differently".

When I hear the song I feel a certain almost muscle memory/urge to do the song's dance routine.

Yes! When I hear a DC song in public, I can't help but to perform the moves, even in public!

Before whenever I heard those songs it feels so ordinary but when I learned a dance routine through Dance Central, it made me feel alive [and] ready to dance and party all I want. The feeling of enjoyment and happiness whenever I heard those songs.

I never danced before the first game released, and as I danced, my iTunes library grew a lot, I came to like more hip-hop, R&B. . . . I never cared about these songs before. . . . When I listen to a song like this, dancing is what comes first to my mind, I begin to imagine the moves that could fit, the expressions a body can translate the song into.

Note that many players describe what feels like an involuntary conditioned response, whether it be wanting to dance, internally rehearsing the choreography, actually enacting the moves, or re-experiencing the affect associated with gameplay.

Other respondents focused more on describing a change in conscious listening technique or musical comprehension/interpretation. (In the next chapter I discuss the relationship between listening technique and dance technique in more detail.)

> Yes. More in tune to counting out the routine in my head when I hear the song.

> I pay more attention to the beat of the song when I learn the routine by heart.

> If it's a song I already know, I start to hear it for its music and beat rather than its lyrics.

> I feel like I understand the music better.

> Yes, because through the moves, I understand the story of the song.

> Very much so, there are some songs I would have just not taken the time to know.

Two of the five "no" answers included descriptions of a transformed musical experience that the respondent did not classify as "hearing differently":

> I don't hear it differently, I just see the dance in my head now!

> I don't hear the song differently, but I may begin to appreciate it more and I may even download the song and listen to it in my leisure time.

While none of the responses to this question suggested that learning a dance routine might negatively impact one's subsequent listening experience, some forum posts and responses to other questions did raise this possibility. Players have strong opinions about game choreography, and it stands to reason that when they dislike a particular routine, those negative associations could also stick to a song. We might be tempted to assume that players are less likely to repeat routines that they do not enjoy, in which case these transformative effects could be less pronounced. However, those who play in social and/or competitive situations must often accommodate others' song selections, and some commit themselves to mastering all available routines for the sake of goal-oriented "completion" or getting their money's worth from a game. Think back to the player who complained that the *Dance Central* choreography had made "Low" into a "feminent, girly song," and consider what it might feel like for him to internally rehearse that "girly" choreography every time "Low" plays on the radio.

Dance games provide a kind of sensory matchmaking service, bringing hearing and kinesthesia together in a congenial atmosphere and helping them get to know each other and discover how much they already have in common. By creating links between music and choreography, dance games inculcate powerful sound/body connections for people without prior dance training, as well as inviting dancers of all experience levels to channel particular listening experiences by playing through choreographers' kinesthetic transcriptions. The games teach players how to sense like a dancer, and lead many to reflect on and develop that new embodied understanding by engaging with a community of practice (Hamera 2007). As we saw in Chapter 2, at times this process of proprioceptive interaction involves exploring movement styles and listening orientations that clash with players' embodied sense of self. Playing dance games offers constant reminders that the human body is not a mass-produced technical interface like a traditional game controller, nor a playback device that repeats the same material the same way again and again. Interacting with sound—especially musical sound—always means interacting with culture, including one's own cumulative embodied experience. The "effects" that so often serve as a hallmark of interactivity may play out through the channels of that embodied experience, beyond the confines of console hardware and game code.

In a sense, dance games really are musical instrument games. The instrument in question is the human body, and the games use guided listening exercises to teach people how to play music through their own bodies. Players' bodies are not generating the musical sound that comes through the speakers, but they are nonetheless making music—creating distinctive forms of musical experience for themselves and others by kinesthetically amplifying particular sonic structures. Performing these kinesthetic transcriptions is a way of organizing one's perception of sound by aligning multiple sensory channels. Musicians who play instruments also learn to map musical sounds to kinesthetic practice; like a dancer who hears a song on the radio and "can't help but think of the moves," a pianist who hears a recording of a song she knows how to play will have a virtual kinesthetic experience of playing it with her own hands. Players' performances also impact the musical experiences of non-dancers. Watching and listening is not the same kind of musical experience as dancing or playing an instrument oneself, but it is quite different from listening to a song without perceiving a corresponding moving body. Elsewhere I've discussed how music-oriented video games recall older media formats that domesticated popular, public, and professional musical repertoires by converting them into a playable format for amateurs at home—a history that ranges from parlor piano sheet music transcriptions of concert hall repertoires to music-minus-one recordings and karaoke machines (Miller 2012).

Dance games offer experiential lessons in multisensory musicality. They suggest that popular music tracks are playable interactive systems like games, and human bodies are playable musical interfaces like instruments. Taking a broader view, dance games demonstrate the potential of multimodal approaches to interactive audio design: how articulating sound to kinesthetic practice can reorient perception, and how people bring that experience to other everyday practices of listening, looking, and moving. These games model a version of "interactive audio" that recalls Massumi's assertion that "potential for interaction" resides in the sensory capacities of idiosyncratic, particular living bodies. Dance games can help us recognize "interactivity" in experiences that harness music to drive sensory transformations and social interactions, circulating intense feeling across bodies and leaving traces that structure future circulations (Kassabian 2013:xii; see also Gibbs 2010).

As we draw on these principles to consider particular instances of multisensory interactivity, we should not lose sight of the complex articulations of sound and kinesthetic repertoire with other cultural formations, including identity categories that are experienced through the body (Sterne and Akiyama 2012:545, Born 2012:165). "Reacting to someone else's reaction to audio" isn't only about channeling that person's analysis of musical structure; as I showed in Chapter 2, it may mean feeling out an embodied experience marked by gender, race, sexual orientation, or cultural background. In the *Dance Central* context, "interactive audio" involves music and dance that grew out of urban African American, Caribbean, and Latino youth cultures. The "teacher" voice that guides players through the rehearsal mode is marked by a black vernacular accent and vocabulary, the choreographers are mostly people of color, and the governing dance aesthetic might best be located at the intersection of contemporary hip-hop and queer club culture. The game's kinesthetic transcriptions were not produced through an automated technical procedure that converts sound waves into the code that animates dancing characters; they were made by humans with individual personal histories and distinctive styles as choreographers, dancers, and teachers. In the next two chapters, I turn to a closer analysis of how game choreographers link listening technique to dance technique, and how their labor situates them as cultural intermediaries.

CHAPTER 4

Practice, Practice, Practice

In the many contexts that dance technique is offered as a medium for learning, or a mode of enquiry, and where this is not necessarily a means to "become" a dancer, then what is it for? (Stanton 2011:88)

How do dance games teach players to dance, and to value dance? Two short stories about teaching, learning, and evaluative standards will help set the stage for an investigation of these linked questions. At their core, both stories are about what it means to dance like a gamer.

I. A CLASSROOM STORY

I visit an undergraduate dance studies seminar to talk about dance games. We push the tables and chairs to the margins of the classroom, hook up my Xbox to the digital projector, close the window shades, turn off the overhead lights, and start the class session with a half hour of playing *Dance Central*. There are six women and one man in the class; all have some formal dance training, but only the male student identifies himself as a gamer. None have played *Dance Central* before. The students are giggly and a little self-conscious, but they dance with enthusiasm. We all do the game routines together, though the Kinect only tracks two of us at a time; we take turns serving as the tracked bodies, trading off between songs. When the game serves up silly photos snapped during the "freestyle" interlude in each song, there's a big burst of laughter every time. At the end of the session I ask the students about their strategies for following the routines. A few tell me that the basic moves and patterns of movement combinations are familiar to them from hip-hop or jazz dance classes. Several seem unclear on whether the Kinect was really tracking or evaluating their moves; they wonder how the game calculated the scores that were displayed at the end of each song.

Now the lone student who claimed substantial gaming experience speaks up. He noticed right away that there were tiered evaluations for each move, indicated by the words Almost, Nice, or Flawless materializing under the screen dancer's feet. After following the screen dancer to get a sense of the key moves at the beginning of each song, he shifted his attention to the scrolling flashcards at the edge of the screen, knowing they would help him anticipate repeated material. He also kept an eye on the accumulating numerical score in the corner of the screen; drawing on his prior experience with *Guitar Hero*, he looked and listened for cues that might indicate special opportunities to earn bonus points, such as the occasional gold flashcards. He observed that the game did not simply allocate a certain number of points for each move but lavishly rewarded long streaks of Flawless moves. Accordingly, he used the freestyle interludes to practice combinations that he knew would be returning, the better to earn these bonuses. The other students look at him with raised eyebrows and cocked heads. Several say they did not even see the flashcards or the words under the dancer's feet.

II. A TALENT SHOW STORY

I receive an email from a colleague at another university. He writes about a performance at a student talent show:

> One of the acts was a dance routine that I'm convinced the student learned from Dance Central or some other dance game. Among other things, one could tell that she learned each component of her dance as a discrete movement with little sense of the interconnection between moves into an integrated routine, much less develop follow-through between the moves. More than anything else, one had a sense that she was orienting herself toward the kinect and was afraid to move out of camera range. It was very very strange, but I suspect has become a common post-Xbox sight.

I am reminded of a term I encountered during my *Guitar Hero* research: "lrn-2reeltar," the shorthand coinage that players used to refer to derisive comments from those who challenged them to repeat their blistering solos on a real guitar (Miller 2012:94). That discourse was rooted in the authenticity paradigms of live rock performance and disciplined classical virtuosity, strongly inflected by related ideologies of masculinity. My colleague's observations trace the contours of a parallel discourse for dance games: We might call it "lrn2reeldanz." I have seen it before, in the reviews that questioned whether game systems could tell the difference between dancing and flailing (see Chapter 1). But it is often invoked by devoted players, too. For instance, in a *Dance Central* forum thread on "Requests, Suggestions, & Features Feedback": "It would be amazing if players who *actually dance* are given higher points than those who do the 'space invader'" (menorche, posted to DanceCentral.com 2011b).

How do dance games transmit dance technique, compile dance repertoires, and represent particular dance histories? What kinds of dance do they teach, and what kinds *can* they teach, at the level of technical affordances? What standards of "realness" are in play here? Both *Just Dance* and *Dance Central* aim to conjure the experience of social, popular dance practices that are at odds with the very idea of choreographic fixity and disciplined technique. Yet as the score-oriented seminar student immediately observed, they also adhere to a traditional game model that focuses on quantifiable achievements, posing well-defined challenges and evaluating players' success in meeting them. It would be very difficult to design a scoring system that allowed for a wide range of variability in players' performances yet still seemed to give fair, consistent evaluations—let alone the kind of fine-grained feedback that could serve the additional design goal of showing off the performance capabilities of a motion-tracking system (see Chapter 1). Thus both *Just Dance* and *Dance Central* model dance paradigms that prize technical specificity and consistent execution, and they both present dance pedagogy systems organized around a repertoire of fixed choreographic works.

In this chapter I offer a working definition of technique, compare dance game pedagogy to typical studio pedagogy, and provide close readings of an example from each game franchise: "Apache (Jump on It)" from *Just Dance 3*, and "Crank That" from *Dance Central*. In addition to demonstrating some general principles of technical pedagogy and kinesthetic transcription in dance games, these two examples show how the games remediate existing song-and-dance repertoires with complex histories of circulation. The production and reception of the dance game versions of "Apache (Jump On It)" and "Crank That" show us game developers and players engaged in the work that lies at the heart of performance studies: "to take seriously the repertoire of embodied practices as an important system of knowing and transmitting knowledge" (Taylor 2003:26).

DEVELOPING TECHNIQUE/MATERIALIZING INTERFACES

Can dance games teach technique? Engaging with this question requires a working definition of technique, one that attends to the term's entwined connotations of both practiced action and achieved accomplishment. Technique is something people do, that exists in the process of the doing, yet also something people desire, strive for, and ultimately claim as a possession. I propose that developing technique entails repetitive practice of an embodied/material-oriented action, with the aim of reaching a point where this particular technique no longer requires constant conscious attention and may be employed in the service of a creative project. (This formulation incorporates elements from a long chain of theories of practical knowledge, e.g., Mauss 1992 [1934], Polanyi 2015 [1958], Shusterman 1999, Hahn 2007, O'Connor 2007, Pakes 2009.) Creative projects that rely on technique are forms of craft; in aesthetic terms, craft often privileges signs of "the hand of the maker," a synecdoche for a body animated by technique. Note that this working definition relies on the principle that repetition is an engine of change. It also implies the existence of evaluative standards, built into the concept of "skills."

Developing technique requires feedback mechanisms and reflection: Are you getting better at this? How do you know? Technique implies learning by trial and error; if there were never any errors, or if you always understood at the outset what caused them, then there would be nothing to gain from repetitive practice. Of course, there are sometimes happy coincidences between individual aptitude and evaluative standards; we say someone is "a natural" if she or he demonstrates technical proficiency without practice and reflection, a phenomenon that also drives concepts of talent and genius. But there is nothing natural about technique—or, rather, "technique" and "nature" exist in a dynamic tension, each helping to constitute the other. In this regard, the idea of technique is closely related to the idea of culture (Boellstorff 2008:54–57).

The evaluative standards for a given technique are a matter of cultural consensus within a community of practice. But, crucially, the feedback mechanisms that drive the development of technical proficiency operate through a practitioner's in-the-moment material engagement, whether or not external or after-the-fact assessment also comes into play (cf. Brinner 1995, Berger 1999). In her ethnographic work on embodied knowledge in glassblowing, Erin O'Connor describes her own early efforts to gather up molten glass for a goblet using terms that could just as easily describe a novice dancer struggling to keep up with complex choreography: "I was seized by a type of stage-fright: my body could not anticipate the right moment. Consequently, I looked for it. . . . I could feel the rapid movement of my eyes—it made me even more nervous—they couldn't keep the tempo, were not the proper organ, could not anticipate, but waited to receive" (2007:133). O'Connor writes vividly about how these processes of consciously "reading the glass" gave way to the "non-reflective anticipation" that characterizes a proficient glassblower's habitus. In time she learned to practice glassblowing techniques without constantly assessing the molten glass; she suggests that explicit evaluative reading of the material "may be the mark of a novice" rather than "an operative mechanism of proficiency" (131). As she explains, "This is the defining exercise of apprenticeship: the apprentice fashions her practice by making an implicit technique explicit, improving and re-aligning that technique with its intended purpose, and allowing the revised technique to again recede into unconsciousness" (130). O'Connor is describing not only the craft of glassblowing but a Foucauldian technology of the self, the transformative crafting of one's own embodied disposition, which "implies certain modes of training and modification of individuals, not only in the obvious sense of acquiring certain skills but also in the sense of acquiring certain attitudes" (Foucault 1988:18). In the case of dance apprenticeship, the "molten glass" is the dancer's own body, and studio training "deploys two Foucauldian technologies: those producing a 'reformed' and disciplined body, adapted to regimes of high culture aesthetics and/or the state, and those of self-fashioning" (Hamera 2007:30).

Susan Foster defines "dance techniques" as "systematic programs of instruction . . . for studying the perceived body, organizing the information it presents and correlating it with demonstrative and ideal bodies." Training in a given technique inculcates a specific "body typography," a way of mapping various body areas and conceiving of their kinesthetic capacities and proper relationships to one another. The "ideal body" is constructed according to the aesthetic standards of a given style and informed by observations of other dancers' bodies; the "perceived body" derives from phenomenological reflection on one's own multisensory embodied experience. The "demonstrative body" mediates the relationship between ideal and perceived bodies "by exemplifying correct or incorrect movement. . . . [It] displays itself in the body of the teacher, and sometimes in one's own image in the mirror and in the bodies of other students in the class and their mirror images" (Foster 1992:483). Foster observes that dance training entails constant comparisons of perceived, demonstrative, and ideal bodies, which tend to reveal "areas of bodily resistance or incapacity" and "produce highly distorted, often obsessive images of the perceived body" (484). This comparative orientation highlights the social nature of technique: In addition to being something individuals practice and claim as their own, technique organizes relationships among practitioners. As Judith Hamera argues, dance technique offers "templates for sociality, by rendering bodies readable, and by organizing the relationships in which these readings can occur. . . . [T]he vocabulary and tropes unique to various techniques organize dancers and audiences into rhetorical, interpretive communities across multiple dimensions of difference" (Hamera 2007:19, 23). In communities of practice, body typographies and templates for sociality are closely intertwined.

Technique is intimate. It manifests an evolving relationship between your intentional consciousness and your material, whether that material is breath/molten glass, hand/knife/carrot, leg-muscles/hamstring/hip-socket, or fingers/keyboard. And all these slashes imply another important concept for our consideration of technique: They designate interfaces, which are zones of material contact, intentional transmission, and technical mediation. When a technique recedes from explicit consciousness, an interface fades out with it. When we are attending carefully to technique, an interface materializes.

My argument here builds from the phenomenology of practical knowledge but also dovetails with theories of the interface from software studies. In the realm of theories of embodied knowledge acquisition and theories of human-computer interaction (HCI), interfaces imply "control allegories"—as the Kinect's "You are the controller" tagline reminds us (Galloway 2012:30; cf. Blaine 2005, Chun 2011). A player's review of *Dance Central 2* shows how dance games articulate connections among concepts of control, technique, body-as-interface, and embodied-knowledge-as-achievement:

> I like to rock out around the house to all the hits, but I am pretty sure my actual moves are a little, um, uncontrolled. SO, I was really excited to have a way to practice some

actual dance moves in the privacy of my own home. . . . In this game, the Kinect can practically detect if your wrist or ankle is turned the wrong way. You would never get that kind of precision-tracking with Just Dance 3, which is frustrating when you want to be appropriately punished or rewarded for the accuracy of your performance. So, with Dance Central, you will get docked if your hip is slightly misaligned, if you're not leaning back enough, etc. That may sound annoying, but it's actually great, because when you DO nail it, you'll feel the difference, and feel like a bad-ass. (Amazon.com 2013a)

Dance technique materializes the dancer's body as an interface. Consider your own body: What would it mean to experience it as a zone of material contact, intentional transmission, and technical mediation? In dance games, the "playable body" is the interface between the player's intention and the choreography she is learning. A choreographed routine is like an unfamiliar instrument or tool. It must be comprehended through embodied engagement using acquired techniques, and it will in turn reconfigure the body that takes it up. It is the object of the techniques of proprioceptive interactivity that dance games inculcate (see Chapter 3). Susan Broadhurst has made a similar argument about digital performance practices more broadly; building on Merleau-Ponty, she writes, "In digital practices, instrumentation is mutually implicated with the body in an epistemological sense. . . . To have experience, to get used to an instrument, is to incorporate that instrument into the body. . . . Instruments appropriated by embodied experience become part of that altered body experience in the world" (2007:186). How does this process work for dance games? How do players learn the techniques required to comprehend game choreography and incorporate it into "an altered body experience in the world"? With some theoretical scaffolding in place, let us turn to practice, and to pragmatic considerations of dance pedagogy and game design.

DANCE PEDAGOGY: STUDIO PRACTICE

The *Dance Central* development team learned about dance pedagogy by consulting with the choreographers hired to create and perform the game routines and by having them teach classes at Harmonix. As lead designer Matt Boch recounted in a convention panel discussion, "We were making a game that was a little outside the comfort zone of a lot of people who were working on it, in terms of their dance skills. We had dance classes and tried to really jump into the whole thing" (Boch 2012). These in-house experiences strongly influenced the design of the first *Dance Central* game, which was "very indebted to the process that you go through learning a dance in a dance class" (Boch and Miller 2012). To understand how *Dance Central* gameplay works, then, we need to know something about the process that it models: studio dance pedagogy. I brought my own experience with studio dance classes to my gameplay and will draw on it here in an effort to show how my comprehension of dance game pedagogy unfolded.

Like the *Dance Central* choreographers I interviewed, I grew up taking several kinds of studio dance classes, including ballet, tap, and jazz. Studio dance pedagogy varies widely depending on style and individual instructor, but it is possible to sketch some common basic features. My 10 years of childhood dance classes took place in multiple studios spread across several different regions of the United States, but they all drew students into the same kind of built environment—a large, brightly lit room with special flooring and at least one full wall of mirrors—and they all employed the same basic format. During the first part of the class we learned and practiced individual elements of a choreographic lexicon through intensive repetition; then we gradually built up these elements into increasingly complex combinations. These combinations were anchored to actual or imagined musical phrase structures through the frequent use of eight-counts or similar verbalized/sung indicators of tempo and meter. Imagine a teacher counting you into the beginning of a combination by saying "five, six, seven, eight" to indicate the pace of the moves, and organizing collections of moves into groups that align with these eight-count phrases. The *Dance Central* rehearsal-mode teacher voice counts players into combinations in exactly this way, and *Dance Central* choreographers Marcos Aguirre and Chanel Thompson playfully refer to this teaching practice in their Twitter handles, @mea5678 and @miss5678.

As my cohort of dance students approached one of our periodic public performances, we would begin learning extended sequences of combinations, associated with specific music, and our teacher would begin to put more emphasis on interpretive nuance. Preparing repertoire for a dance recital, we relied on musical structure and distinctive sonic elements as memory aids: following those eight-count phrases, or listening for cues like the entrance of a particular instrument, shifting dynamics and tempo, or song lyrics. In this process we crossed the conventional line that divides learning technique from learning choreography, akin to the difference between practicing short exercises in every key on a musical instrument and learning pieces credited to individual composers. In both music and dance contexts, this line is fuzzy in practice. Both composers and choreographers create *études*—study pieces that are designed to cultivate technique but also become part of performance repertoires and are treated as artistic works. On the flip side, rehearsing and performing a particular work inevitably contributes to the cumulative technique that a dancer will bring to the next work.

Throughout this learning process each dancer also continually developed her own conscious proprioception and personal body image by comparing her body to the other bodies in the room. The teacher often stood at the front of the room facing a mirrored wall; this allowed us to observe her movements from both the front and the back and to move in the same direction when following along, mapping our right legs to her right leg, and so on. The mirror also made for abundant sightlines and opportunities for surreptitious observation. The teacher could observe the whole class, but it was hard to tell whom she was watching; we could observe each other in the same way. As for observing ourselves in the mirror, we learned to adopt an attitude of analytical detachment—or at least to give that impression. This mirror was not for fixing one's hair or admiring/deploring one's leotard-clad figure; it was a technical feedback mechanism for checking one's form or a visual aid for observing the teacher.

Like studio classes, dance games rely heavily on repetition to teach technique. But due to the song-driven nature of the core gameplay design, that repetition must somehow be folded into full speed dancing-along. Moreover, routines must not feel so repetitive as to be boring, and the complete choreographic lexicon must be substantial and ever-growing, since novelty and variety drive the sale of new repertoire. These considerations structure the central orienting challenge for game choreographers. It is a special class of the level-design task at the core of traditional game development: The play experience should be just hard enough that players are always working at the edge of their competence, experiencing the visceral pleasures of total engagement coupled with progression-oriented motivation to continue (Csikszentmihalyi 1991, Gee 2004:71). How do you cultivate cumulative dance technique through repertoire, collapsing the traditional distinction between skill-and-drill repetition of technical exercises and rehearsing choreographic works for performance? How do you use repetition, variety, and feedback to manage players' affective responses so they will keep coming back for more?

GAME PEDAGOGY: STREAMING CHOREOGRAPHY AND KINESTHETIC LAG

Dance games are built around musical playlists, and the fundamental unit of gameplay is the song. In this regard, *Just Dance* and *Dance Central* share a core design imperative: Players should be able to select a song and start dancing immediately, allowing for brief sessions of casual, accessible, social gameplay as well as longer sets built from multiple songs. This requirement poses significant challenges for integrating dance pedagogy into gameplay because players must learn choreography at full speed and tackle a whole song's worth of choreography in one go. Players have to dance in time to the music, since the game scoring systems rely on tracking their changing physical positions against a timeline; if they are perpetually behind the beat, they won't receive full credit for their moves. They may also experience visceral discomfort from the out-of-sync clash of kinesthetic, visual, and auditory sensations, coupled with anxiety about their dance competence and whether or not they "have rhythm."

The basic structure of dance games seems to imply that choreography should stream into players' bodies in the same way that music and video stream into their auditory and visual systems. You can listen to a new song or watch an unfamiliar video in real time and your powers of perception will keep up. Repeated listening or viewing will feel different, but the first time doesn't feel like a failure. It is the streaming technology that is more likely to fail—to stutter or freeze, due to bandwidth limitations or other technical glitches. Human auditory and visual systems are supposed to be lag-free; signs to the contrary are classified as serious system malfunctions, hallmarks of disability. But playing dance games potentially entails severe kinesthetic lag. There is no sensory/motor channel that allows for seamless perception and physical enactment of an incoming stream of kinesthetic data in real time—yet this is what players are supposed to be doing.

Just Dance and Dance Central put forward different solutions to these problems, but they manifest some shared pedagogical strategies. Give players patterns to follow and teach them how to anticipate some upcoming moves. Offer them occasional respite from the task of anticipation, creating cycles of suspense and release. Tie these patterns to musical structure; make repeating phrases, verses, and choruses work for you, so that choreographic repetition paints a faithful portrait of a popular song rather than feeling like a tedious technical drill. Incorporate some form of progression across your playlist, gradually adding new and more difficult moves. Find ways to motivate players to perform individual songs repeatedly. Augment the model dancing body that moves in time with the music with a graphic notation system that telegraphs upcoming material. And finally—perhaps counterintuitively—limit the feedback that you provide to players. Beginners will not dance well; don't let them know how badly they are doing. This is a crucial difference from studio dance classes. Dance games do not give players a mirror, even though they frequently invite players to imagine one as they sync up with a screen dancer.

Like the Guitar Hero and Rock Band games, Just Dance and Dance Central draw on a sight-reading paradigm familiar from the world of Western art music, one that relies on prescriptive notation and the principle that it is possible to "read ahead" of the actions your body is performing. This is an unusual modality for dance pedagogy. That is not to say that dance is never notated; to the contrary, notation has played a role in dance transmission in many traditions for centuries. Bench draws connections between 18th-century Feuillet notation and 21st-century motion capture, noting that both technologies create "bodies of data"; she argues that in both systems, "motion can be captured, circulated, and mapped because the body has first been rendered an invisible producer of data and movement has been decomposed into combinable units" (2009:52–53). However, in practical terms, dance notation systems most often serve as memory aids for material already learned or as archival technologies for works deemed worthy of preservation. They rarely play a prominent role in the early stages of learning a new technique, style, or particular choreographic work. That is, dance notation systems typically function as descriptive rather than prescriptive (see Nettl 1983:65–81), working as a supplement to living, embodied memory and relying on a foundation of technique taught in body-to-body contexts.

To some degree this is true of all notation systems for embodied techniques and repertoires, including the staff notation used in the Western art music tradition. But there are important differences in how notation systems are employed. For instance, orchestral musicians use sheet music for the first read-through of a new piece, continually annotate it, and keep using it as a reference in performance contexts; there are no analogous initial "read-throughs" from graphic notation systems in the world of Western concert dance, and there is no practical way for dancers to refer to notation during performances (except in the case of experimental multimedia works). For pedagogical purposes, video recordings of dancing bodies might seem to have richer affordances than graphic notation systems, including the capacity for rewind, replay, and slow-motion playback. However, video offers a radically limited sensorium, both over-privileging vision and constraining it through cinematographic framing (Dodds 2001). As many dance scholars have shown, other sensory channels play a key role in dance pedagogy and in cultivating kinesthetic awareness in a particular style (e.g., Foster 1992, Hahn 2007). Moreover, in contrast to graphic notation systems, watching a video of another dancer does not allow for "reading ahead." And finally, from the practical standpoint of sightlines and display technologies, standard dance studio infrastructure and the expectation that dancing might involve turning one's head present numerous obstacles to using visual notation systems or video examples as the primary channels for teaching choreography in a studio class. Dancers move around, and their sightlines move with them. A display screen would also disrupt dancers' access to the mirror wall, an interactive visual technology that has already been fully integrated into studio pedagogy.

Console games organize players' bodies quite differently, placing players in front of a display screen and working from the premise that they will maintain near-constant visual contact with that screen. Dance games capitalize on this fixed-gaze orientation, incorporating multiple forms of notation: prescriptive notation in the form of scrolling icons, juxtaposed with descriptive notation in the form of a video-recorded or animated dancing body. Music can also function as a form of cross-modal prescriptive notation in dance games. As discussed in Chapter 3, game routines present kinesthetic transcriptions of popular songs; since players often know a song before encountering the corresponding dance routine, as they work through a new routine they can "listen ahead," anticipating choreographic patterning through their knowledge of musical structure. As a player explained,

> You can tell where the song is going, especially if you know the songs. Like, oh, they're going to go back to this move again, and you're a little more prepared the next time. Especially for songs I know—or even if you don't, you can kind of tell. They're all pop songs, so you can see where they're going. You're like, okay, they're going to do this arm motion again. . . . The fun moves were the technically slightly more advanced, but the ones that you could pull off the first time. They were fun, I feel like, when they matched the song or when it confirmed your expectations for what it might be. (Adam, postgameplay interview, July 19, 2013)

Just Dance and *Dance Central* each offer a repertoire of tightly integrated musical/choreographic works and a teaching/learning model that relies on synchronous kinesthetic imitation and anticipatory reading/listening. The two franchises diverge largely on the issue of technical feedback, stemming from the different perceptual affordances of their platforms. *Just Dance* was designed to track a single handheld Wii remote; it could not assess or offer feedback on the motion of any other part of a player's body. By comparison, the Kinect offered a detection system that was almost too good, creating a design/marketing quandary: *Dance Central* was supposed to show off the superior motion-tracking capacities of the Kinect, but that meant it would potentially hold players to a standard of technical precision set too high for a dancing-along-in-real-time situation, especially for players without previous dance training. The musicians among my readers are well positioned to understand the problem: Imagine you are learning a new piece in an ensemble situation—either playing along by ear or sight-reading from notation—and someone is giving you constant negative feedback for every intonation problem, missed note, or failure to observe dynamic markings, when you are just trying to keep up with the tempo and get an overall feel for the piece.

In fact, Harmonix developers had already tackled exactly this problem in designing the *Guitar Hero* and *Rock Band* games, and they had solved it by giving players a radically simplified technical pathway to achieving "the feeling of making music"— a sense of visceral responsibility for the generation of pre-recorded musical sounds (Miller 2012:97). *Just Dance* employs much the same solution as *Guitar Hero*: The Wii reads the motion of one handheld controller and credits the player with a full-body performance, just as *Guitar Hero* can receive an input of one button-press and reward the player with the sound of a perfectly executed guitar riff. *Just Dance* cannot play the "real moves" through the player's body in the same way that *Guitar Hero* can play "real music" through the speakers, but it can at least refrain from drawing players' attention to the gap between their performance and that of the screen dancer. That is, in a striking deviation from most studio dance training, *Just Dance* strategically discourages comparisons between the perceived body and the demonstrative body.

There is no obvious way to apply this principle in a game like *Dance Central*, where full-body motion detection is a core technical feature that operates in a mutually reinforcing relationship with the core game concept of "authentic dance." One might imagine a special game scoring setting that is more forgiving, intended for the first run-through when a dancer is "marking it," but it would be difficult to determine exactly how forgiving it should be in order to accommodate a range of player abilities. *Dance Central* addresses this problem by offering each routine at four different difficulty levels, gradually incorporating more technically challenging moves and increasing the pace of choreographic variation. However, there is still no explicit accommodation for a "marking it" run-through of any version. Instead, the designers opted to limit negative feedback, so the first pass through a routine is not a miserable experience, and to build in "progression" elements that encourage repetitive practice, mastery, and "cycles of expertise" structured by a graded curriculum (Gee 2006:180).

Dance Central also offers a rehearsal mode, modeled closely on typical studio pedagogy. Players practice one move at a time, must attempt each move several times before they can move on to the next one, and are encouraged to "watch and learn" rather than mirroring new moves right away (see Chapter 1). At the start of a rehearsal session, the voiceover instructor says, "If you've got this move on lock, go ahead and bust it out and we'll move on. Otherwise just watch first, and *then* try. 5, 6, 7, 8 . . ." In a review for Videogamer.com, Jamin Smith described rehearsal mode as "like having your very own choreographer explain the routine to you." She neatly tied this invocation of the privilege of private, personally tailored dance lessons to the idea of "real dance":

> Each move is slowed down and explained in detail, and once learnt you'll be asked to put them all together in a recap routine. It's more than just a tutorial, though, it's the practice required to tackle a song on higher difficulties (which in my case was anything above easy). It's the learning process you'll need to go through to be any good at the game. Ultimately, it's what real dancers do every time they're given a new routine. (Smith 2010)

However, many players never use the rehearsal mode. They might simply find it tedious; dance games are marketed to "casual" gamers, who are presumed to be less invested in technical mastery and high scores. But there are other reasons to skip the rehearsal breakdowns. Rehearsal mode only works for one player at a time, a significant constraint for social gameplay sessions. If you're looking for a workout, the frequent pauses in rehearsal mode make it hard to keep your heartrate up. And, as Smith's review implies, experienced gamers often eschew tutorial modes; a core principle of contemporary game design dictates that good games cultivate learning-by-doing in the course of play, without requiring separate didactic exercises (Gee 2008). Thus the *Dance Central* choreographers and designers had to negotiate a clash of pedagogical paradigms. They could not assume that players would be willing to engage in "watch and learn" skill-and-drill dance training; they could advertise the rehearsal mode as a value-added feature for mastery-oriented players but had to design for satisfying "dancing along" experiences as well.

As we move on to consider each franchise's dance pedagogy in more detail, it is important to bear in mind the market forces that structured Ubisoft's and Harmonix's efforts to distribute choreography as an interactive entertainment product for a mass audience. For instance, introducing *Dance Central* to the market a year after *Just Dance*, the Harmonix developers had to highlight the Kinect's perceptual powers and their game's "real dance" bona fides in order to differentiate the two franchises, but they also had to match *Just Dance*'s promise of instantly accessible, social gameplay. Meanwhile, the Ubisoft developers continued to play to their franchise's established strengths: releasing new repertoire quickly and deemphasizing technical mastery in favor of shameless exuberance. While the *Dance Central* choreographers, animators, and playtesters might spend months recording multiple versions of a routine, smoothing the transitions in rehearsal-mode breakdowns of subroutines, and fine-tuning the motion detection and scoring systems, the *Just Dance* team put their production resources into creating unique settings, costuming, and characters for each song. In effect, each *Just Dance* game playlist consists of a series of interactive music videos, often loaded with intertextual references to a song's original music video or related media. In *Dance Central*, the choreography is the only element unique to each song; players can perform every song using the same screen dancer, costume, and dance venue, or switch up any of these elements from a fixed menu of options. These design choices created a vicious circle in terms of choreographic labor: *Dance Central*'s long-term commercial viability as a game franchise and platform for selling downloadable content relied on choreographic novelty, but its labor-intensive production processes and the perceptual limitations of the Kinect significantly constrained Harmonix's ability to meet player demand for new repertoire (see Chapter 5).

Just Dance and *Dance Central* represent different solutions to the same design conundrum: how to capture the spirit of free-wheeling, improvisatory club dancing while teaching players to perform pre-choreographed works. Their approaches to technique and repertoire and their divergent production processes recall two other dance contexts that involve the repetitive practice of fixed choreographic works: *Just Dance* models the domestic practice of learning a dance from a music video (Peters and Seier 2009), and *Dance Central* models a studio dance class experience. To different degrees, both franchises also use their scoring systems, multiplayer options, and dance scenarios to invoke a dance-competition paradigm: You learn, practice, and polish your moves at home or in a studio class, then compete with other dancers in social dance situations, in ritualized "battles" drawn from hip-hop culture and fighting games, or on reality TV. Close analysis of an example drawn from each franchise will show how *Just Dance* and *Dance Central* build on established dance transmission paradigms as they create and present sight-readable choreography, teach players practices of anticipation, capitalize on the structural and cultural affordances of licensed popular songs, and associate gameplay with other meaningful dance, music, and media experiences.

REMEDIATING HIP-HOP, TAKE ONE: *JUST DANCE*'S "APACHE"

"Apache (Jump on It)" was originally released by the Sugarhill Gang in 1981 and is a canonical early hip-hop track. The Sugarhill MCs rap over a cover of "Apache," a 1973 funk instrumental by the Incredible Bongo Band that features a melodic hook and lengthy percussion break that came to be strongly associated with hip-hop b-boy culture (Schloss 2006). "Apache" indexes a complex history of sampling and remediation; the Incredible Bongo Band track is itself a funk cover of a 1960 release by the British rock band The Shadows, and the hook and break from the 1973 version have been sampled by dozens of hip-hop artists over several decades.

The *Just Dance* version of "Apache" was part of the playlist for *Just Dance 3*, released 30 years after the Sugarhill album. The game includes a shortened version of the song, cutting a verse but otherwise preserving the musical structure, including a long percussion break. *Just Dance* sets "Apache" in a stylized urban street tableau, with sidewalks eerily empty of human life (see Figure 4.1). A male screen dancer in ersatz pow-wow regalia is green-screened into the scene. He wears a feathered headdress, bright breastplate over a bare torso, and fringed loincloth and leggings. The headdress bounces with every move, a spectacular racial marker that recalls the silhouetted hairstyles that designate other *Just Dance* screen dancers as racial bodies (see Chapter 2). Meanwhile, the fluttering fringes of his costume also index the real-world physics of an authentically human body, a dancer captured on video rather than created through digital animation. As with all the *Just Dance* screen dancers, the exposed skin on this "Apache" dancer's body glows white; in this case it is also marked with bright red "war paint" that connotes an Indian-face performance and a red mask over the eyes referencing the 1950s television series *The Lone Ranger*. He dances against the backdrop of a building wall covered in layered graffiti that depicts stereos and speaker towers stacked into stylized totem poles. Echoing the Sugarhill lyrics, which mention Tonto, Jesse James, and the Lone Ranger catchprases "kemo sabe" and "Hi Ho Silver," the game scenario merges standard hip-hop tropes with colonialist fantasies of Native American dance and cowboy/Indian relations. *Just Dance*'s "Apache" thus remediates what was already a doubly racialized performance: a blackface/Indian-face, urban/primitive, markedly masculine dancing warrior.

The game choreography for "Apache" generally breaks down into a series of eight-counts in which players repeat a single move, with symmetrical variations.

Figure 4.1: A player-produced video of the *Just Dance 3* routine for "Apache (Jump On It)" (AverageAsianDude 2013). (Screenshot by the author.)

For example, the routine begins with an arm gesture that can be performed in an upward or downward direction, pumping open palms toward the sky or pressing them toward the floor. The first two eight-counts of music introduce this material:

up-up-down-down / up-up-down-down // up-up-down-down / up-up-down-down

The dancer is oriented to the right throughout. This might lead to an expectation that the next two 8-counts will repeat the same material to the left. However, there is a change in the music here, and the choreography tracks that change, introducing a new move with the dancer facing forward and alternating right/left rather than up/down. The repetition structure parallels that of the first two 8-counts:

left-left-right-right / left-left-right-right // left-left-right-right / left-left-right-right

The following structural map of the first half of *Just Dance*'s "Apache" gives a feel for the pace of choreographic variation in this routine. Each letter refers to an 8-count of music that features a single distinctive move performed with symmetrical variations. The moves generally combine stock gestures from the coyboys-and-Indians repertoire with simple stepping footwork; in addition to the cartoonish rain dance that opens the routine, the choreography incorporates references to lassos, war whoops, shooting arrows, scanning the horizon, and applying a whip to a horse.

intro	A A B B
interruption	X
intro reprise	A
hook/chorus	C D C E C D C E
transition	F/G F/G
verse 1	H H I I*
interruption	X
intro reprise	A
hook/chorus	C D C E C D C E

X is a "lookout" gesture, pegged to the entry of the vocals with a series of emphatic "Oh!" exclamations; it breaks the usual pattern of symmetrical variation, with the dancer scanning the horizon to right, left, right, and then pausing to reset for the return of the A material. C is a series of muscleman arm-flexing poses performed at half-time, matching the rhythm of the song's signature melodic hook, interspersed with D and E, war-whoop and horse-whipping gestures that return to the normal base tempo of the choreography with the "Jump on it!" chorus lyrics. The entrance of the first verse is marked by a sudden shift to toprocking (H), a foundational b-boy step: "the upright, rhythmic cross-stepping that precedes 'going down' to perform breakdancing's characteristic floor moves" (Schloss 2006:424). There is no going down to the floor in *Just Dance*, however; the toprocking transitions to I, a hop-hop-clap move that kinesthetically amplifies the "boom boom bap" rhythm that marks "Apache" as a b-boy classic. I* indicates a surprise ending; the last iteration of the symmetrical variation ends with a punching move for the vocal interjection "Big Bank!" The remainder of the song unfolds along the same lines, using these same ten basic moves, with choreographic structure and repetitions closely matching musical structure, punctuated by occasional "surprise" moments tied to song lyrics. Note the gradually increasing pace of choreographic variation: Two 8-counts of music underpin [A A], then [C D], then eventually [F/G F/G] before the pace resets to a relaxed [H H] as the verse begins.

This structural overview shows how choreographic repetition organizes the player's unfolding experience of both learning the dance at a technical level and learning how to enjoy it. Repetition not only regulates the arc of the learning curve but also sets the stage for signature flourishes of choreographic novelty, which function like "Easter egg" content in other games: discoverable, collectible surprises designed to provide periodic bursts of delight. In *Just Dance*, such moments are often designated as Gold Moves, which yield bonus points if performed correctly. Gold Moves typically link choreography to musical content or broader pop-culture contexts in a way that gives players a thrill of discovery coupled with the satisfaction of confirmed expectations. For example, *Just Dance*'s "Apache" establishes orderly repetitions of short combinations with symmetrical variations (right and left, forward and back, up and down . . .), then disrupts them with a little choreographic gift wrapped in visual magic; a golden bow materializes in the hands of the screen dancer, and he shoots off an arrow. This moment takes place three-quarters of the way through the routine; players have already learned the basic choreographic lexicon for this song and are repeating familiar combinations. The bow appears with the lyrical exhortation "Hit it gang!", the screen dancer and player let the arrow fly in perfect time with the synth stab that marks the transition to the extended percussion break, and a burst of golden light fills the screen. The bow and arrow appear for less than two seconds, as though the game is asking, "Are you still paying attention?" In addition to keeping players alert for visual surprises, such moments also cue them to listen carefully, anticipating musical material that could generate other one-off moves.

These moves constitute playful secrets that can afford a sense of intimate connection to the game repertoire and motivate sharing it with the uninitiated. Here we have social scaffolding for repeat play-throughs of a routine, associated with the promise of new and different pleasures in future gameplay episodes. Having discovered this golden bow and arrow, players can anticipate and delight in witnessing their friends' initial rush of surprise while also raking in bonus points by taking a pattern-breaking move in stride. While *Just Dance* eschews the skill-and-drill rehearsal-mode breakdowns that signal *Dance Central*'s investment in mastery, *Just Dance* players still engage in repetitive practice and may take an interest in improving their scores, skills, and fluency.

The technical affordances of the Wii impact the learning experience in *Just Dance*, including players' potential approaches to repeated practice. Because the Wii only tracks the motion of one hand, players have considerable latitude in their learning strategies. For instance, they could choose to simply "mark" the routine on the first reading, putting most of their energies into watching the screen dancer, while tracking the broad outlines of arm gestures and directional shifts with one hand. After learning to fluently feel the form of the whole routine, they could focus on arm gestures in detail over several repetitions, internalizing patterns of upper-body motion and letting them recede from attention before adding in the footwork. Or they could opt out of the footwork entirely—an option that accommodates both confined gameplay spaces and players with limited lower-body mobility. The game's scoring system potentially grants full credit for any of these approaches. *Dance Central*'s full-body motion detection system does not support these learning strategies. For example, one player told me she wished *Dance Central* would allow her to learn upper and lower body moves separately before combining them, as she was used to doing in some studio dance classes. I asked, "Why couldn't you do that in the learning process here?" She replied, "You could, but he [the voiceover dance teacher in rehearsal mode] always is yelling at you for not getting it right. So each move you have to do the hands and the feet correctly or else he yells at you and says that you didn't do it right, and then you feel bad" (post-gameplay interview, July 19, 2013).

Just Dance thus lends itself to a dance pedagogy grounded in "simming," a term Scott Magelssen borrowed from online gaming culture and adapted to describe learning experiences that involve participatory performance. Simming is "a bounded action that bears performative reference to another action, which is or stands to become more legitimate or weighty in another time and context" (Magelssen 2014:4). *Just Dance* particularly accommodates "learner-driving simming," wherein participants "make choices based on the knowledge they have coproduced with the institution" (78). "Marking it" on the first run-through or dividing up the learning process over different zones of one's body are choices of this kind.

Magelssen also notes that simming environments frequently encourage "playing against type" in experiential learning contexts. He describes his own experience as a white man invited to occupy the role of a Native American in a "living museum" setting, attending to the fraught implications of "the unmatched body witnessing another's histories and cultures." As Magelssen notes, "these disparities between bodies and experiences both pose representational and historiographical dilemmas, as well as offer promising opportunities for bodily or kinesthetic learning about those whose lives are or were different from our own" (2014:25). These observations resonate with the "Apache" example, where gameplay involves direct bodily engagement with layers of racialized choreography, iconography, sounds, and lyrics. These materials are the museum artifacts that make up *Just Dance*'s experiential museum of pop culture history (cf. Miller 2008b). Where did they come from? Where do they lead people as they circulate? JD3's "Apache" is more than an archive of dance moves that kinesthetically amplify the structural features of a particular musical track; it also indexes other repertoires and histories, and recirculates as an artifact in other archives, such as YouTube.

Joe Schloss cites the Incredible Bongo Band's "Apache" as one of a corpus of songs that are "valued as 'frameworks' for the act of b-boying, because they combine practical factors that facilitate the particular dance style (including fast tempos, loud drums, rhythmic horn passages, and breaks) with socio-historical associations that place any given performance in the context of b-boy history" (2006:418). "Apache" and other songs in this corpus "allow dancers to develop the ability to react instantaneously to each in a manner that reproduces the aesthetic principles of the b-boy community" (421). The Sugarhill Gang are themselves icons of hip-hop history, and "Apache (Jump On It)" is a classic track. When other hip-hop artists sample either version of "Apache," the song's signature sonic elements index both the 1970s funk roots of b-boy dance culture and the Sugarhill Gang's status as MCs a decade later, at the dawn of the commercialization of rap music. This double line of reference is important for understanding the possible significance of including "Apache (Jump On It)" in a dance game. B-boying and MCing are two of the expressive practices that comprise the traditional "four elements" of old-school hip-hop culture (along with DJing and writing graffiti). A DJ might include the Incredible Bongo Band's "Apache" in a mix to supply a musical foundation for further layers of performance by b-boys, MCs, or both.

The Sugarhill Gang were MCs, not b-boys; there is no canonical dance routine that matches their version of "Apache." Even if there were, it probably could not find a place in either *Just Dance* or *Dance Central*. The floor moves, inversions, and spins that are emblematic of the b-boy repertoire are technically difficult, requiring strength, stamina, and an appetite for bruises. This wouldn't necessarily preclude including one such routine as a challenge for advanced players (though one could imagine the legal department raising concerns about neck injuries). However, in addition to considerations of difficulty, many of these moves cannot be performed while holding a Wii remote, cannot be accurately tracked by the Kinect sensor, and would be difficult to learn by mirroring a screen dancer because they break the player's visual connection with the screen.

If the *Just Dance* choreography for "Apache" referenced neither its three-decade history as a sonic showcase for breakdancers nor any signature stage or music-video choreography by the Sugarhill MCs, where did it come from? We have seen that many of the moves reference the cowboys-and-Indians scenario in the lyrics, as well as incorporating recognizable b-boy footwork. Like the screen dancer's costume and the totem-pole/speaker-tower graffiti, a few moves seem to signify a double racial caricature, melding Indian-face with hip-hop-inflected blackface. For instance, the opening move—arms raised over the head, palms pulsing downward, torso angled forward at the waist—traces the cartoonish gestural contours of both "rain dance" and hip-hop hype man. But as I browsed gameplay videos of "Apache" on YouTube, I saw that the commenters seemed to know something I didn't. They were judging this routine against a particular model, and found it wanting. What other histories and repertoires could this routine be citing? To find out, I pursued lines of reference through chains of related videos and in the comment threads that constitute diffuse, unruly clouds of metadata for each item in YouTube's idiosyncratic and unstable archive.

The most popular comment on the most-viewed "Apache" gameplay video had garnered 106 thumbs-up and offered a major clue: "You had ONE fuckin' job, Ubisoft . . . put in the damn pelvic thrusts . . ." (comment on AverageAsianDude 2013b, accessed December 28, 2015). What pelvic thrusts? I scrolled down further, and found more complaints: The game routine diverged too much from the version in the 1990s sitcom *The Fresh Prince of Bel Air*.

> comment: One job Ubisoft one job. THE PROPPER FRESH PRINCE DANCE!! [39 thumbs-up]
>
> reply A: it could be will and carlton in the place of that creepy indian
>
> original commenter: such a shame it isn't
>
> reply B: I think the slight movements of hips would be too little for the game to register
>
> original commenter: that's ubisoft's fault

Soon I was watching YouTube clips of Fresh Prince Will Smith and his bourgie cousin Carlton (Alfonso Ribeiro) dancing to "Apache" on a talent-show stage, with studiously serious faces that parodied hip-hop "hard" masculinity. They wore homemade Indian costumes cobbled together from barely modified street clothes and performed a routine that seemed similarly slapdash and unsophisticated—incorporating the war-whoop moves and other elements recognizable from the *Just Dance* routine, along with a botched swing-dance trick that sent Carlton crashing offstage. Here were the pelvic thrusts, individual exaggerated pop-and-freeze moves awkwardly pegged to each note of the song's melodic hook. Will and Carlton popped their hips in not-quite-sync, first toward the audience and then turning toward each other, a homoerotic face-off played for laughs. I remembered that in the *Just Dance* routine this pelvic motion was replaced by muscleman arm flex poses that seemed curiously out of place, a total break from the routine's cowboy/Indian/ b-boy lexicon; now I understood why the commenters complained. But of course the Wii would not be able to read pelvic popping, and the screen dancer's fringed loincloth would also make it hard for players to see and imitate.

Comments and linked videos continued to draw me deeper into this alternative dance-media genealogy for "Apache," bringing me to clips of "The Carlton Dance"—an iconic TV depiction of living-room dancing from the third season of *The Fresh Prince of Bel Air* (episode 10, 1992). Carlton is at home; he looks around to make sure he is alone, then turns on the living room stereo, plucks a white candle from a side table to serve as a microphone, and begins an uninhibited and deeply unhip dance and lip-sync performance of Tom Jones's 1965 breakout hit "It's Not

Unusual." Will comes in and watches in horror until Carlton realizes he has an audience, shamefacedly turns off the music, and hands over the candle, his emasculation complete. Some of the signature moves from this dance, too, appear in both the *Fresh Prince* "Apache" and the *Just Dance* version—most notably an arm gesture in which parallel forearms trace frenetic arcs from side to side (see Figure 4.2).

I kept following the chain of videos and watched Alfonso Ribeiro reprise both dances in 2014 as a competitor on *Dancing with the Stars*, where his Carlton and "Apache" references helped him become the season 19 champion. The competition generated a burst of Carlton Dance nostalgia and created a platform for Ribeiro to speak to the entertainment media about the Carlton role and the origins of the dance:

> I played a character that was as far from myself as possible. . . . I had never heard of Tom Jones. . . . I grew up in the Bronx; I was a hip-hop kid. The Carlton Dance was created when it said in the script: "Carlton dances." It was never even intended to be funny; it was just that he was dancing. The dance is ultimately Courteney Cox in the Bruce Springsteen video "Dancing in the Dark"; that's the basis. Or in Eddie

Figure 4.2: A "Carlton Dance" reference. Detail from AverageAsianDude 2013. (Screenshot by the author.)

Murphy's "Delirious" video, "The White Man Dance" as he called it. And I said, "That is the corniest dance on the planet that I know of, so why don't I do that?" (Holmes 2015)

Two weeks before Ribeiro's winning performance on the season finale, Sugarhill Gang MC Big Bank Hank died of cancer. As people searched for "Apache" videos online in response to these events, they found both the *Just Dance* gameplay videos uploaded three years earlier and clips of 1980s television footage of the Sugarhill Gang performing the song in feathered headdresses. Viewers contributed new layers of comments to both sets of videos, referencing the Carlton Dance and offering "Rest in Peace" respects to Hank.

Just Dance's "Apache" places the game in this lineage—embedded in the social history of home dancing, including the media circulation history of hip-hop and other racialized kinesthetic repertoires trickling out to suburban living rooms and talent shows through teenagers' participatory performances of their pop-culture engagements. In the gameplay context "Apache" is still a song that calls dancers to the floor, an index of habitus and a means of transmitting it to new dancing bodies. But here it transmits not b-boy habitus but a different dance, a different set of bodily dispositions, celebrating awkwardness and sincere enthusiasm and attaching that affect to comically unpolished racial caricature. In fact, as Ribeiro's comments on the Carlton Dance reveal, *Just Dance*'s "Apache" stages a triple racial caricature: not just blackface and Indian-face, but "the White Man Dance" as well, "the corniest dance on the planet."

Just Dance's "Apache" betrays no signs of ironic critique; it seems to offer players an opportunity to participate in racialized mis-performances so naïve that they can feel innocent. In online circulation, though, this cluster of "Apache" videos has generated a buzz of race-talk—an unruly comment trail of arguments about racism, minstrelsy, and appropriation, including the issue of how performers might mean no harm yet still inflict injury. For example, amid the many *Fresh Prince*-related comments on the most-viewed *Just Dance* gameplay video:

comment: Ummm, racist?

reply A: no it isnt

reply B: Doesn't seem like the song is going against a race. . Oh well . .

reply C: apache is a native American tribe. so actually not racist

original commenter: oh ok, but is it still kind of offensive for native Americans?

reply A2: no because the song is actually called apache if you didnt notice

comment: I find this very offensive to native Americans because I am one my self and this is not how we dance it's the opposite of how we dance

reply: Just dance uses random characters for dancing sometimes they look like the singer sometimes they don't. This is not saying "Native Americans dance like this" it's just one of Just Dances' characters he's in other videos just saying not trying to start a fight

original commenter: Ik [I know] but I thought this was just kinda fucked

The 330 comments on this video included several other viewers simply identifying themselves as Native American: "Im an Apache indian," "I'm an Yaqui Native," "Choctaw indian" (comments on AverageAsianDude 2013b, accessed December 28, 2015).

The most popular YouTube clip of the 1980s Sugarhill television performance, uploaded without attribution in October 2009 and viewed more than 1.5 million times over the next six years, is captioned

Seminal 80s rap group performing an American Indian minstrel show

(Killer song though . . .)

(zacha83 2009; see Figure 4.3.)

Many commenters echo the uploader's assessment, including its ambivalent quality. For instance, in 2015 one viewer wrote "holy crap this is racist," generating a series of replies that sum up many of the rhetorical positions I encountered across other "Apache" comment threads:

reply A: You could view it as a parody of The Lone Ranger series from the 1960s, which was probably a bit unenlightened regarding American Indians. So it's reflecting the TV show rather than real Indian culture. Or old cowboy movies. Stuff made by white Americans, being mocked and cheekily celebrated. You could just view it as a bit of fun. There weren't many black Indians as far as I know. They're not supposed to be representing real Indians. Just the silly stereotype with the "Unga!" and head dresses. It's a rap video after all, not supposed to be a documentary. "Apache" was a pre-existing song that the Gang must've thought would make a good tune for a rap. The associated "Cowboys and Indians" stuff came along with it, Sugarhill didn't invent that. As far as the American Indians go, they've been pretty fucked over by white Americans since not long after they got there. Of all the many things they have to genuinely complain about, I don't think a Sugarhill Gang video is the worst. Their deliberate genocide, germ warfare, scalping (which the whites invented as a system of claiming bounty), their massive inequality in quality of life today, and current human rights abuses, are all more important. American Indians have plenty of real grievances. There's no need to go looking for problems where no malice was intended, and no harm was done. It's just a rap video.

reply B: Allow me to state that in the reverse. Yes, they do have bigger grievances, this was a good song (that was my era), but it's still racist.

reply C: BLACK PEOPLE CANT BE RACIST

Figure 4.3: The Sugarhill Gang's "Apache (Jump On It)" circulating on YouTube. (Screenshot by the author.)

reply C2: i was joking

reply D: Not nearly as racist as the tv show that inspired it. If anything, this is a satirical swipe at that show.

reply E: Imitating an image that the white man put out there about Native Americans. Who made those crazy westerns? Not a black man. Black man didn't have his own movie studios back then.

reply F: They're just black men mixed with Native American mixing tribal beats with rap. What's so racist about that? By the way racism is the extremist belief that one race is better than all others races. How is this racist?

reply B2: Ok, how about grossly inappropriate. Do I really have to spell this out people? Would you do this at a pow wow? Anyway, I'm not just pointing fingers here. I used to be a DJ and this was one of our most popular songs, so yes I participated, now regretfully.

BTW "tonto" spanish for idiot, don't know what it means in any First Nations languages.

My apologies to my FN brothers (and sisters).

(Comments on zacha83 2009, accessed December 28, 2015)

As in this thread, some of the arguments I encountered turned on the question of whether black performers can be racist, or whether they should get a free pass for performances of racial caricature, as though parallel histories of oppression justify and neutralize hip-hop renditions of Indian-face. Others showed commenters comparing and contrasting ideas about blackness and indigeneity that circulate in different national and post-colonial contexts, and making "different times" arguments; they justified *Just Dance*'s Indian-face as racial drag faithful to its historical antecedents, as represented by both the Sugarhill Gang and *The Fresh Prince of Bel Air*.

REMEDIATING HIP-HOP, TAKE TWO: *DANCE CENTRAL'S* "CRANK THAT"

Dance Central offers a complementary remediation story, one that illustrates how this game franchise attempted to link hip-hop authenticity and the circulatory energy of viral media to gameplay mechanics that feature skill-and-drill dance pedagogy. Soulja Boy's 2007 hit "Crank That" was a design touchstone for *Dance Central*. Lead designer Matt Boch often mentioned it when telling the franchise's birth story to industry journalists and convention audiences. I first heard him mention it during a PAX East developers' panel titled "Finding the Soul of Your Game": "Working on a dance game, you have a fair amount of dance culture to draw from. I try to get my inspiration from real-world examples of dance as much as possible. Early on in the game, in prototyping the game that would become *Dance Central*, I was dead set on the game being able to teach you 'Crank That' by Soulja Boy, which was blowing up at the time. I felt like if we were going to make a successful dance game, it had to be able to do that" (Boch 2012).

What made "Crank That" such an important point of inspiration, emblematic of the developing "soul" of *Dance Central*? It was a song about a dance, and it "blew up" through the circulation of "social dance-media" (Bench 2010). The "Crank That" music video and the numerous video remixes and parodies that it spawned offered an early example of a dance craze going viral in the Web 2.0 era. "Crank That" had first attracted an audience via Soulja Boy's MySpace page, where he posted the song in February 2007 "as the soundtrack to another group's homemade dance video" (Driscoll 2013); as Kevin Driscoll notes, various "crank dat" songs and moves had been spreading through the "snap music" corner of the hip-hop world for some time. Soulja Boy was soon "discovered" and signed by Interscope Records, with "Crank That" becoming the lead single for his debut album.

The official music video, released by Interscope in the summer of 2007, offered ample visual demonstrations of the dance and placed it in a particular social context, even as the video's circulation brought it to audiences far removed from the milieu of a Mississippi high school student who produced his tracks using Fruity Loops and uploaded them to Soundclick and MySpace. The video depicts the process in which it participates, telling the story of a dance going viral and an artist being discovered. It opens with a record executive learning of the latest street dance craze from small children; he traces the dance back to Soulja Boy and tracks him down to offer him a record deal. We see the dance circulating online and on cell phones, performed by people of all ages in everyday urban settings, and by Soulja Boy and other hip-hop artists for adulatory crowds.

Notably, this video depicts the "Crank That" dance sweeping through an exclusively African American social world, from the record executive to the dancing traffic cop to the senior citizens creakily rising off a park bench to crank their wrists. The implication is that viewers who are watching and sharing this official music video through YouTube are participating in a second-order viral circulation, after the "Crank That" song and dance have already been saturated with hip-hop authenticity through street-level circulation in black popular culture. To say that *Dance Central* had to be able to teach players "Crank That" is to invoke an aspirational alliance with hip-hop, with viral media circulation, and with raw, edgy content. (The song is filled with sexual entendres, including the controversial exhortation to "superman that ho"; the inclusion of this kind of song accounts for *Dance Central*'s "T for Teen" rating, which distinguishes it from the family-friendly *Just Dance* series.) This strategic alliance is part and parcel of *Dance Central*'s adoption of a venerable music industry business model: repackaging African American music and dance for mass distribution to global markets.

Like every song in the *Dance Central* catalog, "Crank That" presented its assigned game choreographer with particular constraints. The game routine had to incorporate the signature dance sequence from the video, kinesthetically amplify lyrics that implied particular moves (e.g., "Robocop," "Jock," "Superman"), and follow the structure of the song, which involves numerous repetitions of the hook. Due to its prior circulation with a dance already attached, "Crank That" imposed major limitations on the choreographer's choice of movement vocabulary. Because the song was a huge hit that could help drive sales of the entire game, the game routine also had to be relatively easy to perform, so it would be accessible to the widest possible range of players. (It was eventually classified as a "Moderate" song, a difficulty level of 3 out of 7.) These circumstances make "Crank That" an excellent case study for a consideration of technical pedagogy in *Dance Central*. How did the game choreographer, Devin Woolridge, reverse-engineer the "Crank That" dance so that he could build it up across three different difficulty levels in the game?

Table 4.1 shows how repetition and variation drive the pedagogical process in *Dance Central*. The move names are taken from the flashcards that scroll up the edge of the screen; each card represents one 4-count of music. Often a highlighted arm or leg on the card icon cues attention to a particular moving part; players learn to expect that the same motion might immediately be repeated on the opposite side of the body or in the other direction. In the case of the Crank Dat move,

Table 4.1: DEVELOPING VARIATIONS IN *DANCE CENTRAL'S* "CRANK THAT"

EASY = 7 moves	MEDIUM = 10 moves	HARD = 15 moves
Lean & Rock x3 [L]	Lean & Rock x2 [L]	Jump Off
[R]	[R]	Lean & Rock [R]
[L]	Kneeslapper	Kneeslapper
Supah Man	Supah Man	Supah Man
Crank Dat x4 [LRLR]	Crank Dat x4 [LRLR]	Crank Dat x4 [LRLR]
------------------------	------------------------	------------------------
Lean & Rock x2 [L]	Lean & Rock x2 [L]	Jump Off
[R]	[R]	Lean & Rock [R]
Supah Man	Supah Man	Supah Man
Robocop	Robocop	Robocop
Show 'Em Up x4 [RLRL]	Jock	Jock
	Push Pop	Push Pop
	Jock	Lean & Rock [R]
	Push Pop	Lean Left Crank
Punch Out x4	Punch Out x4	Crank Dat Still
		Tough Guy
		Punch Out
		Cocky
Don't Hate x4 [RLRL]	Show 'Em Up x2 [R]	Show 'Em Up x2 [R]
	[L]	[L]
	Don't Hate x2 [R]	Don't Hate x2 [R]
	[L]	[L]
------------------------	------------------------	------------------------
[Double chorus:	[Double chorus:	[Double chorus:
repeat first 4 8-counts x2]	repeat first 4 8-counts x2]	repeat first 4 8-counts x2]
------------------------	------------------------	------------------------
Freestyle: 4 8-counts	Freestyle: 4 8-counts	Freestyle: 4 8-counts
------------------------	------------------------	------------------------
[Double chorus:	[Double chorus:	[Double chorus:
repeat first 4 8-counts x2]	repeat first 8 4-counts x2]	repeat first 4 8-counts x2]
Lean & Rock x4 [LRLR]	Lean & Rock x4 [LRLR]	Lean & Rock x4 [LRLR]
Finishing Move	Finishing Move	Finishing Move

the icon includes a prominent arrow indicating the direction of motion for the signature lateral hop (see Figure 4.4). These icons help to construct a "body typography . . . governing the proper relations of [body] areas"; such typographies are then "put in motion by performing sequences of movement usually designated by the demonstrative body of the teacher," a role played by the screen dancer in dance games (Foster 1992:483).

Figure 4.4: Move icons, constructing a body typography and teaching players to anticipate patterned choreography. Detail from a player-produced video of the *Dance Central* routine for "Crank That" (Only Music Gaming 2015). Note the player's silhouette in the recognition window next to the Supah Man flashcard. (Screenshot by the author.)

In the Zumba classes at my local YMCA, my teachers attempted to accomplish the same kind of body-typography cueing in the course of full-speed, synchronous-imitation transmission of a new routine by raising one index finger and pointing to the body part that was about to begin executing a new move: follow this foot! Inevitably, many of us would also mirror the pointing gesture, mistaking it for part of the choreography. In *Dance Central*, the flashcards take over the role of the index finger, placing body typography cues in a perceptual channel that runs parallel to the model performance provided by the demonstrative body. One player also suggested that the flashcards compensate for the absence of a mirror:

> I do rely on flashcards quite a bit to get a feel for what the next move is, versus before with choreography and learning it in a studio, it really was more just muscle memory. Like I knew my arm was down here, and all of a sudden, the next move, I stick my arm up in this way, then I push my leg out. And that happens a lot with repetition and seeing yourself in the mirror. That helps a lot. But when you don't have that feedback, when you just have the game telling you what you're doing right or what you're doing wrong

and you can't see yourself, then you end up having to rely on other things: mainly the flashcards, because you see them move and then you see the position of the body and you're like, "Okay, that's where that move starts." (Riffraff, recorded phone interview, August 24, 2011)

Working through the available difficulty levels in sequence, players experience arcs of delayed gratification. For example, note how the two 8-counts of choreography for the opening hook develop over the three difficulty levels. The viral choreography for "Crank That" presented a level-design problem for the game version because the very first move is the most difficult one in the whole routine: a jump start, crossing and uncrossing the feet and then slapping one heel behind the back. In the *Dance Central* version, this opening move is withheld until the "Hard" difficulty level. On "Easy," the routine opens with a simple shift-weight-and-snap move, the Lean & Rock, repeated three times in alternating directions. This warm-up eases players into the variation tempo of this difficulty level and sets the stage for two signature moves from the viral routine, the Supah Man and the Crank Dat, both of which are synched with the corresponding song lyrics: a satisfying confirmation of expectations. On "Medium," players still start with two Lean & Rocks but add in one more element from the viral routine: the Kneeslapper. Moving up to "Hard" for the first time, players finally get the opening Jump Off, which makes for an exciting adrenaline burst: at last, the real routine! And a flurry of nerves: If this very first move is so much harder, then what will the rest be like? After a moment in the comfort zone of repeating the Crank Dat four times, the variation tempo takes off: a new move for each 4-count, eschewing even right/left repeats. Newly introduced moves flesh out lyrics about Soulja Boy's fighting prowess: the Tough Guy, Punch Out, and Cocky. After 12 4-counts at this pace of variation, players get a half-time reprieve with left/right repeats of Show 'Em Up and Don't Hate; then they Jump Off again as the hook returns, repeating several times to close out the song.

In the music video, these repetitions of the hook support repeated demonstrations of the dance as it travels across various bodies and contexts. In the game, where the screen dancer and setting don't change, one might think that so many verbatim repeats of the same choreography could feel tedious. But structural charts can be misleading when it comes to accounting for the unfolding experience of dancing through a routine. The chart for "Crank That" offers a straightforward and complete inventory of a relatively simple dance; at the hardest difficulty level, the choreography encompasses 15 moves, assembled in a modest number of combinations. The choreography for the hook at the start of the song repeats another four times without variation at the end. But as I encounter these verbatim repeats as a dancing player, there are indeed variations in my experience, and there is room for significant variation in my dancing. After the freestyle section, going into the final double chorus, I can release the effort of anticipating what will happen next in the routine and attend to the feeling of my body joyfully and vigorously moving without explicit instruction, a flow experience akin to a runner's high. If I suddenly stopped and stood still, I know I would keep feeling the Crank Dat hops; my proprioceptive system has locked onto the choreo. Yet I do not feel like an automaton. I am specifically embodied, feeling the bounce of my feet against my living room floor, the faint twinge of an old hamstring injury, the ragged breath of effort.

I release my visual focus, too—I look around, check out the on-screen background dancers and the details of my score, become more aware of my friend dancing next to me. I synch up with her micro-timing as we Lean & Rock; suddenly it feels like we are dancing together instead of in parallel. I think about technique: This time can I really connect hand and foot on the heel slap behind my back instead of just marking the gesture? Can my jumps be higher? I consider what I'm doing between the frames, smooth the transitions, try out alternative weight options with my feet, feel myself moving through three dimensions instead of performing as a stuttering freeze-frame silhouette that meets the perceptual demands of the Kinect. I'm no longer "marking" the choreography; I'm dancing, and fluently feeling the form of the song. And I'm listening: I'm noticing the ticking hi-hat that pushes new energy through the chorus the second time. I'm thinking about teenagers making dance music at home, unzipping downloaded folders chock-full of drum samples— the EDM equivalent of a giant box of crayons. I'm remembering that new Crayola smell and wondering what Soulja Boy is up to these days. And then I'm striking the finishing pose: Supah Man forward, toward the camera, freeze on one foot. I have pulled out the 20 virtual pins that tacked me to the screen dancer's skeleton; now I cast my own shadow. All this transpires across four repetitions of "the same" choreographic material.

CONCLUSION: PLAYABLE DANCE AND REAL DANCE

What kinds of dance do dance games teach? Presentational dance: forward-facing, mirroring a screen dancer and framed by the invisible mirror-borders of the screen, which also delineate the perceptual frame of the motion-sensing system. Legible dance: a semaphore vocabulary of well-defined gestures that create shadowbox-theater silhouettes, easy for the game system to read and easy for players and their human audiences to comprehend as kinesthetic transcription of lyrics, musical elements, and related cultural references. Modular dance: choreography built up from two-beat or four-beat moves that kinesthetically amplify the metrical structures of popular dance music, lend themselves to symmetrical variations, and are easy to chain together or remix, like an EDM producer's collection of drum samples. Popular dance: basic steps culled from the big-tent genres of disco, house, hip-hop, salsa, and aerobics, a choreographic lingua franca established through several decades of club dancing, television dance shows, music videos, and school- or gym-based dance classes. Referential, nostalgic dance: choreography that samples, commemorates, and canonizes old dance crazes and hit songs. Social dance: not social as in partner-dancing but social as in social media, where relational infrastructure develops laterally in the course of parallel play. Dancing side by side (virtually or actually) while oriented toward the same screen, bodies never touch yet accrue intimate, embodied, mutual knowledge through practicing the same technique and repertoire. Learnable dance: choreography that deploys repetition and novelty in the service of creating cycles of challenge, practice, tests of mastery, and affirmations of success. Playable dance, in two senses: dance as a playlist of pre-recorded choreographic works to be played back through one's body, but also dance as a collection of mini-games, with rules and stakes different from those of club dance, dance class, or stage dance contexts.

Both *Just Dance* and *Dance Central* materialize bodies and popular songs as playable interfaces, and cultivate technique through multisensory engagement with those interfaces. The resulting gameplay experiences rely on cumulative practice, trial and error, anticipation and realization, and comparative reflection—comparisons across repetitions of choreography and across the virtual and actual dancing bodies who enact those repetitions. Dance game playlists are collections of proprioception *études*, driven by hybrid dance transmission modalities that combine elements drawn from studio dance pedagogy, home-dance practices, prescriptive music notation systems, and game level-design principles, each informed by particular ideologies of skill and mastery. The games incorporate elements of discipline—including the self-regulating discipline required by self-fashioning projects—but always framed in terms of experimental, voluntary play: "simming" discipline, one might say (Magelssen 2014).

Through their engagements with existing popular music and dance repertoires and associated histories of circulation, dance games also posit an aspirational relationship between virtual dance and "real dance." The terms and stakes of this realness can shape-shift in different dancing and gaming contexts. This chapter has explored the forms of racialized realness that inform both *Just Dance*'s "Apache" and *Dance Central*'s "Crank That": the realness of "street" dances authenticated by their circulation through black urban social life and the mirror-image realness of sincere, intimate, and unabashedly awkward domestic dancing, coded white. This twinned constellation guided Carlton's "White Man Dance" performances on *The Fresh Prince of Bel Air*, as Alfonso Ribeiro explained, and aids players in navigating their dance game experiences. Dance games also foreground ideas of realness predicated on digital/analog and automaton/human dichotomies, which have their own racialized dimensions (see, e.g., Weheliye 2002, Chun 2009). This kind of realness is closely associated with dancerly "flow," "groove," or "flavor"—qualities of movement that cannot be assessed by the game systems, that only humans can embody and verify. Flow is a sign of a player's capacity to go beyond simming, a proof of both genuine individual expression and fluent competence in an established style.

When my colleague wrote to me about the fragmented, jittery talent-show dance performance he had witnessed—"a dance routine that I'm convinced the student learned from *Dance Central* or some other dance game. . . . very very strange"—I wrote back right away:

I actually haven't seen a lot of Dance Central players dance like that, but it's certainly possible that the system could encourage it in terms of giving a high score to that style of performance—and that a player might not realize the mismatch between their own dance style and the more fluid performance of the motion-captured animated dancer, since players mostly don't see themselves on screen. The game designers count on players to "fill in" the choreography with their received knowledge of dance culture (just as they counted on Guitar Hero players to physically perform like rock guitarists even though in that case the game couldn't acknowledge those performances).

Upon further consideration, I realized that dance games push this model a step further than *Guitar Hero*. They present the tantalizing prospect of one-upping a game on its own turf. *Guitar Hero* celebrates a model of heroic, improvisatory, virtuosic musicianship that can't be practiced in the context of gameplay, where players read transcribed guitar solos from notation and hear someone else's performance come out of the speakers. Dance games present the possibility that players can really dance—with flow, with individual creative expression. But if they do, the scoring algorithm will never be the wiser. The game systems continually prove themselves inadequate to the task of evaluating real dance, and that very inadequacy helps define realness and reinforce its value. To put it another way, while *Guitar Hero* perpetuates rock authenticity by positioning players as always falling just short of genuine guitar heroism, dance games perpetuate dance authenticity by positioning machines as forever falling short of human powers of recognition, judgment, embodied presence, and analog flow. "Real dance" materializes between the frames, eluding machinic perception and assessment:

menorche: It would be great if there was a way to reward players who have so much more "groove" when doing a song, as opposed to those who barely move and hit the "keyframes" at the right time. Perhaps it is a Kinect sensor issue, but it would be amazing if players who *actually dance* are given higher points than those who do the "space invader". The best example I can give is this guy: http://www.youtube.com/watch?v=59W NkSpUmek [rosroskof's performance of "Lapdance," discussed in Chapter 2]

Lauson1ex: Haha, the "space invader." I laughed.

Incidentally, this is our fellow [forum] member Oblitt. His moves are incredible.

Ironically, despite your suggestion, it seems like the game punishes him more than it rewards him for his "groove." It's just like if Dance Central *requires* you to do robotic moves in order to give you good scores. I, myself, am quite confident on the Dance Central routines in order to put my own *flavor* to them and still get Gold Stars, but songs like "Because Of You" just seem impossible to me to nail Gold Stars unless I perform the dance moves in a robotic away; the aforementioned "space invader" syndrome. (DanceCentral.com 2011b)

Dance games thus teach "real dance" by leading players to search their own and others' performances for signs of expression that evade the gaze and interpretive powers of the game system. This search is a self-fashioning project, highlighting the ways that dance technique intersects with the layered, iterative acquisition of other embodied skills and attitudes.

The idea of "real dance," like the idea of technique more generally, always points forward and backward: projecting an ideal to be achieved through practice while also referring back to authentic sources. This chapter has addressed some of those sources, in the form of choreographies that circulated across media platforms and among watching, listening, dancing bodies for years before being remediated in dance games. In the next chapter I turn to the human representatives of "real dance" who made these remediations possible, the dancers whose features are blurred out in *Just Dance*'s music video scenarios and whose traces linger in the motion-capture code that pulls the strings of *Dance Central*'s animated characters. Their own ideas about "real dance" inform their embodied and affective labor at the intersection of the professional dance world and the game industry, the creative-economy niche where they work simultaneously as choreographers, dancers, teachers, developers, promoters, and cultural intermediaries.

CHAPTER 5
Choreographic Labor, FTFO

In the months leading up to the release of *Just Dance 2*, Ubisoft posted a series of "backstage" videos to its Just Dance UK channel on YouTube. The third video is titled "Meet the dancers" (Just Dance UK 2010). At the opening, a young white woman leans against a mirrored wall. She is hip and sophisticated, wearing stylish street clothes; her heavy eyeliner and shaggy bleach-blonde hair with dark roots contribute to a look that walks the line between edgy and chic. Screen text identifies her as "Julia: Lead choreographer JustDance2." Speaking French, she alludes to her work on the first *Just Dance* game and outlines some new features for the sequel. The video provides subtitles in slightly unidiomatic British English: "One new development in this game is the two-player mode, which is really brilliant, because two or even four people can play. There are also a lot of different dance styles, a lot of variety. It's really a pride of knowing that my movements, my choreography, are being danced by kids and adults around the world. It's really a pleasure" (see Figure 5.1).

The opening of Beyoncé's 2003 hit "Crazy in Love" swells to fill the soundtrack—it is a faithful cover version of the song, suggesting that Ubisoft did not secure rights for the original. For about 20 seconds we see Julia dancing in a spacious studio, flooded with light and lined with mirrors. She is alone in the room; there is no game production technology in sight, and she is not holding a Wii remote. This is a depiction of a dancer "just dancing," or perhaps engaged in the creative process of crafting choreography. Occasionally a TV screen showing the matching *Just Dance 2* gameplay video for "Crazy in Love" appears on the right side of the frame. The routine includes some recognizable elements from the Beyoncé music video, including several variations on a strutting walk, along with booty pops shown in profile on the "Uh oh" chorus.

The video cuts to a second choreographer, identified as Zack, who stands against a tree in a forest or thickly wooded park. Zack is a young black man wearing a blue chambray work shirt, fully buttoned to the neck. He too looks stylish, with a shaved

Figure 5.1: *Just Dance 2* choreographer Julia, presented in a "Meet the dancers" video (Just Dance UK 2010). (Screenshot by the author.)

Figure 5.2: *Just Dance 2* choreographer Zack, presented in a "Meet the dancers" video (Just Dance UK 2010). (Screenshot by the author.)

head and meticulously minimalist goatee, but his relatively plain clothes and diffident speaking style telegraph more earnestness than edginess. As he speaks, the video shows clips of him performing some dance moves amid the foliage (see Figure 5.2).

> I think when people dance with JD, they let themselves go. They relax, they enjoy themselves: it's a game that lets you dance and learn dance movements without even realizing it, something you can do with your family, your mates, your friends, whoever! At the end

of the day, it's all about having a good time together. The James Brown choreography was a bit complicated to do. My only brief was that it needed to be inspired by James Brown and that it was important to keep the essence of his dancing. So I did that, and also added a bit of my own style to bring it up to date, and that's it, the final result is in the game. (spoken in French; quotation from English subtitles)

Zack briefly dances amid the trees to James Brown's "I Feel Good" (1965) before an abrupt cut to a new choreographer and setting. Now a different young black man leans against a railing, standing on the outdoor mezzanine of an industrial building that overlooks a dense urban area. The identifying screen text simply says "Twins." This choreographer wears black sunglasses, a graphic T-shirt, and a black denim jacket with the sleeves turned up (see Figure 5.3). He tousles his spiked Afro with one hand as he says (in French), "Really, the only thing I know is dance, it's been like that since I was born." The video cuts to short clips of him dancing to Kris Kross's debut single "Jump" (1992), joined by his twin brother. Their matching hip-hop moves are framed by the cinderblock hallways of the industrial building. Occasionally the corresponding two-player gameplay routine appears in an inset box in the corner. He continues speaking over the dance clips:

We both lose ourselves in it: it's an obligation, a discipline, a way of life. Seeing as Just Dance 1 had just come out, I tried it and thought it was cool. I played it all night and liked it a lot, so I said okay. We go for a style that's a bit mad, playing on our cartoon side, but at the same time, we still had to respect the fact that it's a dance game for people who know or don't know how to dance. It was wicked, I loved every minute. (quotation from English subtitles)

Figure 5.3: *Just Dance 2* choreographer: one of the Twins (unnamed), presented in a "Meet the dancers" video (Just Dance UK 2010). (Screenshot by the author.)

This three-and-a-half minute video is packed with allusions to disparate dance styles, contexts, ideologies, and archetypal characters. Julia is a polished professional studio dancer/choreographer who still knows how to have fun. Zack presents dance as natural, intuitive, accessible, and social. The Twins personify gritty urban cool; they describe dance as a birthright and an all-encompassing "way of life," associated with a hip-hop ethos. There are multiple versions of dance authenticity in play here—dance as studio art, as natural/universal human behavior, and as street culture, each presented with gendered/racialized dimensions. But there are also common threads. All three featured songs are major hits by African American artists; they span nearly four decades of popular music history and carry nostalgia value for multiple generations of players. Julia and the Twins present two versions of dancerly discipline: the flexible, versatile (white) studio dancer who can work in any style, and the born-to-dance (black) hip-hop brothers who describe dance like a religious faith with its own rigorous ethical code. Meanwhile, Zack and the Twins offer up contrasting versions of dancerly black masculinity: One version is naturalized, non-threatening, and radiates feel-good warmth, while the other is spectacular, powerful, and cool. Both function as authentic representatives of transnational black culture, willing and able to make James Brown and hip-hop accessible to a broad audience that includes "people who don't know how to dance." Finally, all the choreographers refer to their personal styles, asserting individual creative authorship within the constraints of game production. Notably, while the video is titled "Meet the dancers," these artists all represent the combined role of dancer-choreographer, with its connotations of expressive agency and personal authenticity—in contrast to most dancers in popular music videos, who perform someone else's choreographic work to back up a star musician. Through their words and their dancing affect, Julia, Zack, and the Twins also all declare that they take pleasure in their work.

This kind of video functions not only as a promotional device to attract new players but also as a gathering place and topic of conversation for experienced players—what Steve Jones calls a "paratext," part of the "transmedia, multidimensional grid of possibilities surrounding any given game" (2008:10). The YouTube video was posted in advance of the game release, but many comments appeared well after the release date, written by people who had already played *Just Dance 2*. The vast majority of comments are in English, and many express surprise that the choreographers are speaking French. Most commenters focus on the Twins; many remark on their sex appeal, and several display insider knowledge by referring to them by their first names and explaining other details.

Jacqueline Rodriguez: It's LES TWINS!!! Speaking French *faint* they are fine

ChinaDoll Brooklyn: .mhmmm , them twins is hella sexy !

BeautyV11: Larry(LEFT) Laurent(RIGHT)

numra25: i love seeing les twins in real life dancing to this song =D i knew it was them as soon as i saw the characters and the dance lol andy smith: afro dude is wearing his pants backward

Devin Spencer: You guys didnt know the song les twins are dancing to is one of the reasons why their pants are backwards. . . it was the craze when the song came out. . also their older brothers made them wear them backwards when they got in trouble.

Kwazhia Keliswright: I figured Les Twins did Jump because of the Afros in the video game. . . .
(comments on Just Dance UK 2010, accessed November 14, 2015)

Promotional media featuring game choreographers highlight one of the distinctive qualities of dance games, as compared to most other video games. Dance games privilege the idea that there are actual human bodies at the beginning and end of the chain of technical mediations that links game development and player experiences, and that the bodies at both ends are *really doing* the action modeled by the gameplay. They are not shooting fake guns, driving fake cars, or playing fake guitars, but actually dancing. Notice the way that YouTube commenters call out their recognition of the original bodies behind the blank-faced silhouettes in *Just Dance 2*, eroticize them, and place them in a real-life dance-historical context. Like recording artists, dance game choreographers function "both as object[s] of fantasy, identification, and commerce and as skilled working subject[s] integrated into legal and economic structures" (Stahl 2013:3). They lay claim to particular versions of dance authenticity through their embodied and affective labor, and players participate in the process of legitimizing these claims both through kinesthetic practice—learning to dance—and through discourse.

This chapter builds on the discussion of technique, pedagogy, remediation, and realness in Chapter 4 to investigate the nature of choreographic labor in dance games. How do game companies incorporate professional choreographers into their industry—as cultural consultants, developers, content generators, and promoters—and how do game choreographers feel about their own work? As we have seen, dance games raise questions about what counts as "real dance," and about how players can determine whether they are achieving this aspirational standard. Choreographers are charged with defining and representing "real dance" through their own realness, not only as legitimately skilled dancers but also as flesh-and-blood humans who can reach across time, space, and layers of digital mediation to impart their kinesthetic energy into players' bodies.

In addition to crafting and performing the routines that appear in dance games, choreographers teach game developers about dance culture and dance pedagogy, negotiate the affordances of game technologies, participate in the "quality assurance" (QA) playtesting that establishes evaluation standards for players' performances, represent the games in promotional media, and interact directly with players via social media, conventions, and tournaments. This is an unusual range of roles for a game-industry professional. Game development companies employ many voice actors, motion-capture actors, and musicians, but these workers typically remain behind the scenes and have limited participation in game development beyond their role as studio performers. Game choreographers thus function as mediators between popular dance culture and gamer culture as well as between the game industry and players. More generally, they are part of the cadre of creative workers who "exemplify the individual autonomy promised (in different registers) by democratic and neoliberal ideology and institutions as well as the routine subordination of individuals demanded in and by liberal market society" (Stahl 2013:5).

As Jennifer Smith Maguire writes, following Bourdieu, "Shaping tastes and matching things to people require that cultural intermediaries frame particular practices and products as worthy of their claimed value, involving them in constructing repertoires of cultural legitimacy. Consequently, cultural intermediaries are not simply taste makers; they are professional taste makers and 'authorities of legitimation'" (2014:21, Bourdieu 1990:96). Like the personal trainers who are the focus of Smith Maguire's work, game choreographers draw on "their personal lives, bodies and tastes as crucial occupational resources" as they "help to educate consumers in a particular view of the body as a vehicle of self-expression and a focal point for consumption" (Smith Maguire 2008:219, 212). These educational projects are baked into each dance game's approach to technical pedagogy, at the level of basic gameplay mechanics. Game choreographers also advance the same projects through extensive affective labor in support of the games, whether it be through their contributions to "behind the scenes" promotional materials or their personal interaction with players. Like many culture workers, they are engaged in the business of managing other people's emotions, particularly their emotions about their bodies.

This chapter focuses on the perspectives of two *Dance Central* choreographers, Marcos Aguirre and Chanel Thompson, who shared reflections about their years of work on the franchise when I interviewed them in 2015 (Aguirre and Miller 2015, Thompson and Miller 2015). As dance professionals, Aguirre and Thompson routinely juggle a collection of distinct and overlapping gigs as choreographers, performers, and teachers; they are navigating the neoliberal regime of flexible/precarious labor, which has entailed "a shift of the artist's position from the periphery of society—occupying a bohemian or genius outsider status—into the very center and limelight of current economic and employment practices" (Kolb 2013:41, following Hardt and Negri 2000). Like the majority of the *Dance Central* choreographers, Thompson and Aguirre are people of color engaged in the business of performing racialized, gendered, and classed repertoires in industries structured by systemic discrimination and inequity. They should also be recognized as game developers in their own right, rather than simply generators of content that others capture, transcode, and integrate into games. While they both disavowed any deep knowledge of game development technology at the level of programming, animation, or hardware design, their accounts of their work at Harmonix demonstrate that they and their fellow choreographers substantially shaped the terms of other developers' and players' interactions with the Kinect as "a supple system [that does] a sort of social/emotional 'dance' with the end user" (Isbister and Höök 2009:4).

In addition to featuring Aguirre's and Thompson's personal accounts, I draw on choreographer perspectives gleaned from official promotional media, player-produced media, and web-based interactions between players and choreographers, which take place in game forums, on Twitter, and in YouTube comment threads. (I attempted to secure interviews with *Just Dance* choreographers and additional *Dance Central* choreographers, but was unsuccessful.) In all of these contexts, game choreographers are speaking as professionals with contractual obligations to promote particular products, and in the case of company-produced promotional videos their commentary might be scripted or significantly edited. Nevertheless, I believe we have something to learn from the way game choreographers talk about dance and the way their respective companies choose to deploy them for promotional purposes—not only lessons about the construction of dance authenticity but also insight into "how the reproduction of consumer economies rests on the personal, affective investments of their promoters" (Smith Maguire 2014:23).

Aguirre and Thompson were deeply engaged interview participants, generous with their time and ideas. Our conversations resonated with Giselinde Kuipers's observation that while interviews with cultural intermediaries "often are very 'frontstage' affairs," they can also be rich sources of collaboratively generated ethnographic data. As Kuipers writes, the ethnographic interview is "a genre that cultural intermediaries understand: a conversation in which meanings and values are discussed, dissected and co-produced" (2014:55). In the course of their work at Harmonix and their discussions with me, Aguirre and Thompson were keenly aware of their role as ambassadors not just for *Dance Central* but for dance itself, particularly as a means of experiencing popular music in global circulation. They each presented their work as a form of advocacy for dance and as a means of fulfilling a personal obligation to share a gift. In what follows, I will provide a brief profile of each choreographer and then interweave their reflections on several key themes that run through this book, including their ideas about dance technique, interface affordances, digital transmission of embodied repertoires, gender performance, cultural appropriation, and playable/workable bodies.

MARCOS AGUIRRE, A.K.A. DAMON REBELL, A.K.A. DZANIELLA NANI

Marcos Aguirre was one of two full-time, in-house staff choreographers recruited by Harmonix Music Systems very early in the *Dance Central* development process. During this period, around 2009–2010, multiple game companies were at work on closely guarded projects to create launch games for the Kinect. I followed Aguirre's official promotional work and interactions with players via social media across the life of the *Dance Central* franchise, beginning with the commercial release of the original *Dance Central* in the fall of 2010 (see Figure 5.4). By the time *Dance Central 3* was released in fall 2012, Aguirre had moved from Boston to Los Angeles

Figure 5.4: Marcos Aguirre in the motion-capture studio, juxtaposed with Emilia performing his choreography. Still from a behind-the-scenes promotional video (Harmonix Music Systems 2011b). (Screenshot by the author.)

to pursue the next phase of his dance career. In the summer of 2015 I initiated email correspondence with him and he graciously agreed to a phone interview. We spoke for an hour as he walked through the sweltering streets of Los Angeles and I sat in my dining room in Providence, Rhode Island. In the virtual third space of our conversation, we shared in the productive challenge of communicating about our embodied experience with *Dance Central* without recourse to body language.

Aguirre grew up in the Boston area, where he did most of his dance training, performing, and teaching until making his move to Los Angeles. When I emailed to ask him how he would prefer to be described in this book, he wrote, "I'm originally from Methuen, MA. Sassy Puerto Rican is fine though lol." Aguirre and his fellow in-house choreographer Francisca "Frenchy" Hernandez played an enormous role in developing the *Dance Central* franchise, serving as the resident dance and dance-music experts in a company that had for years focused on a rock music performance paradigm. Senior producer Naoko Takamoto described the initial choreographer recruiting process to *Polygon* writer Russ Pitts:

> We put up flyers at studios. We told friends. But it was super-secret. I can't believe that they didn't even run away when they saw us. . . . We were like, "Hi! We work for a video game company. Come meet us in this basement kitchen where there's going to be a camera set up and just dance for us. It's totally cool. Totally not sketchy. Can you sign all this paperwork for us?" It was super shady to them. Marcos was like, "Uh . . . alright? I guess? You want me to dance here?" For the people who are internal, we wanted to get people who also had a good design brain. . . . We needed people who were generalists. Those two are very much . . . they have their own style, but they've studied forever and they take from different types of choreography. They're not pop-and-lockers, but they use it

in their choreography. There's some jazz. They just pull from everything. That was really important for us, to make sure the game is balanced. They also teach a lot. That was really important to us, that we could have people who could teach people who are here how to dance and be more comfortable. (Pitts 2012)

At Harmonix, Aguirre and Hernandez taught dance workshops, explained how studio dance classes work, and shared their pedagogical strategies for creating accessible, pleasurable learning experiences for dance students with widely varying levels of experience. They also put the Kinect through its paces, drawing on the full stylistic range of their own dance training to determine what choreographic vocabulary could be tracked by this new technology, which was itself still actively in development.

In effect, Hernandez and Aguirre co-constructed the affordances of the Kinect. Their work involved not only determining what the Kinect could and couldn't do, but what they wanted it to be able to do to accommodate particular dance styles, teaching modalities, and musical selections. The task of crafting choreography for any given song involved a complex triangulation process, as choreographers drew on their understanding of the Kinect's technical capacities and constraints; their expectations about players' dance competence, tastes, and desires; and their own creative inclinations—all of which shifted substantially across several years of iterative development work on three major game editions. As this process unfolded, Hernandez and Aguirre also influenced the stylistic range of the franchise by drawing on their personal and professional networks in the Boston-area dance world to assemble a team of "external" choreographers who worked as independent contractors, charged with creating routines for particular songs. Aguirre, Hernandez, and several of the external choreographers also routinely participated in the playtesting process used to fine-tune the motion-detection/scoring mechanisms for each track.

Aguirre is the credited choreographer for over 60 *Dance Central* tracks, spanning the three main game editions and additional downloadable content (DLC). Frenchy Hernandez is credited with the next-largest number of tracks, at about 30. Six external choreographers made major, sustained contributions across multiple game editions, each choreographing between 10 and 25 tracks: Chanel Thompson, Devin Woolridge, Ricardo Foster Jr., Kunle Oladehin, Spikey Soria, and Torey Nelson, each of whom was selected with an eye to strengthening a particular stylistic register in *Dance Central*. Takamoto's rundown of their contributions often dwells on confluences of gender and genre:

This time we wanted to get people who had more specialties, who were a little more . . . they're all still generalists, but they definitely have the things that they're interested in. That's when we got Chanel Thompson. Chanel has a huge cheerleading influence. She does actually girly, but still androgynous . . . not too sexy kind of stuff, because a lot of guys weren't into doing that. She does "androgynous tough girl" stuff really amazingly. We got Devin, and Devin just has this big energy. If you ever saw Phunk Phenomenon [competing on *America's Best Dance Crew*], they look like they're going to beat you up. It's awesome. Ricardo . . . he can do everything. He's an extraordinarily graceful dancer, but he can also crump your face off. . . . Then, last year, we hired Torey Nelson and Spikey Soria. Spikey's just another beautiful version of how more girls dance. We wanted more variety in girls. Torey's . . . I don't know. He's really earthy and really hip-hop. I don't know how else . . . he makes it look really easy. And we have Kunle Oladehin, who's popping, locking, but does hip-hop really well, and R&B stuff really well. (Pitts 2012)

Two additional choreographers each contributed a handful of tracks and a dose of prestige: Nick DeMoura, a member of the Boston-area dance network who rose to international prominence as Justin Bieber's tour choreographer, and celebrity choreographer Aakomon "AJ" Jones, who choreographed four Usher tracks in connection with Usher's endorsement of *Dance Central 3* (HarmonixMusic.com 2013).

The choreographers' names appear prominently in the playlist menu screens for the *Dance Central* games, and players routinely discuss their individual styles on the player forums (see Chapter 3). In most cases, the person who choreographed a given song also did the corresponding motion-capture performance work. As Aguirre explained, "For choreography, each choreographer definitely got to shoot their own thing, unless they were not available. Then one of us, usually it would be me or Frenchy, would learn the choreography and do it for the motion capture." As described in Chapter 2, each song in *Dance Central* is associated with a particular default screen dancer drawn from the game's collection of characters, though players have an opportunity to switch characters before they start the track. In terms of matching motion-capture performers to the designated default screen dancer for a particular song, Aguirre said, "When it comes to specific characters, anybody could've been anybody." This principle of variability certainly held true for Aguirre's own choreographic work, since he created so many routines; if his performances had always been mapped onto a single character, that character would be the default dancer for a disproportionate percentage of the *Dance Central* catalog. However, some other choreographers did become closely associated with particular screen dancers. For instance, if a song's default character was Taye, many players came to assume that the motion-capture performance and choreography were both by Chanel Thompson (discussed further below).

Aguirre initially heard about the job opportunity at Harmonix by word of mouth, through one of the dance studios where he was teaching at the time. In our conversation he described his teaching portfolio as "everything based around hip-hop," but he noted that "I fuse my style a lot. . . . I took modern and ballet in school and grew up doing jazz and jazz funk and dancehall and some house. . . . The studio put it under hip-hop, but for me it was just a dance class. You never knew what you were going to get when you came in and took my class. . . . For me it's just movement, movement to music." This flexible approach to stylistic categories also seemed to structure Aguirre's understanding of gender performance; "masculine" and "feminine" were just two more conventional movement styles, with arbitrary

Figure 5.5: Marcos Aguirre: @mea5678 Twitter profile photo, December 2015. (Screenshot by the author.)

boundaries constructed through comparison to other styles. "You can always make something feminine or make something masculine or make it look like another gender or make it no gender. . . . I think it comes from just being comfortable with yourself, and owning it. . . . It's just all about learning and experiencing something new, learning what your body can do" (see Chapter 2).

In preparation for our conversation, I had explored Aguirre's personal and professional social media channels on YouTube, Twitter, and Instagram, where he sometimes employed two alternative names (see Figures 5.5 and 5.6). As he explained via email,

> They are more like character performers. Damon Rebell is an edgy, darker alter ego I've created for video projects and stage performances. I've recently started getting him into the burlesque side of the dance art world. Dzaniella Nani is my "female" alter ego. She's an overall entertainer living her own life and career, dabbling in stand-up comedy, music and acting. Also getting her into burlesque shows as well. I look at it like I'm just her manager or something. Get her the auditions, gigs and [she] even has her own social media sites. Definitely a different way for me to be and stay creative, and challenged. (I've never done drag before!!!)

Figure 5.6: Dzaniella Nani's Instagram page, December 2015. (Screenshot by the author.)

Aguirre's development of these alternative characters sheds light on his approach to game choreography and dance technique, and it resonates with the "playable bodies" concept at the heart of this book. Aguirre has created his own avatars, mixed-reality performers who manifest as both digital and fleshed-out bodies. He has pieced them together out of materials drawn from his acquired stylistic repertoire and aspects of his own personality, a process that requires both intimate reflection and strategic, entrepreneurial creativity.

CHANEL THOMPSON, A.K.A. MISS 5678

Chanel Thompson was among the first "external" choreographers hired for *Dance Central*. She was part of the core team from the beginning of the franchise, working on *Dance Central, Dance Central 2, Dance Central 3*, and the download-only spinoff game *Dance Central Spotlight*. By the time I met her in the summer of 2015, I was already familiar with her signature high-energy personal warmth from following her interactions with players in social media contexts for the previous four years. (See Figures 5.7 and 5.8.)

Figure 5.7: Chanel Thompson in a behind-the-scenes promotional video (Harmonix Music Systems 2011b). (Screenshot by the author.)

Figure 5.8: Chanel Thompson at our interview, August 2015. (Photograph by the author.)

I interviewed Thompson during her lunch hour on the roof deck of an office building in Boston's financial district; in our first few minutes together, I watched her charm her way through several layers of building security in the process of getting me a visitor badge. Thompson is a pragmatic problem solver and strikingly charismatic, qualities that she has cultivated in the course of simultaneously pursuing three demanding lines of work: a full-time administrative job at a brokerage firm, numerous dance-related professional projects, and raising a daughter. She has adopted an entrepreneurial and network-oriented approach to her work in the dance world and ultimately aims to weave together the strands of her career by offering financial planning services to other dancers. As she explained,

CHANEL THOMPSON: Dancers, we don't have stability. It's still not a stable career. It's much like the DJ, it's much like the artist, it's much like the hairstylist and the barber.
KM: Who rent a chair.
THOMPSON: That's right. You don't have a 401(k), it's not a corporate job. You don't have mutual funds, you don't have health benefits. And for the most part when you get with these [touring musical] artists and you dance professionally, or even with Harmonix, the contract could be a wonderful contract, but when you're dancing, you have to be able to manage your money. Because you don't know when the next gig's going to come along. So if you don't properly manage your money then you're going to be overzealous and not be able to take care of your business. There's so many more things that play into dance. How do you brand yourself, how do you promote yourself? What's your business? What do you offer?

At the time of our conversation, Thompson was not actively working for Harmonix, having recently completed an intensive period of choreography, motion-capture, and QA ("quality assurance" playtesting) to produce downloadable tracks for *Dance Central Spotlight*—repertoire that was gradually released to consumers over a period of several months. We did not talk in detail about her contract arrangements, but I gathered that they involved a non-compete agreement that restricted her from doing choreographic work for other digital games but did not stand in the way of teaching dance classes, taking on clients for private coaching, or performing. I brought a series of open-ended questions to our meeting, some focusing on technical aspects of game production and others on her professional history in the dance world. She gravitated to the topic of choreographic labor, including the generally precarious position of professional performing artists and her own investment in creating a personal artistic legacy through her work on *Dance Central*.

Thompson's account of her background emphasized her international experience, cosmopolitan versatility, and affinity for high-energy, spectacular, and technically precise dance styles:

I am a United States Air Force brat, so I spent five years in Texas, two years in Germany, four years in England, and the main duration of the rest of that, from sophomore year of high school to senior year, in Medford and Boston. . . . I have backgrounds in hip-hop basics, a little bit of street jazz, a little bit of vogueing and waacking type of movement, and 18 years of cheerleading: all of its technique, teaching, All-Star, competitive, and just every aspect of cheerleading, the dance aspect as well. I'm focusing right now on dancehall and dancehall workouts.

At the moment when she first started working on *Dance Central*, Thompson was "doing what I normally do—booking dancers, dancing back-up and doing choreography for artists and dance teams. Artist and dancer development." She described some of her gigs, including performing with acts associated with reggaeton producer Noriega, and "working with affiliates of [*America's Best Dance Crew* competitors] Phunk Phenomenon, and some of the dancers that now dance for Beyoncé on tour."

Throughout our conversation Thompson emphasized the themes of performance energy and "clean" technical execution:

A lot of people come and ask me to either clean their dance team up or clean their dancer up or clean their artist up, or perfect what they're doing and add to it. It's an energy. . . . You have 30 seconds when you get on the stage, or when you do anything, that has to do with dance or performing. You have 30 seconds to capture that person's attention, and most of that is all energy. And if you don't have it [as a teacher], you're not setting a tone, they're not going to pick it up, they're not going to do it the way you're doing it. So you have to set the tone, starting with your energy.

Thompson is clearly a big believer in affective contagion. She described striving to transmit her own intense energy to students and clients so that they would "feel the way that I feel": "If I have high energy, you're going to have high energy. Because I'm showing you that's what I have, so you're going to emulate that with the same energy, or start to feel that way, be inspired by that." This concept of transmittable personal energy dovetails with ideas about liveness and the special potential of body-to-body transmission contexts, whether in dance performance or dance pedagogy (cf. Gibbs 2010). But how could Thompson square these values with the layers of technical mediation involved in *Dance Central*? What was it like to have her energetic performances captured as a data set that would be folded into a complex digital animation process? For a dancer, this might seem to be the ultimate form of alienated labor.

KM: You have a very charismatic personality, and I can imagine that in person it's very easy to transmit that [energy]. So how did it feel to be attempting to find ways to transmit that through 40 glowing bulbs on your body?

THOMPSON: Just remembering why I'm doing it. I think anybody that's doing anything that they're passionate about, if they have a reason why they're doing it, they're going to do it full-out. As Marcos [Aguirre] would say—I don't know if you have any censorship on swearing—as he always says, FTFO, full the fuck out, you know what I mean, you gotta go full out. And a lot of the times when you're in your [motion-capture] suit, that energy comes across, and when you get to watch what your energy level is, whether it's on video or whether you're looking at yourself with the [LED] lights on, you can tell how much energy you have to project in your routine or your choreography. Because otherwise it reads as boring, or it reads as low-energy. So that's why you have to have that energy up, and be charismatic, exciting. And go into character, or go into whatever mode you get into in order to portray whatever you're trying to portray for that choreography. There's times where like for example Marcos and Frenchy would have very sensual or very passionate emotion when they dance, and you could feel that, they would make the facial expressions and all that.

The *Dance Central* motion capture process does not record dancers' facial expressions; having donned an LED-covered suit hundreds of times, Thompson knew very well that there is no direct data link between game choreographers' studio performances and the screen dancers' animated faces. Yet she still believed that the *feeling* of those embodied expressions somehow made its way from the studio to players' living rooms. I will return to these intertwined issues of motion-captured kinesthetic labor and choreographer/player affective relations below.

Players strongly associate Chanel Thompson both with the game character Taye (the only adult African American female character) and with the playfully authoritative dance-teacher persona indexed by her Twitter handle, @miss5678. She has traveled widely to promote the *Dance Central* games at conventions, where she often engages in a kind of cosplay-as-herself; she adopts elements of Taye's sartorial style and dances with fans like a flesh-and-blood version of the character, while also clearly projecting her own professional identity as a dancer/choreographer/teacher. Her young daughter sometimes accompanies her, hanging out with game staff and players on the *Dance Central* stage at industry events. Thompson confirmed that many players assume her daughter was the inspiration or perhaps even the motion-capture performer for the game character Lil T, presented as Taye's younger sister— "Absolutely, and she'd come dressed as Lil T. But in actuality, Frenchy [Hernandez] is Lil T and I'm Taye" (see Figure 5.9). Meanwhile, Thompson's daughter also engaged with *Dance Central* from the production side, experiencing it as part of her mother's professional life:

My daughter is such a Harmonix baby, she's one of those babies that spent a lot of time during choreography sessions and choreography review, motion capture, filter testing, and meetings. . . . She is the kid that spent her afternoons and her summers, when she's supposed to be on vacation, watching mommy grind for the bigger picture, which is choreography to reach the world. And that's what we did. She was able to be a part of that process and see that process.

Figure 5.9: Character sketch of Lil T and Taye. Still from a behind-the-scenes promotional video (Harmonix Music Systems 2011a). (Screenshot by the author.)

During our conversation, Thompson often connected her role as a parent with her "bigger picture" mission; she expressed pride at the prospect of leaving her daughter an artistic legacy, and she described the motivating force of her commitment to being a good provider and securing long-term financial stability for her family.

Through her statements in official promotional materials as well as her embodied presence in the predominantly white and male space of game conventions, Thompson served Harmonix not only as a choreographer but also as a spokesperson for diversity and inclusion. As discussed in Chapter 2, a promotional video for *Dance Central 2* features her assertion that "If I can see someone that acts like me, talks like me, dances like me, I'm more likely to be more comfortable in who I am self-esteem-wise" (Harmonix Music Systems 2011a). Her position as a mother gives this claim special force, potentially appealing to other parents—particularly other parents raising daughters of color in a mediascape structured by racism and sexism. In our conversation, she expanded on this statement with reference to both the game industry and the professional dance world:

> You've got [choreographers] Frenchy, myself, Spikey, three girls—and [producer] Naoko, who's like the mastermind and a great friend—who were able to do the choreography and

be the characters, and it's us, it's our personalities, it's completely us to a T. And to be able to have this across the world, and people will accept it and love it—and it's mainstream and corporate too, you know what I mean, and we're the ones doing it. It's hard, it's a male-dominated industry. To be able to do that and carry your own and be like, "Yeah, I did this," and have men doing our choreography and having confidence doing it—it's awesome. It's a sense of leadership. So when I say this person looks like me, acts like me, it's great because I can identify. A lot of times we can't identify, so we're scrambling around—and dancers specifically, they're scrambling around looking for identity in their dance, especially when they are a dancer or instructor or choreographer, they are looking for what their niche is. And sometimes they can't identify. So when you can do that, that's special, it's great. . . . I think being able to identify is what I was most connected to, that I could identify with myself, that [Taye] is me, and being able to do it for thousands and thousands of people.

BREAK IT DOWN: AFFORDANCES, CONSTRAINTS, AND CHOREOGRAPHIC AGENCY

When Marcos Aguirre and Frenchy Hernandez began working on the choreographic content for the first *Dance Central* game, they adapted the iterative, experimental strategies that dancers habitually bring to their own bodily training to the new context of iterative game development and experimental prospecting of the Kinect's affordances. Lead designer Matt Boch explained some of the parameters that guided the choreographers' work:

> The development of the Dance Central choreographic vocabulary was really a collaboration between [lead producer] Naoko Takamoto, Marcos and Frenchy, who are our two internal choreographers, and myself. During prototyping, I got to the point of, okay, there's four-beat moves, and they're all going to have names, they're going to have flashcards. But the exact nature of what the choreographic style was going to be like and what process we were going to go through to achieve that choreographic style was something that was pretty—I guess that happened just in that context. (Boch and Miller 2012)

Aguirre and Hernandez were responsible for defining and naming many of the four-beat moves in the *Dance Central* lexicon. This was a key piece of curricular development work, creating the scaffolding for the game's dance pedagogy. Many move names simply describe actions (Prep & Spin), cite standard steps taught in studio classes (Jazz Square), or borrow established terms from popular media and social dance contexts (Booty Pop). However, just as often, Aguirre and Hernandez chose names that cue a particular bodily comportment, often inflected by gender or ethnicity (Diva, Rival Walk, Latino), or names closely linked to song lyrics, encouraging players to listen their way through the choreography (see Chapters 3 and 4).

As they added moves to the lexicon, named them, and considered where they would fit into a graded curriculum organized by difficulty, Hernandez and Aguirre also tailored each move to suit a modular choreographic style. This approach made it relatively straightforward to create tiered difficulty options for each routine and to build up the pace of choreographic variation across those difficulty levels. It also provided the core infrastructure for the game's interactive rehearsal mode (originally called "Break It Down"), where the teaching/learning process progresses from single-move skill-and-drill to rehearsal of short subroutines. In addition to structuring *Dance Central*'s pedagogy, modular choreography reduced the amount of motion-capture work that would otherwise have been required to support the rehearsal mode; the animation team could chain together motion-capture performances of individual moves into a variety of skill-and-drill sequences with reasonably smooth animated transitions between moves.

Aguirre and I spoke at length about the process of working out the terms of this choreographic style and its associated technical pedagogy.

KM: How do you think "Break It Down" mode compared to the way that you would be teaching in a studio class?

AGUIRRE: It was definitely interesting. To try to break that down without having people physically there to ask you questions—we had to kind of be in people's minds and guess what would they ask. How can we make this as simple as possible so people can just pick it up and understand clearly without us physically being there? . . . I was able to teach different age groups growing up, I taught a lot of kids, so the easier levels, it was kind of like going through that phase of teaching with the kids and then building it up from there.

KM: I noticed that you are responsible for the very first set of warm-up songs in the very first game, those are all credited to you. It seems like a lot of thought must have gone into what could be possible from those particular songs.

AGUIRRE: Yeah, you know, you would think making up choreography would be super easy, and it is when you do it for a regular class. But when it comes to the game, there's so much more that needs to be thought out. And the fact that we had to name every single dance move—it was like, oh my God, we have to really, really break it down! It wasn't just putting movements together and making sure it *felt good*, it was putting movements together and making sure it *made sense*, make sure it's repetitive, and we have to take it through different levels—so it's repetitive so people can catch on, but challenging, and we want people to come back and do it again for better scores.

KM: Were there certain kinds of moves that you felt like you couldn't include— or that you especially wanted to include—because of what the motion capture could do, or what the Kinect could read?

AGUIRRE: Oh yeah, definitely. It was so new, and while I was working on the game [the Kinect] was still being made, so it was kind of like still working through it. Doing turns, and anything that had your back towards the camera, was difficult to read. So it would hold us back from doing something that we would naturally want to do. We would have to think, what's the next best thing that we could do, to make it feel the same, but not exactly turn or have our back towards the camera. Because if you think about it, if you have your back towards the camera for too long, how is the player going to see what they have to do? They have to look back at the TV, like what am I doing?! And then from there they can easily be discouraged and just not want to do it.

KM: When I was starting to play through, I realized it also would be this marker of difficulty, like if there was a spin or turn I'd be like, "Oh, all right, now that shows I'm doing something that's a little harder."

AGUIRRE: See, I'm just a person who likes to push the envelope as far as I can. You can see towards the end of the game, if you play through it, you start seeing a few more turns. After a lot of development we were able to do that, have your back towards the camera—we kind of figured it out.

Chanel Thompson also described this impulse to "push the envelope." I came to understand that the moves I had experienced as markers of progressive technical difficulty were often also markers of a choreographer's sense of creative agency and personal style.

THOMPSON: I would get in trouble for doing stuff on the floor. But I didn't care, and I'd be like nope, we're doing it, oh well! Let's get up real quick. It was a challenge at first, but then it was a triumph after. . . . Floor work, or turns. . . . I was trying to do leaps, high kicks, and they were like, "No," and I was like, "Come on!"

KM: I was just thinking about you this morning when I was doing the jumping lunges for "Firework" [Katy Perry, 2010].

THOMPSON: [laughter] Sorry!

While Thompson focused on the Kinect's perceptual limitations with respect to some of the expansive, high-energy, athletic moves from her cheerleading repertoire, Aguirre told me about the technical obstacles to including the smaller-scale, subtle wrist and hip movements that were an important part of his own personal style:

Anything that was too small, like if you're trying to rotate your wrist or something, you can't really get scored that way. It was the little nuances like that. Or anything that had very small movements, or things that were too fast, just didn't read well. And sometimes the hips could get tricky. And I love moving my hips! I have always moved my hips. We just had to keep on trying different ways: if we do something with the hips, just add an arm to it so it's more readable.

Aguirre is referring to the limitations of the Kinect, not those of the motion-capture system that supported the transfer of game choreography from his performing body to that of an animated screen dancer. The motion-capture system could and did collect performance data corresponding to three-dimensional hip movements and some wrist movements; it could not capture more subtle hand and finger movements, but these could be added in the final stages of the animation process (Pitts 2012). However, as Aguirre and Thompson explain, the choreographers did not simply don LED-covered suits and dance as they usually would, offering up representative samples of the particular genres they had been hired to embody. Instead, they had to anticipate players' eventual experiences in front of the Kinect and decide whether to present them with moves that the Kinect would not be able to evaluate.

Strictly from the standpoint of user-experience design, this is a terrible idea. It runs the risk of undermining players' confidence in the scoring system, drawing attention to the limitations of the interface that the game was designed to sell, and disrupting the sense of communicative agency at the heart of traditional interactivity—the sense that the game system will reliably recognize and respond to player inputs. Choreographers therefore had to adopt an advocacy position on behalf of particular kinds of moves, making the case for including them in the game despite these risks, and sometimes working out strategic compromises like combining an undetectable move that was crucial to their own conception of the choreography with another gesture that would drive the scoring. For Aguirre, these choreographic strategies for gaming the system often came into play in the realm of gendered movement styles, one of his areas of specialization as a dancer. At the time of our interview Aguirre had only recently begun professional work as a drag performer, but he told me that he had always been drawn to feminine movement styles, which he associated with creative risk-taking:

> When it comes to me, I do a little bit of everything, but [growing up] I fell into the category of doing more feminine movement. I grew up loving Britney [Spears] and Janet [Jackson], so that's what inspired me to want to move, because I like to push the envelope and take risks. When we were going through the interview process, they were only supposed to hire one choreographer, one in-house choreographer, but I think it made more sense to hire a male and a female, and that's why me and Frenchy were hired. . . . Since I dabble in both masculine and feminine, I had to figure out that balance.

Aguirre choreographed all eight Lady Gaga tracks in the *Dance Central* catalog, in addition to songs by Janet Jackson, Mary J. Blige, the Spice Girls, Paula Abdul, and numerous other female artists. He also collaborated with Frenchy Hernandez on the choreography for Rihanna's "Rude Boy," which choreographers and players regularly used as a touchstone in discussions of "feminine" routines. While in theory there is no reason that a track by a female musician would require a markedly feminine game routine, these are musical artists with established histories of gendered dance performance, circulated through music videos and tour performances. In general, Aguirre felt a responsibility to create routines that felt true to the music, which meant both meeting fans' expectations and educating newcomers appropriately, so they could "feel more authentic with it. . . . Don't just make up movement that doesn't even go to it!" His choreography for these tracks by iconic female artists reflects his commitment to transmitting the gendered movement styles that he learned as a child dancing along with music videos—even when the nature of these styles presented technical difficulties for the game development process and stirred up gender trouble for some players.

As I discussed in Chapter 2, many players experience feminine routines as viscerally transgressive. Both Aguirre and Thompson observed that performing hip or arm motions often posed threats to a player's sense of masculinity. Moreover, as Aguirre pointed out, *Dance Central* choreography often doubles down on these types of motion, combining them, because the Kinect recognizes arm movement so much better than hip movement. Recall that choreographer Ricardo Foster Jr. shared this information as an insider tip for a player's video blog. He encouraged players to experiment with a masculine approach to arm movement, suggesting that it might neutralize their discomfort with the pelvic motion in songs like "Rude Boy": "You can flip it. . . . Really whip it down [*demonstrates with arms*]. The Kinect still sees that you're doing the movement and still reads you as a 'Flawless' score. You just gotta make sure that everything is clear and precise. So you can focus more on the arms, and be more of a—bam!—masculine, dominant effect" (MightyMeCreative 2011a; see Chapter 2). This advice is true to Aguirre's dictum that a skilled dancer "can always make something feminine or make something masculine or make it look like another gender or make it no gender." It also aligns masculinity with agentive choices about performance style, and with mastery of "clear and precise" technique.

Thompson made a similar link between gendered performance styles and technical mastery. During our interview, I broached the topic of men "not always feeling totally comfortable with the moves that they're doing." Thompson replied,

> Oh no they're not! Not with "Rude Boy," I'll tell you that! . . . It goes both ways. Some guys will do it and feel awkward because they feel like it's a chick move, or a girl move, and they'll feel awkward. But they'll goof off and laugh, and at that moment they don't take themselves as serious. Which is okay, to lighten up. Then there's times where they don't realize they *have* moves. And they're like, "Oh, shit, I can do this." (Excuse my language!) Sometimes with guys, it's almost like food, you don't know whether you like it until you taste it and try. . . . And they'll realize, "Oh, I can do this, I can do this full-out. I didn't even know I can move like this." So it goes both ways: sometimes they're uncomfortable because they feel that it might be more of a female movement, and then there's times when they're doing it and didn't realize they could. So there is a reward in both. Mainly the takeaway is if I can do this, I can do more stuff. Or, let me not take myself so seriously and lighten up, and be with their friends, cracking up laughing, because they're doing "Rude Boy" or something that has to do with arms. . . . Most guys that are not into dance and they do this for the first time, they're not comfortable

with all that, they're not ready for that type of movement yet. Or they're not familiar with it, shall I say.

KM: And if they turn out to actually be really good at it, maybe for some of them that might also be a little scary.

THOMPSON: [laughter] They might like it! And they might be like, "Hey, wait a minute, let me show you what I can do!" I've had guys come in, they don't dance and then they do Dance Central, and once they do Dance Central they're like, "Oh, I dance now." . . . I love to hear those stories: "I never used to dance at the school dance, I never used to dance at weddings. But I do now." That's the part that I love. And they don't care what it is, whether it's a female move, a manly move, whatever, they'll just do it.

KM: What do you think gets them to that point, where suddenly it doesn't matter and they're no longer saying, "Oh, this move doesn't feel right for me"?

THOMPSON: Just the fact that when they can get the choreography correctly. . . . Like, I'll be honest, Ricardo [Foster Jr.], we still work together, I dance for his company. As complex or difficult as sometimes the movement can be for me, once I get it, I'm excited and I feel rewarded. Because I've got the choreography, I understand it, and now I can actually perform it. . . . People get past the fact that it was something hard for them, and then they actually get to accomplish it.

Note Thompson's emphasis on the challenge-and-reward cycle of mastering an unfamiliar choreographic style, both for players and for herself as a dance professional. Like Aguirre, she also draws attention to the pleasure of discovery: being surprised by what one's body can do. These are affective strategies for managing not only the challenges of flexible gender performance but also the challenges of flexible labor: learning to be whomever you need to be for the task at hand, by adopting techniques of bodily discipline and self-motivation that figure versatility as the ultimate accomplishment. Susan Foster refers to this approach to technique as the construction of a dancer's "hired body," which she argues is "built at a great distance from the self [and] reduces it to a pragmatic merchant of movement proffering whatever look appeals at the moment." Foster warns that the "hired body" "proscribes a relational self whose desire to empathize predominates over its need for display" (Foster 1992:494–95). Thompson's far more positive account exemplifies "an orientation toward agency that is focused on ongoing adaptation, adjustment, improvisation, and developing wiles for surviving, thriving, and transcending the world as it presents itself," in line with a long history of "public-sphere femininity" in the United States (Berlant 2008:2). Thompson shows how she makes sense of her own experience as a "hired body" and also demonstrates how framing this flexibility as a matter of voluntary play rather than compulsory labor might aid in sustaining one's sense of self and expressive agency—finding ways to "own it." This is one of the skills that *Dance Central* cultivates, for its makers as well as its players.

Dance games raise a host of questions about "owning" dance, at the level of intellectual property as well as that of personal expressive agency. Choreographic
works have been eligible for copyright protection in the United States since the
1976 Copyright Act, as long as they are "fixed in any tangible medium of expression, now known or later developed, from which they can be perceived, reproduced, or otherwise communicated, either directly or with the aid of a machine
or device" (US Code Title 17, Section 102). However, as Joi Michelle Lakes notes,
"the Act itself and the rules set forth by the Copyright Office do not state what
constitutes expressive, copyrightable material in a choreographic work," resulting in "ambiguity between what is eligible for copyright and what should remain
in the public domain" (2005:1831). One of the few cases that did result in published rulings, *Horgan v. MacMillan* 1986, dealt with the question of whether a
book that included performance photographs infringed the copyright for George
Balanchine's choreography of "The Nutcracker" (*Horgan v. MacMillan*, 789 F.2d
157 [2nd Circuit 1986]). The district court found in favor of the defendant, relying on the principle that "choreography is the flow of steps in a ballet, which could
not be reproduced from the still photographs in the book." But the Second Circuit
Court of Appeals disagreed, ruling that the district court had applied an incorrect
test for infringement, and remanded the case back to the lower court. (The parties
subsequently settled out of court.)

In their ruling, the Second Circuit relied heavily on the definition of choreography in the 1984 Compendium of Copyright Office Practices. The Compendium
defined choreography as "the composition and arrangement of dance movements
and patterns. . . . Dance is static and kinetic successions of bodily movement in
certain rhythmic and spatial relationships." The Compendium guidelines explicitly
exclude "social dance steps and simple routines" from copyright protection, stating that they "may be utilized as the choreographer's basic material in much the
same way that words are the writer's basic material" (Section 450, cited in *Horgan v.
MacMillan* 1986). As Anthea Kraut observes, this rationale is grounded in a
value distinction: "The flat exclusion of participatory dance forms not designed
for presentation on the proscenium stage mirrors and inscribes into law the hierarchies between different modes of dance that have long characterized the field"
(2009:77). Kraut also unpacks the implications of one early case in which a choreographer did assert copyright: Hanya Holm's 1952 copyright registration for the
choreography in the musical *Kiss Me, Kate*, made "tangible" via Labanotation. Kraut
shows how "granting the choreographer property rights necessitated papering over
the nonautonomous and non-original aspects of the choreographic process: its collaborations, borrowings, appropriations, and vitally, its dependence on the labor of
racialized others" (93).

The hazy distinction between "basic material" and original creative work, as
well as the role of "flow" in choreographic expression, can only be clarified through

additional case law. But given these ambiguities in the law, and the considerable financial resources required to go to court, very few choreographers have ever sued for infringement; most do not register their works with the Copyright Office (Haye 2011). Instead, choreographers have "relied on contracts and developed a unique set of community standards which governed copying and unauthorized performances of their works. . . . These customs and contracts allowed for flexible enforcement of norms in a community that understood dance and its peculiarities" (Lakes 2005:1830, 1833).

New media technologies have vastly increased the options for fixing choreography in a tangible medium over the last few decades, and increasing corporate investment in dance as commercial entertainment have changed the financial stakes of these issues for choreographers and the publishing companies who often hold the rights to their works (Lakes 2005:1840; see also Haye 2011, on the Belgian choreographer Anne Teresa De Keersmaeker's allegations that Beyoncé appropriated her choreography). Dance game developers employ choreographers specifically to create original choreographic works that can be "fixed in a tangible medium" through video and/or motion-capture technologies and sold on a vast commercial scale, an enterprise that implicitly relies on choreographic copyright and seems tailor-made to generate situations that will test the law. The situation is particularly complex when dance games remediate existing choreography; for at least one song, the viral hit "Gangnam Style" (PSY, 2012), Harmonix Music Systems did formally secure the rights to choreography in addition to licensing the music (Pitts 2012). In most cases, however, due to the modular character of game choreography, the routines in these games might seem to fall into the hazy no man's land between "social dance steps and simple routines" and "original choreographic works" in a high-art paradigm.

Meanwhile, motion-capture and animation technologies have the potential to change the terms of infringement tests by collecting, archiving, and representing movement data in new ways. For instance, Lakes argues that paying more attention to "flow" as a defining attribute of creative expression could help clarify "when a work moves from public domain steps to copyrightable expressive choreography" (2005:1847). She proposes defining a choreographic work as "a choreographer's expression represented by the planned flow of one or more dancer's movement in time through body positions and spatial arrangements" (1858), but she has little to say about the kinds of evidence that might represent "flow" in a court case. She also draws attention to the limits and risks of video notation. In addition to problematic issues related to camera positioning, framing, and the reduction of three-dimensional movement to two-dimensional images, video "may capture a dancer's mistake or unintended addition" and "only extends protection to 'what is disclosed therein,'" according to the 1984 Compendium guidelines (1855). Motion-capture data potentially presents a far richer and more detailed form of fixed notation of choreographic works, in a format that better lends itself to quantitative analysis and the comparative tests on which infringement suits turn.

I spoke with Thompson and Aguirre about these questions of ownership, authorship, appropriation, and originality, asking them each the same starting question: "Can you remember what it felt like to you the first time you saw your motion mapped onto a character?" I anticipated that game choreographers might feel ambivalent about the motion-capture process, which skims a layer of data from their embodied performances to facilitate the production and circulation of dance as a consumable commodity. Might this feel like a form of theft, or an obscuring of their individual creative work? But their responses went in the opposite direction:

AGUIRRE: Oh my God, it was surreal. Just looking back at it, it was like, "Oh my God, I can tell that's me, I can tell that was my movement, and it looks so real." Like, "Oh, this is really happening." But I think throughout the whole entire process it didn't feel real until we actually saw people playing the game. And that was at the E3 convention when it was exposed to the world and everyone got to play, and it was like all ages, everything, everything! I was like, "Wow, this is really, really something."

THOMPSON: The first time I saw my choreography was "I Gotta Feeling," by the Black Eyed Peas. That was the first time I was able to see what the character was doing. It just motivated me more: that I was doing what my passion was, what my gift is. I'm able to have this opportunity to show people what my gift is, through dance. And when I saw that, I was like "Okay, I want more, I want to do more." It motivated me to do more choreography and to learn, to realize that all these things I did before are aligning themselves and paying off, because this is going to touch and reach millions of people that play this game. So that was my experience and my feeling that I got: I was like, "Oh my God, this is gonna be on all these people, they're gonna play this game and they're gonna love this song." Because it's a hot record, you know.

KM: So it still feels like you, like some piece of you reaching them, even though there are all these layers between?

THOMPSON: Oh yeah. I mean, I heard it yesterday in the office, it happened to be in a commercial on TV. I heard it and immediately I started doing one of the moves for it, the Tell It. And I still get that feeling, anytime I hear any of our songs for our game, anything I worked on, it always brings me back to when I was starting it or doing it or mocapping it or playing it with a fan or playing it with my coworkers. And it's always a great feeling, a warm feeling, like "Oh wow, I did that."

Thompson's warm memories resonate with Harmony Bench's observation that "motion capture is inherently nostalgic, resolutely oriented toward the archive." Bench shows how this archival orientation has often been associated with "a rhetoric of loss (of the body)" (2009:35). But Thompson and Aguirre do not talk about motion capture in terms of loss; instead, they focus on transmission, explaining how this archive functions to spread their creative work into new bodies. Note how Aguirre's recollection of seeing his performance mapped onto a character moves swiftly from the "surreal" experience of recognizing his own movement in the animated dancer to the "real" of seeing that same movement embodied by players at the E3 convention. Thompson, too, repeatedly emphasized her pride in seeing her choreography "on all these people."

We know that the screen dancers in *Just Dance* and *Dance Central* were not designed to function like conventional game avatars; as I have discussed in earlier chapters, if anything the control chain runs in the opposite direction, as players submit their own bodies to choreographic puppeteering. But suppose instead that we imagine the screen dancer as *an avatar of the choreographer*, a way for someone like Chanel Thompson to project herself into a geographically distributed massively multiplayer world and interact with its inhabitants where they live, in their own fleshly bodies and built environments. This is how Thompson and Aguirre seemed to conceive of their work on *Dance Central*: not as the alienation of their labor through work-for-hire intellectual property arrangements and a motion-capture process that reduces their dancing bodies to data sets, but rather as a virtual extension of their usual choreographic, teaching, and performance work, one that had allowed them to make intimate, personal connections with dancers and dance audiences on a heretofore unimaginable scale. For example, Thompson described watching an online video of "a little boy in Singapore.... He must've been four or five, and he was playing the game full out, fluid, meaning he knew every move, and he knew how to score. And everyone was watching him, the entire mall was watching this little boy play. And that was one of those sappy moments where I got emotional." Aguirre also emphasized the global reach of the games:

> You know, people come out here to L.A. to dance.... People come here working on visas from all over the world, Russia, China, Japan. Knowing that we were able to build something for those people, and more people, who can't even take a dance class outside of their living room, we were able to *bring that to them*—nothing beats that, you know what I mean? ... And it's almost like we're there with you, because it is our movement, and sometimes it's our voices. It was a way to be there without being there. Or a way to make them feel like they're a part of something, I feel. And if I can't go to everyone individually and teach them something, there's the game, and it's almost just as good.

In these accounts, dance games do not simply extract the essence of dancers' performances and convert them into commodities; rather, they allow for choreography-at-a-distance. Dance games integrate archive and repertoire in a way that perfectly exemplifies Rebecca Schneider's argument that archives are constituted through "live practices of access" and "built for live encounter with privileged remains" (2011:108). Their "architectures of access" (104) strongly imply that the point of archiving a particular repertoire is to support future embodied performance, rather than detached critical analysis or reverent contemplation of "preserved" material traces from the past. Dance games thus present parallels with heritage projects that aim to support transmission rather than preservation, as well as experiential learning contexts like living history museums (Magelssen 2014). In this framework, game choreographers play the role of culture-bearers, representatives of particular dance repertoires and communities who are engaged in a kind of heritage work and are personally invested in the outcome of that work. For Aguirre and Thompson, player performances are the evidence of their success, proving that their choreographic and pedagogical work really can make it through layers of technological mediation and global commercial circulation to reach other dancing bodies.

But if game choreographers are functioning in part as culture-bearers, they are also clearly engaged as culture-sellers, raising sensitive questions about the appropriation and commercial exploitation of dance styles that emerged in African American, Latina/o, and queer social worlds (see DeFrantz 2012, Bragin 2014, Salkind 2016). In a brief speculative essay about *Dance Central*, Derek Burrill and Melissa Blanco Borelli note that "a Marxist analysis might suggest these bodies operate as alienated labor" and ask, "What does it mean when the labor of a proper flesh-encased choreographer of color is morphed into and onto a white avatar? Is this a version of cyber-racial-appropriation? . . . What kind of historical erasures of the importance and significance of social dance in specific communities is happening through the virtual world of a kinetic utopia that *Dance Central* celebrates?" (2014:438–39). I brought up these issues with project director Matt Boch, and subsequently with Marcos Aguirre.

KM: One of the critiques someone could make is that this game puts people in a position—white people—where they can learn, or think that they're learning, something about embodied black experience without having contact with actual black people.

MATT BOCH: Interesting question. I guess my thoughts about that are twofold, like one: I believe that you are interacting with the people who made the game. . . . I don't think communication necessarily has to be direct. . . . But I guess the desire is to be authentic to the material. And so if the song is a pop song, we want to have an authentic pop routine. If the song is a hip-hop classic from the '90s, you want to have classic hip-hop moves from the '90s. Because that's what the choreographers want to do and that's what feels best for the song. . . . And while I can see the ways in which that is racialized in some cases, I think the song set and move set of Dance Central is broad enough to encompass things that have come out of all sorts of various subcultures. (Boch and Miller 2012)

KM: Sometimes people ask me about whether these games are making some kind of cultural appropriation possible, like an Elvis thing, teaching white people to do these moves that they wouldn't learn in their own cultural context. . . . If somebody were to make a criticism and be like, you're teaching people hip-hop moves that belong to someone else's culture, and they shouldn't feel entitled to those moves—how would you respond to that?

AGUIRRE: Well, that's kind of hard. It's not like we—nothing's being taken. Everything comes from somewhere, everything is inspired by something. A lot of moves we've learned growing up, and it's kind of like just being spread. I mean everyone should learn the basics, and the basics come from someone, but it's not like we're taking credit for those basics, I mean obviously it comes from somewhere. . . . Everybody just wants to learn something, and you have to learn it from somewhere. Some people don't even have the resources to learn exactly where things come from.

KM: Do you think that the game teaches people anything about where some of these moves come from?

AGUIRRE: I believe it does, actually. Some of the movements, we made up a lot of move names but if there was something specific that we knew already has a name to it, that name was used. . . . I mean, people can always Google.

Boch's response hinged on the idea of authenticity, both in terms of dance style and in terms of authentic interaction between choreographers of color and the players who learn their routines. Aguirre's response rejected the idea that dance should be the exclusive cultural property of any particular community, but he also took care to emphasize that these repertoires do have specific histories, and that he and his fellow choreographers were not attempting to claim personal credit for moves that were already in circulation.

In general, Aguirre and Thompson discussed their choreographic and peda-gogical work in terms of a "culture of sharing" in the dance community (Lakes 2005:1833). Both referred to dance as a gift, and described feeling a calling to share that gift. When I asked Aguirre, "What would you want [readers of this book] to know about your experience as a choreographer and what you personally brought to these games, if you could talk to them directly?" he replied,

> I want people to understand that every time we made up a choreo or pulled something together to build this project, from day one until now, we always had the people in our mind. Like it was never just about us. . . . We don't want people to give up, and we want people to keep pushing, and really learn something from this game. Something that they are proud of, something that they feel accomplished with. And for me, it was just the greatest gift for me that I could give to someone else. Because for me it was amazing to be able to do something that I feel is going to make someone else better, or help someone in some sort of way, whatever it may be, physically, mentally, spiritually. If it helps you, then I feel happy about what I did.

Thompson described her choreographic work on the games as "a legacy": "What are you leaving behind? What are people going to remember most about you? The choreography that you did is special because you designed it, you did it, and it's your gift, and people love that gift, and they appreciate it and support it and respect it." Neither choreographer expressed concern about who exactly might be the recipi-ent of these gifts, nor that they could be misused. Thompson told me, "Dance is universal." Aguirre told me, "Dance does something to your soul. . . . It just takes me somewhere, somewhere unexplainable, somewhere magical. There's nothing better."

While this gift paradigm does not resolve the thorny questions about appropriation and commodification that dance games raise, it does shed light on how choreographers imagine their own positions in this process and their relationships to players. The idea of dance as gift allows them to maintain a sense of personal dignity and autonomy, as generous teachers and talented artists. Giving a gift forestalls appropriation; you can't appropriate something that has been freely given to you, and the ethics of gift economies also dictate that gifts incur obligations. Thompson described other labor situations in which dancers are treated as service workers, like the barber who rents a chair; she told me that working on *Dance Central* was different, and she described players as fans and students rather than as customers: "The fact that my choreography is all the way in Singapore. . . .You only see this with, like, Michael Jackson or Beyoncé and Tina Turner and Janet Jackson, all those artists who get to go and tour all over the world and hear people who listen to their songs say their words, recite their words." She suggested that dance games functioned like a karaoke system that featured the artistry of dancers rather than musicians— "something that shows us off and represents us," encouraging fans to "emulate an artist." Meanwhile, she invoked the circuit of reciprocal gift-giving in describing her ongoing relationship with fans through social media:

> People will inbox me [on Twitter] and say, "Hey, I needed you to say that today." Whether it's an inspirational quote, a motivational quote, or whether it's like, I just went and had Taco Loco—they needed that little quirky or goofy thing I said. And I love that. I love that I still get to connect with those fans, because they really don't know how much they helped me and my family, by supporting this. And they're a part of it: that's what I really feel like, they supported this and they're a part of it too.

Aguirre and Thompson each referred to their work on *Dance Central* as the greatest professional accomplishment of their careers to date, and they vividly described their pride and satisfaction in seeing their choreography performed by players around the world. What can we learn from taking them at their word? Clearly, game choreographers have a continuing vested interest in the success of the products they helped produce, and expressing dissatisfaction with their contract arrangements could jeopardize their future professional opportunities in the game industry. For example, Thompson and Aguirre might well have preferred to retain rights to their choreography and receive royalties on every track Harmonix sold rather than creating routines on a work-for-hire basis—but they did not communicate any such preference to me. At the same time, it would be a mistake to discount everything they *did* communicate to me as boosterism scripted by a marketing department. Arguing from my own professional position as an ethnographer, I would contend that anyone interested in developing a critical analysis of the culture industries should seek to understand how people like Thompson and Aguirre have made sense of their own work, for both intellectual and ethical reasons. We all labor in the context of structural limitations, and we all deserve respectful consideration of our expressions of agency in those contexts—recognition of our capacity for "free movement within a more rigid structure," as Salen and Zimmerman characterize the nature of play (2004:583), and recognition that such movement can sometimes alter the structures themselves.

Talking with Thompson and Aguirre about their experiences helped me understand how differently *Just Dance* and *Dance Central* represent the dancing bodies that they employ. *Just Dance* presents "real bodies," captured by video, but renders them faceless and highly stylized; their silhouettes afford just enough detail to allow for escapist identity play while also functioning as a dynamic notation system meant to get players' mirror neurons firing (Parkin 2010, see Chapter 1). *Dance Central* presents animated bodies based on motion capture of human dancing bodies, and infuses the animated bodies with "realness" not only by making them specific characters with distinctive voices and personalities, but by linking them back to staff choreographers who are prominently credited for each routine. While some *Just Dance* choreographers and studio dancers have occasionally appeared in behind-the-scenes promotional media (as in the video described at the start of this chapter), the games do not include choreographer credits for individual songs. Instead, *Just Dance*'s choreographers function more like the anonymous studio musicians who have long performed in a work-for-hire capacity on albums for big-name stars (see Stahl 2013).

These varying labor and credit arrangements matter. As Anthea Kraut writes, "We need to remain alert to the particularized relations of power that inhere in contests for credit and ownership" and how these contests reveal "the impossibility of disentangling economic, cultural, and racial capital" (2009:93–94). Dance games are part of an advancing wave of virtual reality technologies that rely on the capture, commodification, and digital distribution of embodied practices. These technologies portend increased demand for specialists in the kinesthetic arts, workers who will not only perform particular repertoires for motion-capture systems but also develop virtual training systems that will teach users the embodied techniques required to interact with "natural" gestural interfaces. It behooves us to attend to the evolving industry practices and legal frameworks that will govern these forms of choreographic labor and establish "architectures of access" for corporeal knowledge (Schneider 2011:104).

CONCLUSION: WORKING THE PLAYABLE BODY

As I conducted background research on dance game choreographers, I regularly encountered the video compilations that they have assembled to represent themselves in the professional dance world. These highlight reels cut from stage performances to commercials to studio settings, dance classes, and competitions, showing bodies that are seemingly capable of anything that might be asked of them. They zoom in on moments when their protagonists display technical virtuosity, break away from the ensemble for a brief star turn, or appear in contexts that elevate their own status through association with celebrity artists, prestigious cultural institutions, or powerful corporations. And every so often, a game character appears: a digital body animated by the choreographer's creative, embodied, and affective labor, included in the video as simply one more representative instance of the choreographer's own versatile body.

Watching these highlight reels and talking with Marcos Aguirre and Chanel Thompson about their work, my thoughts turned back to the question of "avatar relations" in dance games, and about how screen dancers might function not as game avatars but as labor avatars. In addition to affording Aguirre and Thompson a tremendous sense of accomplishment by serving as virtual performers and teachers of their archived choreography, the *Dance Central* screen dancers draw players into gameplay situations that hint at the challenges of pursuing a dance career. Thompson's dictum that professional performers "have 30 seconds to set the tone" highlights the affinities between the competitive settings of dance battles, team competitions, dance reality shows, and the virtual stage conjured by the Kinect in players' living rooms. Dance games urge players to go FTFO for the length of a single song and then stand panting to await their scores. They channel the emotional highs and lows of competitive audition settings, but with different stakes; because they are games, "the consequences of the activity are negotiable" (Juul 2005:36). For dance professionals, the grind of high-stakes auditions, the risk of injury, and the demand for constant FTFO energy can be exhausting; the requirements for performing both protean versatility and star-power individuality can leave dancers "scrambling around" for a sense of self, as Thompson put it.

Dance Central does not engage directly with these issues of precarious labor; the screen dancers never pull a hamstring during a routine, nor do we see them juggling day-job shifts, childcare, auditions, and teaching a few Zumba classes down at the local gym. But the teaching, learning, and performance orientations modeled by the series obliquely reference game choreographers' professional experience, including the rehearsal techniques and emotional strategies they have deployed to structure their own careers. The rehearsal-mode teacher voice, with its encouraging exhortations mingled with occasional undermining criticisms, models the internal voice of many aspiring professional dancers: "Try it three times now. . . . Practice makes perfect. . . . Careful now! . . . I guess you put your own interpretation on that one. . . . This game is lying! . . . Yo, you got formal training or something?" Perhaps *Dance Central*'s teacher has no human body because he is the voice inside the screen dancer's head, a voice that constantly, adaptively remixes a stream of pre-recorded expressions of praise, criticism, and technical instruction. Practice, practice, practice, to make the body playable, workable, and hireable.

CHAPTER 6
Intimate Media

Body Projects Megamix

D ance is creative expression in an intimate medium. This intimacy resides not simply in the fact that a dancer's own body is the material of expression—the paint, stretched canvas, brushes, and moving brushstrokes all in one—but in the way dance articulates connections and marks breaks within and among bodies. Dance as a "universal language" is a beautiful dream of transcendent, perfect communication, premised on the idea of a universally shared experience of human embodiment. But there is no such universal experience, nor even a stable experience of embodiment for an individual dancer. Like all intimacy, the intimacy of dance is a relational quality, driven by the push and pull of trial and error—what Erica Stanton calls "doing, re-doing, and undoing" (Stanton 2011). Writing about the deeply destabilizing process of "unraveling movement traits or 'comfortable' practice" through dance training, Stanton describes the challenge of negotiating a new relationship with her own center of gravity:

> Even finding a true, vertical mid-line to your stance can feel like a major ordeal—in my first ballet class as an adult, my teacher asked me to stand a little further forward on my feet: my weight was behind my mid-line and the small shift I was required to make felt enormous. After a few weeks of experimenting with a new stance, I was then given feedback by my Cunningham teacher that my weight was too far forward when I was in motion. As a result, for several weeks I felt "all over the place" as new movement patterns were assimilated. I still recall my discomfiture—not so much from the physical or kinaesthetic difficulty—but from the psychological one caused by feeling unusually clumsy and uncoordinated. I felt that I was a lesser dancer and it was not until a year later that the rewards of this healthier alignment came into play. (2011:91)

Dancers cultivate intimacy with their own bodies through processes of estrangement, risk-taking, and miscommunication; they come to understand boundaries by pushing against them and sometimes pushing through them to the point of injury. They build up powerful connections among zones of the body and sensory channels that previously felt distinct, and they take joy in feeling themselves to be more than the sum of these parts. They also know that these connections can weaken or break through repetitive strain, neglect, or the sudden impact of an external force. While "brief moments of 'mastery of the body' or of 'feeling at one with the body'" have a powerful motivating force, "dancers constantly apprehend the discrepancy between what they want to do and what they can do" (Foster 1992:482). Dancers cultivate relationships with other dancers by engaging in these same processes collaboratively, across multiple bodies—attempting to recognize the quality of someone else's intimate process of embodiment and reenact it in their own bodies, and rarely getting it right the first time. (Is this what you meant? Let me try again.) Through processes of recognition and misrecognition, prospecting for sameness and difference, developing technique and sharing repertoire, they cultivate a visceral sense of connection that requires ongoing care, remains vulnerable to injury, and changes over time through cumulative repetition-with-a-difference.

In this final chapter I explore how dance gameplay harnesses the intimate affordances of dance to those of contemporary social media. We have seen how dance gameplay guides players' bodies through rehearsals and performances of uninhibited play, disciplined practice, mastery over technology, kinesthetic listening, experimental identity work, and participatory engagement with popular culture: interlinked body projects driven by dynamics of recognition, control, and consent. This chapter shows how some of these body projects have been mobilized through social media and how dance gameplay configures relationships among other intimate media practices. I also aim to guide readers through a meaning-making process that evokes my research experience: navigating social media feeds, following chains of related videos, jumping across platforms, reading scholarly literature alongside comment threads, contending with idiosyncratic metadata and ephemeral archives, and learning to listen for concord, discord, echoes, and rhymes across these materials. In the performative writing that follows, I employ formal elements and rhetorical conventions borrowed from contemporary social media platforms and content aggregators to weave together research materials, reflective notes, virtual dialogues, and hat-tips to other scholars with passages of more traditional scholarly prose.

UPLOADING: REPETITION WITH A DIFFERENCE

#collaboration #play #performance #public #reciprocity #community

@kiri: Soon after the release of *Dance Central* in 2010, players began uploading videos of their living-room dancing to YouTube. Why? What were they hoping to share or prove? What audience were they hoping to reach?

@Burgess&Green2009: It is important not to fall into the trap of simply assuming that vernacular video is organized primarily around a desire to broadcast the self. (25–26)

@kiri: By the summer of 2011, a core group of about 10 uploaders were regularly posting videos, attracting subscribers, and accumulating substantial viewcounts—not viral-video level, but in the tens of thousands. They interacted with each other and with game choreographers on YouTube and Twitter; some were active on the official *Dance Central* player forums. Their videos became shared points of reference for forum discussions.

@Burgess&Green2009: It is this social network function that is most noticeably absent from most mainstream accounts of amateur and everyday content creation: the idea that the motivation for this activity might have at least as much to do with social network formation or collective play as it does self-promotion. (29)

@kiri: I contacted these uploaders through YouTube; seven of them agreed to participate in interviews, by email or phone. In this section I remix their individual interviews in the form of a virtual group conversation.

KM: What inspired you to start posting your videos on YouTube?

Riffraff: What started it definitely was MightyMeCreative, who was the first one who did it. And I just thought it was a cool thing to do. I'm not going to lie, a little part of it was that I thought that my dancing was good enough for me to get some respect.

twinbladestaff: After my first few weeks of playing Dance Central, I decided to log onto YouTube and search for the actual gameplay itself, only to come across players who filmed themselves via splitscreen! I was impressed that so many were brave enough to post videos of themselves playing the game, having fun no matter how ridiculous it looked. One night I thought about following along and creating my own videos, I remember thinking "i don't care how bad it looks, i'm going to try it out" My first upload/performance was "Weapon of Choice" by Fatboy Slim. I was definitely nervous because I didn't know how I should act in front of the camera, it was my first time. I was thinking "should I be myself or should I fake a smile and pretend i'm having fun" But when you watch the video you can see I was so focused on the routine that I almost looked bored (lol)

Lola: At first I feel pretty nervous of posting it to youtube, but later better and I feel more natural to do any moves at the "freestyles" part in the middle part of each song. My family and friends all support me. They said it is fun to share with other people.

JWMidnight: I'm not really sure why I posted videos. I suppose there weren't too many stars at the time and I wanted to help fill out the songlist from DC.

Riffraff: To be honest with you, only four people in the world know what I do with these videos. That's like personally, that I personally know that I see every day. . . .

Figure 6.1: MightyMeCreative celebrates a five-star living room/YouTube performance (Mighty MeCreative 2011). (Screenshot by the author.)

I just feel that it's a little too much showboating on my end. Like, "Look at me. I'm so cool." At this game. It's a video game. It's a dancing video game. In some way I feel that it's something that I really shouldn't be investing as much of my time in, but I do. Because it's something that I enjoy a lot. And I feel that sometimes maybe I expect people, say, like my parents, will find out about these videos and they'll go, "Well, really? That's what you do in your spare time? Why don't you go get married or something?"

#realdance

KM: What was the most challenging aspect of becoming a good player?

MMC [MightyMeCreative]: I consider myself to be a better "dancer" than "player." I think that's two different things. I don't play the way most people do, fighting to keep their top spots on the leader board with high scores. . . . In my opinion, to be a good dancer, you need to be able to DANCE without flashcards or an avatar; you have to be able to move naturally to the beat, improvise, & freestyle. The "freestyle" is tell-tale right there. Real dancers MUST be able to freestyle & dance without worrying like they look dumb. . . . Though the YouTube DC trend is to put up perfect takes, I'd rather put out my best performance, or an imperfect take because I like my natural reaction to missing a move or not reaching my goal. If I have a very high score, but I have a freestyle or "swagger" that I like better in a lower scoring take, I'll put that one out there.

@DeFrantz2014: [Recognition in hip-hop] includes the *imperative to innovate*; dancers in this idiom must reveal something unprecedented for the dance to arrive with conviction. . . . Hip-hop dance proceeds from an assumption that each individual dancer will fulfill herself through an unprecedented alignment of desire, intention, and action. (236)

Riffraff: I really want to make it look like I'm actually dancing in the game, and not just going through the motions. . . . There are people that I've seen YouTube videos of, people that score really, really high in the game, but I watch their gameplay videos, and they're barely dancing. Like one guy, he essentially gamed the game by learning the angles to hit and which points his body needs to be in. And I watched the gameplay video, and it was like, "That's not dancing. Basically you look like you're in pain." I almost felt a little insulted by it because he scored higher than I did, and I was like, "I busted my ass getting this." And I danced the way it should have been danced. . . . It's really all about flavor. I mean there's a kind of undefinable quality where someone just has attitude. . . . It's that kind of quality, that attitude that strengthens the dance and makes a difference and makes you look like you're dancing and not just like 1 and 2 and 3 and 4 and counting your way through steps. . . . There is that undefinable quality you put into it that makes it more special to you, versus the game, because it doesn't score me any additional points. And sometimes it even costs me points.

JWMidnight: I'd say the most challenging part is letting loose when you're dancing. Some people aren't afraid to act a fool, and they're usually some of the first people to get really good at the game. Needless to say, if you're afraid to move your body, you're not going to be dancing too well.

Riffraff: I have to admit at this point it has become a bit like work in that I do play just to be able to post videos. It's funny, the days that I don't tape a video are the days that I'm actually feeling a little less stressed out. Because I feel like if I tape a video, like I have to make sure I get this one perfectly, and make sure that I put enough flavor in it, make sure I get this little movement just right.

#recognition

@Watkins2010: Affects, as such, are the corporeal instantiation of recognition, the sensations one may feel in being recognized, which accumulate over time, fostering a sense of self-worth. (273)

KM: When you get good at a particular song, do you still watch the flashcards and the avatar while you are dancing?

rosroskof: When people copy/mirror the avatars, they tend to focus on arm and leg movements. But there are subtle movements that can make certain dance moves look a lot better and much more enjoyable to dance. For example, head movement/head tilt, shoulder and hip movements, even the angle of your foot!

KM: How and when do you think you learned to be aware of subtle things like that?

rosroskof: Half the time from the dancers/avatars/performer themselves. And about half the time from other people mimicking the moves (Dance Central videos from other people in youtube).

@Gibbs2010: [We should] rethink mimesis not as simple mimicry or copying dependent on vision (monkey see, monkey do) but as a complex communicative process in which other sensory and affective modalities are centrally involved. What we have to gain from this is a better understanding of the role of mimetic communication in social processes, and especially of the making—and breaking—of social bonds. These form the basis for a sense of "belonging." (191–92)

JWMidnight: Aside from actual dancing its also important to know if the Kinect is picking you up correctly, haha. I started having trouble with really easy moves and I couldn't figure out why. So I started turning on more lights to play, and it still wasn't working. I finally figured out that it was my rather large afro the whole time - the Kinect picked up my 'fro as my head, therefore making my head disproportionate to my body and giving the Kinect trouble recognizing me! I tie down my hair when I play now and it works flawlessly.

@Brown2015: "Racializing surveillance" signals those moments when enactments of surveillance reify boundaries, borders, and bodies along racial lines, and where the outcome is often discriminatory treatment of those who are negatively racialized by such surveillance. (16)

@kiri: This was a known issue during the game development process. Dance Central choreographer Chanel Thompson told me that the Kinect sometimes could not recognize her young daughter: "Her hair was too big, and it would be like, what is that?" The Kinect literally could not read a player with an Afro as a human body—even as Dance Central praised players for technical accuracy by declaring "I see you, I see you!" in an audibly African American voice. JWMidnight seems to take this racialized misrecognition in stride, but one might imagine that such dehumanizing encounters with a purportedly objective machine could motivate players to seek out human recognition and extend it to others: I see you, you see me.

#communityofpractice

KM: Do you watch other people's videos?

twinbladestaff: Absolutely! Those I know who create their own Dance Central videos are quite inspirational (ie. MightyMeCreative, Latty2Cute, SuicideXSqueeze etc.) I always watch with interest and envy. It also pushes me to become better at the routines as I learn a ton from the videos they post.

Lola: I watch other people's videos especially when I miss some particular steps even if I think I do them right. Just questioning myself why I never get it??? And some people do dance very well, I can't stop watching it.

MMC: It's interesting to see the way people interpret the movement - dance is an art form & there is no right or wrong way, but then again with DC, you have those ratings. I never watch screen-only gameplays; that's all about showcasing your score & I'm not into that.

JWMidnight: Most of the time I watch to either learn new DLC or to watch their freestyles! Freestyles are so much fun.

rosroskof: A lot of people would like to see a certain song's choreography before purchasing the DLC.

@Burgess&Green2009: Participation in this self-constituted YouTube "community" relies on various forms of vernacular expertise, combining a critical and literate understanding of the "attention economy" and the affordances of the network with the ability to navigate the social and cultural norms of the community. (98)

KM: How do people find your videos?

Riffraff: A lot of it was just really through tags. . . . A lot of [videos] don't get seen because they have bad SEO [search-engine optimization]. And then if there was a new release of some DLC, downloadable content, then I would go out of my way to make sure that I would do the video right away on the day it came out and then post it because people would be searching—I knew, for a fact, that they would be searching for that song and gameplay for that song. So I'd get the timing, and get more subscribers that way. Of course the odd interaction with Suicide or with MightyMeCreative would help also, like make people aware that I was around. And eventually, as much as I resisted, I had to open a Twitter account and basically give people another option.

KM: Why did you have to start a Twitter account? What was the demand?

Riffraff: There was a bit of clamor for people to get updates on what kind of stuff I was doing. I think part of it also was me being able to keep track of other people's stuff, doing things as well. Most notably the choreographers of the game, the people that run the game at Harmonix.

#feedback

@Lange2008: Video quality is not necessarily the determining factor in terms of how videos affect social networks. Rather, creating and circulating video affectively enacts social relationships between those who make and those who view videos. (368)

KM: How do you feel about the comments you receive?

twinbladestaff: Every single positive comment/feedback I read pushes me to continue on filming Dance Central. It's the support and encouragement that keeps me going.

Riffraff: The feedback is really what kind of keeps you coming back. I mean it's, yeah, I'm not going to lie. It's great getting compliments from people, especially—I feel like it validates all my investment in, or my time in the game, my time putting up the videos, like the extra effort I put into making sure the choreography looks good.

rosroskof: A few friends in the Navy saw my videos on facebook, I get the most interesting feedback from them. Maybe because I work with them in a professional manner and they never expected anything like that from me.

Lola: I feel flattered when I see the good comments. But I welcome for people to give me advice or constructive comments. When I see the unreasonable and disrespectful comments, I usually won't comment nor delete.

MMC: I'm very lucky to receive a majority of good comments & I appreciate them. I really read all of them, but the ones that stand out are the ones that pay attention to detail. Of course I have a few "dislikes" in every video, but that's par for the course. The few comments I delete are deliberately mean-spirited, non-constructive, racial, or sexual, and those commenters get blocked immediately. I know that YouTube is notorious for mean comments & arguing, but I watch my stuff. I'm aware that I have a lot of young fans too. I think that seeing those types of comments only reinforces people to think that it's okay to be insensitive to others. I don't have tolerance for that because I devote a LOT of time & energy into YouTube, and I put myself out there FOR FREE, so I can show whichever I want. It's not free speech, "Get the "F" off my channel!" That's my attitude.

Riffraff: I made it a policy, and it's in the notes of the details of the video, that if there are any mean-spirited or basically bad remarks—not bad remarks. I'm fine with criticism, just not anything malicious. If there's anything of that sort that pops up in the comments, I basically delete your comments and I block you from watching the videos.

KM: You're comfortable censoring the haters.

Riffraff: I am, if only because I think most of the people that do go to these sites tend to watch—they're just there to have a good time, you know. Something that's not supposed to be stressful. . . . It's my rules, and if I don't want to have everyone else have to sift through your negativity, then I'm not going to let it happen.

#winning

KM: When you are having a peak experience with Dance Central—when it is the most fun or engaging—what does it feel like?

Lola: I feel like I am a real dance performer.

MMC: When I finally get 100% & gold stars in a song. That is always my goal, so to achieve that makes me happy. Also, with YouTube: I never get to see how I compare to the avatar until I'm finished filming & editing & putting the split-screen together. I feel really good when it looks like I match the avatar's movement & style. That is what I want people to gain from my videos. I want to show how I interpret the movement to be with my own style, with a lot of energy, and naturally I'm enjoying myself.

@DeFrantz2014: The pleasure of repeated rehearsal as a feature of social exchange enabled by the dance gives way to the pleasure of execution—the aesthetic action underscored by the coolness of preparation. The pleasure of hip-hop dance practice is always visible in performance. This pleasure is aligned with accuracy of performance, with the execution of aesthetic action well done. (235–36)

twinbladestaff: To me it's like a burst of energy runs through my body. It's hard to describe, but it makes me feel good. It usually occurs when i'm performing my favorite routines in front of family or friends or when new music/routines come out (DLCs).

JWMidnight: The most fun I have with DC is with my friends. It's great to see them mess up and goof around with the moves! It's a great feeling, dancing together with friends, especially in the freestyles!

Riffraff: When I invite my coworkers over to play the game—when they throw these shackles off and they're like, "We're just going to have fun. We're all friends here. Who cares? All of us are going to be bad or good at it." And they just let loose. And that makes me the most happy: seeing people just not care about what other people think about what they do. I mean granted, this was in a controlled environment. We're all friends there. We're not dancing on a stage in front of the world. But to them, it's like, you accept me and I accept the fact that I look like an idiot in this game, but who cares? I'm having fun right now and that's all that matters.

@kiri: The uploading body project explores the tension between technical mastery and individual expression as standards of achievement. This is not just a question of "owning" someone else's choreography by imbuing it with personal flavor—it's about staging a competition between human and machinic perception. Uploaders ask their audiences to recognize them in ways that the Kinect can't: This machine says all these performances are the same, but we collectively affirm that they're different. This process implicitly invokes a third possible standard of achievement: developing social relationships online that involve the same kind of reciprocity, trust, and collective pleasure as an intimate dance party with family and friends. Uploaders are playing a dance meta-game that involves a threefold authentication challenge: Prove that you can earn real scores, perform real dance, and participate in a real community.

7/27/2015

"Good start! You've just walked across Central Park!" I'm trying out a "Sweat Mode" playlist in *Just Dance 3*. Between songs, interstitial screens encourage me along. As I dance to Cee Lo and the Pointer Sisters, I contemplate what it means for Central Park to function as a unit of accomplishment: a perfect conflation of data-driven fitness goals and cosmopolitan aspirations.... End of my Sweat playlist. I won a prize! It's a "Jamaican Dance dance mash-up," now unlocked for play. "2000 [sweat drop icons] reached! Well done! You've just run 10 rounds of the Wembley Stadium!" From New York to London: not bad in a day's work of dance play.

@kiri: Ubisoft and Harmonix focused on play and pleasure in marketing their dance games; their titles, packaging, and major advertising campaigns do not overtly revolve around workouts or weight loss. But the first wave of Wii games had already established a connection between motion games and body work.

@Millington2009: Through myriad features that both discipline the body and encourage responsibility, the Wii connects anatamo-political concerns (specifically over individual fitness) with biopolitical anxieties over the wellness of the population as a whole. In effect, the Wii invokes and thus fortifies a governmental form of control. (630)

@kiri: If *Just Dance* and *Dance Central* are figured as dance and music games, then your mission is to learn how to take new kinds of pleasure in popular music, your own moving body, and your social relations. Both *Just Dance* and *Dance Central* promise that according to these terms, *anyone can win*: your game scores might be higher or lower, but there is no "death" or "fail" state, and bad dancing can generate the biggest social wins. But how do the stakes of gameplay shift if we think of dance games as fitness games? Players did considerable work to articulate this connection in online reviews and YouTube videos.

@Gimlin2001: The meanings of the body are neither free-floating in culture nor created solely by individuals, but are embedded in those institutions where culture and individual effort meet. Thus, group forces, commercial interests, professional considerations, and the structures of communities act, as fully as culture and individual negotiation do, to construct the relationship between self and body. (9)

@kiri: Remember Liraella, the Amazon reviewer who praised *Dance Central 3* for letting her work out in private, back in Chapter 1? Let's revisit her review in full.

5.0 out of 5 stars

An amazing game for an exercise beginner!

November 20, 2012

By Liraella

I feel that it's important for people who are more overweight to see real reviews from customers like them. For that reason, I have chosen to disclose that I am a 32 year old woman who presently weighs 270 lbs. I ask that this disclosure be respected for its intended purpose, which is to evidence a true "beginner" review.

My girlfriends know I'm on a mission to lose over 100 pounds, and they always invite me to work out with them—walks, gym, Zumba classes, you name it. But the fact is that I simply cannot keep up. Until now.

Dance Central 3 is an amazingly enjoyable game, even for someone who usually falls behind. This game has easy to follow moves, an awesome rehearsal mode that can even slow moves down so you can properly learn them if needed, and infinite ways to challenge yourself. The first couple times you play it, you may feel a bit lost in some of the moves, but the tracks are kickin' and the moves are realistic, and it makes you want to keep going.

From a fitness standpoint, this game is awesome. It estimates calories burned, tracks how long you've been active during the session, and has playlists that provide continual music to help you keep going. I have terrible knees, and I am always afraid to blow one out. I just hop a little less or "fake" whatever I don't think I can do, and keep going. There are slow songs and songs that will really increase your heart rate. And the best part is that you can turn the "pictures" mode OFF. I'm so grateful that I don't have to be photographed when I'm working out!! This installment also has an option to "level up," so you unlock outfits for your characters over time—another cute way to add variety.

I have always been that one that "won't work out around anyone" because I feel fat, slow, and incapable. But I play this game so often, that I now host Dance Central

KINECT WEIGHT LOSS JOURNEY WEEK 1 WEIGH IN

Figure 6.2: A player-produced "fitness journey" series on YouTube, bringing together *Dance Central* and the competitive weight-loss discourse of the reality television show "The Biggest Loser" (Carr 2011). (Screenshot by the author.)

parties and join in with my friends. I actually now usually play a skill level above my friends because they feel left out like I once used to. I've held small gatherings of up to 10 friends, and everyone has a great time. It was a very well-spent $50 to have a killer time with my pals and on my own.

Dance Central 1 and Dance Central 2 are also awesome games, and they're importable into DC3. I now have over 100 songs to choose from, and for someone who hates repetitive exercise, that's such a blessing. With the dance central games, I'm now active a few days a week for up to two hours, and I finally have a way to be more active with my friends.

The bottom line—don't be intimidated by this game. It's flexible, extremely well done, very fun, and you can keep up with this game. Close the window blinds, turn off the photograph option in the game, crank up the volume, and rock it out! (Liraella 2012)

#testimony

@*kiri*: Liraella's review maintained its top-ranked status on the Amazon product page throughout the years of my research project. By early 2016, it carried the annotation "720 of 722 people found the following review helpful," and had accrued 33 comments. Here's a selection.

> Good luck on your health journey !! and thanks for an inspiring review!

> I need to lose 80 lbs. & I can relate to the knee problem. You've inspired me to go for it & get this game. Keep dancing & having fun & best wishes on your healthy journey.

> (reply from Liraella): Thank you for your support - this is an unbelievably long journey, but I'm learning that it really doesn't have to be torture. I am so happy with the Xbox and this game - it's given me a great start. Best of luck on your new journey!!

> Good luck, this is exactly how I started my journey . . . 1-21-2012, I'm age 34 278lbs, today, 11-27-2012 73lbs GONE, I started with Just Dance, because I have no rhythm whatsoever, doing this at home was the best for me!!!

> I'm right with you Lirella! I'm 55 and HAD to get my weight down. I was too embarrassed to go to a gym, or be seen in public wearing anything that resembled exercise clothes. I got DC2 about a year ago, and just upgraded to DC 3. I try to spend at least 30 minutes a day on it. I still can't dance worth a darn, but I have had to buy lots of new clothes, twice, because of my weight loss.

> As someone who used to weigh 290, I understand COMPLETELY where you are coming from. I love to dance but working out in a gym full of "fit" people was very overwhelming at times. But with this game (and the other two DC games) I never looked at it as working out, I was playing a game and having fun while doing it. It just so happened that I was sweating my behind off.

Thanks for your honest review! I need to also lose 100+ pounds, and when I watch the YouTube clips from the game and I feel like I'd just look stupid panting and struggling to keep up. But I have heard it's great for exercise and this would be a fun way to get in some movement, increase the heart rate and actually burn calories. I think any movement that does that is good movement and if you're like me, who just can't keep an exercise program up, this would work, because it doesn't feel like exercise because it's fun. It may not be the type of program a doctor would approve *eyeroll* but I've seen some of the dances and they are real cardio! keep it up, I'm right behind you!

I also wanted to thank you for such an inspiring review. I get these games to work out also (DC1 & DC2) and at first I would only play it when I was home alone because I was terrified that anyone, even my husband, would see me dancing. Now I get this game out and try to get anyone to play it with me. I did buy this game after reading your review :) I am inspired to continue my weight-loss journey with this fun game.

OMG . . . . what a motivation . . . . you guys ROCK and I hope to join your status soon . . . . I have DC2 and 3 and now I am more motivated than ever to use them . . . . Thanks

Thank you so much, Liraella. You are an inspiration to me. I needed your encouraging message more than you can know!

(comments on Liraella 2012, accessed January 21, 2016)

@*kiri*: While industry reviewers noted that *Just Dance* and *Dance Central* lacked the campaign modes or extended narrative arcs that have traditionally been a mark of quality in gamer culture, these Amazon reviewers demonstrate that dance games are a perfect match for the campaign mode of the "fitness journey." This kind of player-driven discourse also allowed Ubisoft and Harmonix to position themselves as offering support and encouragement for these laudable self-care initiatives: no pressure, but if you want a "sweat mode," calorie-counter feature, or help making social connections with other fitness-oriented players, we're here for you.

@*Millington2009*: As commodities instilled with interactive features that build individualized consumer experiences, active video games in fact may mobilize ideologies of self-expression while contributing to the development of indistinguishable, interchangeable and "desirable" citizens. (638)

#challenge

@*kiri*: Leading up to the release of *Dance Central 2*, Harmonix began to promote the game's fitness affordances via the official *Dance Central* blog and social media channels.

Dance Central Fitness Challenge

Over the past few weeks, Harmonixers and community members have been sharing their Dance Central success stories on how the game has helped them in reaching their individual fitness goals. With the upcoming launch of Dance Central 2 we've decided to kick off a Dance Central Fitness Challenge among members of the Harmonix team! We've split the group up into "Crews" all of which have a variety of fitness goals that range from dropping a few pounds to increasing overall stamina for marathon Dance Central sessions! . . . Want to join our fitness challenge? Try using Dance Central as part of your regular workout routine and share your progress with us on our official Facebook page, Twitter [@Dance_Central], and the forums! To help you get started, you can check out these DanceCentral.com exclusive Fitness Playlists assembled by Dance Central choreographers Frenchy Hernandez and Chanel Thompson! The playlists below are made up of tracks from the original Dance Central and are tailored to work out specific body parts! (DanceCentral.com 2011a)

@*kiri*: Fitness journey narratives began to appear in the regular "Dancer's Spotlight" feature on the *Dance Central* blog, alongside posts about *Dance Central* cosplayers and fan art based on the game characters—a juxtaposition that celebrates self-fashioning body work as individual creative expression.

May Dancer's Spotlight: Meet John

Hello, my name is John Estrada, I am 43 year old Adult Probation Officer living in Brownsville, Texas. I am avid gamer who grew up with Atari to the games today. I own both the PlayStation 4 and Xbox One. Long live gaming! . . . [*A photograph presents "John before his fitness journey," with his belly straining the buttons of his shirt. Another photo includes a trim friend for scale; John looks twice as wide.*] I weighed myself and was shocked how bad I had let myself go. When you see that scale read 460 it hits you like a ton of bricks that you have let yourself get so unhealthy that you may die if you continue down this path. I was very depressed and embarrassed about my weight. Simple things like getting on an airplane were stressful because I would have to ask for an extender just to put my seatbelt on. I knew I had to do something but gyms are not for me. *Dance Central* I had played before and knew I could at least do a few songs and every time in the past I had used it I was sweating. So I started with 4 songs in a row every day. In 3 months I was doing 22 songs in a row. What I realize now is that I stumbled on the perfect novice exercise game because of all the breaks the game gives like freestyle while doing a song and the time it takes to load the next song. For someone in terrible shape like me this was the best way to take baby steps and feel motivated to keep pushing myself with more and more songs. . . . It's easy to give up because of pain but remember that sometimes the pain is from the weight and if you don't push thru it you will always have it regardless of what you do. I do not suffer from any of those old pains now that I have lost the weight. . . . [*Two "after" photos supply evidence of John's transformation. He is sleek and muscular in black athletic gear at what looks like a charity race event, with his arm around a smiling woman in a pink March of Dimes t-shirt—his loving wife? Then he is polished and confident in a shirt and tie in an office setting, chest open, arms hanging at his sides with loosely curled fists, feet planted in a wide stance.*] I was very lucky to have a very supportive wife who helped me this entire year. I really want to thank the people at Harmonix. I am sure when you created this game you did not think people would use it like this. You guys have helped me change my life for the better. For that I will be eternally grateful. (DanceCentral.com 2014)

@kiri: None of the photographs in the post show John playing *Dance Central*. Instead, he provides a playlist that testifies to his embodied experience with the game and models a fitness-oriented listening technique: how to make music work for you by strategically leveraging each song's potential to mobilize your playable body. The playlist also maps out a kind of pilgrimage route, allowing other players to literally follow in John's footsteps as they pursue their own fitness journeys.

PLAYLIST CHALLENGE

"Poker Face" -Lady Gaga (This is the perfect warm up song to get the blood flowing.)

"Super Freak" -Rick James (Unity! This song starts to move you a little more without being too hard.)

"I Gotta Feeling" -The Black Eyed Peas (Great song that starts off slow cardio wise and picks up in the middle.)

"Firework" -Katy Perry (Another example of a song that starts off slow and picks up in the middle.)

"Moves Like Jagger" -Maroon 5 (This song is just one of those songs you just want to dance to so I had to add it to my list.)

"On the Floor" -Jennifer Lopez ft. Pitbull (This song really gets the sweat going and the moves are not to rigorous.)

"Gangam Style" -PSY (I know this song has been done to death but from a weight loss perspective it's the perfect cardio song. You will be out of breath and sweating after this one.)

"Stronger (What Doesn't Kill You)" -Kelly Clarkson (A good song to keep the heart rate up after the last one yet not as hard on you.)

"Sexy and I Know It" -LMFAO (Time to pick up the cardio again and this song helps me do that.)

"OMG" -Usher (Great way to end a workout and use that last bit of energy you have been saving.)
(DanceCentral.com 2014)

#success #failure

@kiri: The disciplining body project converts dance play into productive labor. To say that "anyone can win" at a fitness game is to assert that all players can and should strive to achieve a particular normative standard of physical ability. By the same token, to fail

at a fitness game is a failure of self-discipline and social responsibility. The collaborative pursuit of the disciplining body project across virtual and visceral platforms may call into being an "intimate public" whose participants "feel as though it expresses what is common among them, a subjective likeness that seems to emanate from their history and their ongoing attachments and actions" (Berlant 2008:5).

@Berlant2008: A public is intimate when it foregrounds affective and emotional attachments located in fantasies of the common, the everyday, and a sense of ordinariness, a space where the social world is rich with anonymity and local recognitions, and where challenging and banal conditions of life take place in proximity to the attentions of power but also squarely in the radar of a recognition that can be provided by other humans. (10)

INFRINGING: SURROGATE LABOR
#gameplaynotes #workaround

6/10/2014
This afternoon I went down to my basement for a Just Dance session and found that the batteries were dead in both my Wii Remotes. After a scavenging effort around the house proved fruitless—no luck with half-juiced batteries from bike lights, stereo remotes, clocks, old cameras—I tried to think what another player might do. For me, this session was part of my research plan for the workday. It would be easy enough to swap in another task: read some more critical theory, answer some emails. But suppose I really felt the itch to play, and nothing else would do? Or suppose this was part of my fitness regimen, or my rehearsal plan for the talent show, or my self-promised reward for finishing my taxes? I switched the TV input source over to the decrepit laptop I use for streaming video, opened up YouTube, and searched for "just dance".

The first hit was the Lady Gaga music video, but the rest of the page gave me plenty of game routines to choose from. From the thumbnails, they all seemed to be straightforward captures of game video—that is, what you'd see on screen while playing. No fancy splitscreen editing, nary a human body in sight. I started from the top, with Pitbull's "Timber" (feat. Ke$ha), posted by AverageAsianDude—a DLC track for *Just Dance 2014*, as the video title informed me. I hit play, entered fullscreen mode, and began dancing along with a surreal duo: a cowgirl in an American flag top and red high-heeled boots, partnered by a jiggly panda bear sporting a denim jacket and heavy gold chain, set against a flashing-neon Wild West backdrop. The song's lyrics were displayed karaoke-style in the lower left corner of the screen, white text filling up with color as the track went by: "I have 'em like Miley Cyrus clothes off/Twerking in their bras and thongs. . ./Face down, booty up." But there was no twerking in the choreo. It was a campy hoedown routine: knees up, elbows out, with linked-arm swings and promenade variations for the "Swing your partner round and round" in the chorus. At the end, the cowgirl jumped up on the panda's

Figure 6.3: AverageAsianDude's gameplay video for the *Just Dance 2014* version of Pitbull's "Timber" (AverageAsianDude 2014). (Screenshot by the author.)

back, rodeo-style, pumping one fist like a hype-woman wielding an invisible lasso. Partnerless, with no one to ride, at this point I could only stand back and marvel.

As I browsed through some of the comments and considered the options in the "related videos" queue, I reflected on how this experience was different from actually playing *Just Dance*. It didn't feel like I was missing much. Like many players, I'm not very invested in my *Just Dance* scores and have little confidence in the Wii's capacity to give me meaningful feedback on my dance skills. It was more fun to dance without holding the Wii remote, and the video quality was excellent. I knew that if I wanted to practice the choreography, I'd be able to use YouTube's video controls to pause, rewind, and replay short sections; in the game, I'd have to repeat the entire track. The comments and related videos made me feel like I was right in the middle of an active community of players, yet I hadn't submitted my dancing body to any form of tracking. YouTube would be collecting data and finding ways to monetize my viewing, of course, but I wasn't logged into my personal YouTube account, so this data would be relatively depersonalized. All in all, dancing along with YouTube felt both more private and more social than playing *Just Dance* on the Wii alone in my living room. In many respects it seemed like an improvement on actual gameplay. With every game track just a YouTube search away, why pay extra for a DLC track or buy the next edition of *Just Dance*?

6/11/2014

I revisited the "Timber" video today and noticed a request in the "About" section: "Watch this video to support me," with a YouTube link. I clicked through to find the same gameplay video, this time with no audio, with 110,428 views (as compared to over 7 million for the version with sound). This new "About" section led me further: "why no audio? watch this." I clicked through again, and after I watched a 15-second car insurance ad, a *Just Dance* gameplay video started with the audio track replaced by voiceover from AverageAsianDude. He read out a statement that was also printed in the "About" section:

> Hello everyone, this is AverageAsianDude here. Today I am going to talk about some changes that I am going to make for this channel.
>
> First, let me explain why. If you guys not already known, I am a youtube partner under Maker Studio, what that means is I can upload gameplay videos on youtube and monitize them for some extra money.
>
> But on the 9th of December, youtube flipped the Content ID switch, basically all of the just dance and dance central videos I've uploaded are flagged by the music companies and all of them got blocked in Germany, a few of them got blocked worldwide. I love my german fans but it sucks that the laws in your country is so strict, there is nothing i can do about it.
>
> Anyway, I can no longer earn anything from my videos and i don't think it is right because ubisoft and harmonix, they bought the rights to use the songs in their video games and i can upload those video games so this should be allowed. But it doesn't work like that.
>
> I love dancing and playing Just dance/ dance centrals and I am going to continue making those videos. From now on, I am going to upload a normal video with audio like I always do and after that i am going to upload the same video without the audio this time and you can click on it or open it on another tab and just let it run. That would really help me out a lot. I am not saying you have to do it, but if you really love this channel and want to support it, this is all you have to do. watch the audio video as usual and in the description i will put the link to the video without audio, just open it on another tab or after you finish watching the audio video open that video and let it run for 20 seconds. I really appriciate your support over the years and I love all of my subscribers.
> (AverageAsianDude 2013a)

@kiri: AverageAsianDude's gameplay videos require as much participation from his dancing body as those produced by the uploaders who turn the camera on themselves or employ splitscreen tools. He is really playing the games; we see his moving silhouette when he uses game editions produced for the Kinect, and souvenir photos from his performances pop up on the scoring screen at the end of Dance Central routines. But his videos are not racking up millions of views because of his individual style or technical prowess as a dancer or gamer. While his scores are good, he does not seem particularly invested in showing off his skills or narrating tales

Figure 6.4: AverageAsianDude in a rare on-screen appearance. Detail from the scoring screen at the end of his gameplay video for the *Dance Central 2* version of Mary J. Blige's "Real Love" (AverageAsianDude 2012). (Screenshot by the author.)

of challenge and triumph. In short, AverageAsianDude's videos are not about him. Rather, he is providing a service, through behind-the-scenes labor that requires both dance and media production skills.

AverageAsianDude serves as a surrogate: He provides the necessary physical input to generate gameplay videos that can be circulated like music videos. His viewers can watch, listen, or dance along, as they wish, without buying a game console, software, or DLC tracks; they don't have to rearrange the living room or subject their bodies to tracking. At the same time, AverageAsianDude's videos serve YouTube by attracting ad views, and serve game publishers by providing free publicity and player-community development work on behalf of their products. Like virtually all major corporations today, both Harmonix and Ubisoft actively encourage their players to interact on social media, and company staff have commented approvingly on player-produced gameplay videos. While most gameplay videos across all game genres seem to present clear-cut cases of copyright infringement, game companies have generally seemed more inclined to integrate player-produced material into their marketing strategies than to issue takedown orders. In the case of games built around licensed popular music content, uploaders are doing marketing work that the game publishers themselves might not be able to carry out due to the terms of their licensing agreements with music publishers. Many viewers encounter gameplay videos through searches for song titles and artist names; thus uploaders are effectively using music to promote the games.

AverageAsianDude's request to viewers solicits their active collusion in his infringing, as a way of compensating him for his labor as a surrogate body. He is proposing a collective infringement project through a workaround that games the YouTube business model. He will continue providing his subscribers with videos that include copyrighted music, but will stop monetizing them. In return, he asks that his viewers volunteer their support by pretending to be interested in gameplay videos without music. These videos won't generate automatic Content ID takedown orders, so he can continue to monetize them as original content under the terms of his YouTube Maker Studio partnership; YouTube will pay AverageAsianDude for his viewers' feigned attention. While the game companies could come after him for reproducing copyrighted graphic content, he is betting that they will recognize how this arrangement benefits them as well. This infringing body project links gray-market entrepreneurship with discourses of reciprocity and resistance; AverageAsianDude and his viewer-collaborators will continue to go through the motions of dancing, viewing, listening, and clicking, but will not fully comply with the terms of corporate choreography.

#gameplaynotes #takedown

1/28/16

Today I tried to revisit AverageAsianDude's video for *Just Dance*'s "Apache." The video was gone. I went to his main channel page, where one video thumbnail image stood out from the array: a stark black box with two lines of white text. I knew right away what had happened—I've seen this kind of goodbye video before. The video was titled "Channel Update and bad news." I clicked on it and read the title screen text:

> Channel update: -No more JD videos.</3

Contemplating the pathos of the broken-heart emoticon, I listened to AverageAsianDude make his farewell. At times his voice broke with emotion.

> Hey guys, it's AverageAsianDude here and this is a very much needed channel update. I know that I've been slacking and not doing anything for the past, what seems like forever now, but I've been looking around trying to find a way to do this. But I guess I'm just going to give it to you guys straight. So the deal is, I'm going to stop doing Just Dance videos altogether. So recently Ubisoft themself sent me an email saying that all my videos is going to get taken down by the 28th of January, which is in three days. So yeah, so that's just sort of like the tipping point of the scale for me, because for the past year or so every single video that I put out got copyrighted by the music publishers and then once

in a while I'd get a copyright strike on my channel for using music—that's already in the games in Just Dance, because they use famous songs and stuff, the mainstream songs—and as you guys know, on YouTube if you get three strikes, then that's it, your channel is out, it gets deleted, and I really don't want that. So I don't think I can take the risk anymore, and just like I said Ubisoft personally requested me that I stop doing any videos, because they said it violated some terms between them and the music publishers as well. So I just can't do this anymore, cannot upload any Just Dance-related videos, basically the gameplay. So yeah. But I don't want to stop doing YouTube videos, so I'm going to do something else that I also love, which is Dota 2 videos [image changes to Dota 2 gameplay footage] . . . sort of like League of Legends but not quite, so basically I'm going to just do some highlight videos of the professional matches between the teams in the tournaments and stuff. . . . I feel like this is something that I would like to do and I hope you guys would watch it. If you don't, it's understandable. . . . Anyway I really thank all of you for the continuous support over the three or four years now that I've been doing Just Dance videos. . . . I just cannot thank all of you enough. I have so many subscribers, so many views, approaching nearly one million subscribers now— that's just actually insane, and when I started doing this there was no way that I thought my channel was going to get this big. But then it's sort of all come crashing down, with how YouTube was taking off, and the music industry and publishers, they come in on YouTube and they try to do these things, so it's just inevitable really. And I really cannot blame anyone, the music companies or Ubisoft for doing this to me. I guess I probably knew this was going to happen, nothing is going to last forever, you know. I just hope that you guys will continue to watch my video, and if you enjoy it, you know, keep on sticking around with me and see what's next for me. But if not, then I guess this is farewell. Once again I want to stress that I tremendously appreciate every single one of you for sticking around for this long. I know I've been not really sociable—been very social? socialized?—sociable. I mean, like, I haven't been uploading a lot. I haven't really been doing anything. It's just this thing has really eaten up on me. So you know, new year, new thing for me, new everything, I'm going to try and change. I'm going to be more engaging and do this thing, and yeah. [sigh] Yeah. Thank you guys once again for sticking around. That's it, that's the channel update. Thank you very much. (AverageAsianDude 2016)

Figure 6.5: Loyal viewers mourn the deletion of AverageAsianDude's dance game videos. (Comments on AverageAsianDude 2016; screenshot by the author.)

@Bench2009: Media choreograph bodies; media represent bodily motion according to their protocols and parameters, and then compel dancers to fit themselves into the bodies that have been imagined for them. (279)

@kiri: From an online portfolio page hosted by Cargo Collective, "a personal publishing platform aimed at creating accessible tools and a networked context to enhance the exposure of talented individuals on the Internet" (Cargo Collective 2016):

Joakim Khoury | Art Director & Creative

To promote the Just Dance 3 video game, we created Autodance, a free video app which makes anyone dance, regardless of talent. Record 4 short clips of a friend doing stuff, and Autodance syncs their movement to music, to create a personalised music video. Each video was branded, so everytime a user shares a video, they were essentially sharing an ad. With over 5 million downloads and 2 million shared videos, it seemed to work a treat. As Autodance hit 2 million downloads, Just Dance 3 topped the video games chart for the whole of Europe.

@kiri: Embedded videos provide examples. A man wearing yellow rubber gloves washes dishes at a sink, turns to the camera with a startled "stop filming" gesture, scrubs another plate, then seems to succumb, miming a quick dance move with his arms. We also see him spraying and wiping down a cafeteria table, glancing over his shoulder. Short clips of these movements are repeated and stitched together with a steady visual rhythm, synced to the retro-disco hit "Barbra Streisand" (Duck Sauce, 2010). Closing title screen: "Anyone can Just Dance."

Facts & Figures

With no media spend, Autodance exposed Just Dance 3 to a new audience of millions. And over Christmas 2011, Just Dance 3 became the best-selling video game in Europe.

Results (june 2012) since the release of Autodance, Oct 2011:

App downloads: +5 millions and counting

User-generated videos: 19 millions

Video views (in phone): 56 millions

Total video shares (Facebook and YouTube): 1.6 millions

Facebook likes: 2.5 millions

Facebook comments: 1.6 millions

Submitted videos to YouTube Channel: 450,000 (110,000 made public)

App Store:

No.1 music app in 15 countries

Top 10 (overall) app in 10 countries

App store reviews: 2647 Average score: 4/5

(Khoury 2012)

@kiri: Autodance is Auto-Tune for the moving body: an homage to the "I Am T-Pain" app (Smule 2009), with kinesthetic correction in place of pitch correction. Beginning with *Just Dance 4*, Autodance was an in-game feature for all game editions released for the Xbox and PlayStation consoles, taking advantage of their camera-based motion-sensing systems. (There could be no integrated Autodance for the Wii, which had no camera—though players could use the Autodance app on their phones instead.) This is a telling development choice: as *Just Dance* expanded across platforms, Ubisoft could have used full-body motion detection features in the service of cultivating "real dance" mastery, encroaching on the niche that Harmonix had carved out for *Dance Central*. Instead, they used the cameras to extend *Just Dance*'s intimate social affordances: if it's fun to embarrass yourself in front of a few friends in your living room, why not share that experience with a network of players worldwide? The Autodance feature would also serve to generate content for a proprietary social media channel, an in-game video-sharing platform called JDTV. Autodance and JDTV functioned as enclosure technologies, allowing Ubisoft to

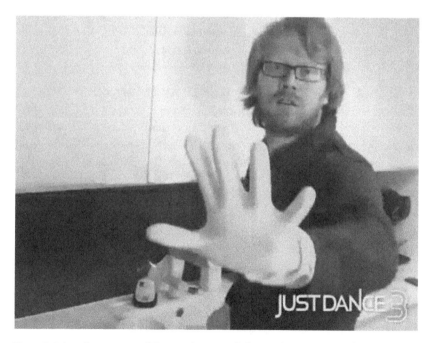

Figure 6.6: Autodance in action (JD3Autodance 2011). (Screenshot by the author.)

fence off and control the production and circulation of gameplay videos. At the same time, they served to promote video-sharing as a natural extension of living-room social gameplay. In effect, Autodance and JDTV constituted an online multiplayer feature for *Just Dance*, based on turn-taking rather than synchronous play.

#gameplaynotes #community #privacy

7/15/15

First day trying out *Just Dance 2014* for the Xbox One, and my first time playing a *Just Dance* game with a camera-based system instead of a Wii remote. I played a few songs and explored some of the integrated social media features, including JDTV, where you can upload gameplay videos and share them with other players immediately after you play. There were over 13,000 videos available, from all over the world—little flag icons indicate national origin for each video. Where these come from: the Autodance videos automatically taken during each play session. They aren't straightforward video clips of your dancing; the frame rate has more of a flipbook feel, deliberately choppy, and short segments are automatically repeated for a playful cut-and-mix effect. This is clearly a one-up on the silly photos that *Dance Central* snaps during Freestyle. I saw the little video camera icon popping up while I was playing, telling me when the Kinect was collecting material, but it is pretty subtle. You get a chance to watch your Autodance video at the end of each song, and from there you can upload your video directly to JDTV. When I watched my own first Autodance video, the ridiculousness made me grin, and the game unlocked a reward badge that said "Made You Smile." This felt really creepy: it destabilized my sense of when the Kinect is watching and when it is not. It also reminded me of street harassment.

@kiri: The Autodancing body project promises that anyone can dance, "regardless of talent," and also that anyone can be *made* to dance, with or without their consent. So why not play along and enjoy it? Autodance promises safety in numbers and in techno-standardized artifice, like an Instagram filter for the moving body. It generates virtual dance that celebrates its own inauthenticity. In contrast to the uploading project, where players submit the idiosyncratic flow of their actual dancing to evaluative comparisons premised on "real dance" standards, the Autodancing project puts everyone on the same level: No one has flow with Autodance. The smoothest and most awkward dancers can meet on the dance floor in perfect stop-motion synchrony, and any movement at all can be converted into dance. It is a cross-sensory pop-culture joke that demonstrates how easy it is to make every body move to the same beat.

BELONGING: NEVER DANCE ALONE

@Bollen2001: One of the defining features of the dance-floor experience is an involving engagement in relations with others. Understanding how relations with

others are negotiated is central to understanding the possibilities and limitations of the dance floor as social context. (292)

@*kiri*: In the summer of 2013, Ubisoft released a two-minute trailer promoting the upcoming release of *Just Dance 2014*. It was distributed through game industry websites and YouTube; I watched it on IGN's YouTube channel (IGN 2013). The trailer opens with a shot of a train rolling through the steel trusswork of an elevated urban transit line. The opening guitar riff of Nicki Minaj's "Starships" (2012) plays over the rumble of the train, and a screen title presents a new feature for this game edition: "World Dancefloor: The First Online Dancing Experience." A train car bearing an American flag decal passes down the track, and we cut to an interior view of a modest city apartment: there's a bay window with a few potted plants (not thriving), and some mismatched basic furniture. (*First apartment out of college, probably a few roommates.*) A screen-text banner in the corner tells us we're in "Brooklyn, New York." A twenty-something African American woman stands facing the camera; she has waist-length braids and wears a loose-fitting yellow crop-top t-shirt, which is falling off one shoulder. She holds up her right hand, palm forward. (*No Wii remote! This trailer is going to be all about new features designed to take advantage of the Xbox One and PlayStation 4 camera systems.*) Cut to the Brooklyn woman's TV, placed against an exposed brick wall, showing a *Just Dance* song selection menu. Screen text tells us where we're headed: "Dance with players around the world!" The text persists as we cut to a quick exterior shot of Notre Dame, then an indoor casual café space where a 20-something white woman wearing an elegantly draped jersey shirt and meticulous makeup walks toward the camera and raises a hand. She's communicating with the game console, we know, but also waving at the woman in Brooklyn. She selects "Starships" from the game menu, and steps back to prepare herself to dance. Cut back to the TV against Brooklyn brick, now showing a screen dancer with *Just Dance*'s signature blank white face and arms. "Starships" is revving up, and she's rocking a Technicolor tutu ensemble, dancing on a candy-colored platform in a cartoon cloudscape. And now the Brooklyn woman dances: cut to her feet, twisting on the floor in pink sneakers, and witness the spectacular swoop of her braids as she sweeps her whole torso in a circle toward the floor. Next scene! "Rio de Janeiro, Brazil": brightly painted apartment buildings are packed tight together on a hillside, with laundry hanging to dry from balconies. Here in the *favela* we don't quite make it inside, but rather follow a group of three young people as they carry a large flatscreen TV through a door and down a flight of cement stairs between buildings. The camera dwells on the last person, marked as Afro-Brazilian by his dark skin tone and chin-length braids; he gestures to unseen friends to come along, too. Then he's dancing in the street next to a woman with much lighter skin and long, straight, light brown hair. Cut back to Paris, where the white Frenchwoman has been joined by an equally chic Afro-Parisian friend. Cut to Tokyo! And now we have split-screen: a young Japanese couple run through neon-lit nighttime streets toward someplace where something fun is about to happen, while the New York woman rides a bright green bicycle through sunny Brooklyn. (*Oh! This is all unfolding at once in different time zones!*) She meets a white friend outside a classic brownstone building, where a flat-screen TV stands on the stoop. We cut rapidly among these four locations; more dancers arrive to join the fun in each scene, and splitscreen effects juxtapose two or four global locations at a time. Now and then the solo screen dancer is included in the mix, too. (*And why not? All these dance spaces are interchangeably utopian and fantastical, and her moving body is what's bringing everyone else together: a choreographic time-space portal.*) Just as Nicki comes back around to the "Starships" chorus, we get a new location: "Mumbai, India," where a young man selects a "Dance With" button on a menu screen, and a screen title promises "Global dance-offs!" In Mumbai, all the dancers are young men, in a huge crowd. (*Even in a cosmopolitan fantasy, there's still no mixed-gender nighttime street dancing in India.*) We see there's a game option for selecting a "Boys vs. Girls" virtual dance-off. Back to the cosmopolitan mashup: Everyone's doing the same choreography, locked into Nicki's beats, performing their difference and togetherness with sweaty exuberance. It's the Brooklyn girls versus the Mumbai boys, but the mixed-gender groups in Rio, Tokyo, and Paris are doing the same dance, too. As the song winds down, the pace of cuts slows with it, and the groups of dancers collapse in laughter and high-fives. We linger in Mumbai, where the TV is in a shop window facing out toward the street; the lettering in the window reads "Beauty Saloon." One of the guys in Mumbai looks to the other with a questioning expression—he gets an enthusiastic thumbs-up, and turns back to the TV to select a button marked "Add as Friend." The guys look back at each other, nod firmly, and high-five: we just made friends with some hot girls in Brooklyn. This scene recedes and becomes one facet of a hybrid globe/disco-ball graphic. The planet full of dancers floats in space, glowing at the center of a milky starscape (*Nicki's starship, "meant to fly!"*). And the parting message, in blocky 3-D letters superimposed over starship/dance-floor Earth:

JUST DANCE 2014

NEVER DANCE ALONE

@kiri: When my copy of *Just Dance 2014* comes in the mail, I tear off the shrink-wrap, put the disc in my Xbox One, and prepare for my World Dancefloor experience. There is online multiplayer—sort of. You can't actually see other people dancing, nor do you interact with them via in-game avatars, as in most online-multiplayer games. But you can *know that you are dancing at the same time*, with your sensing bodies fully synced up. You're generating intimacy and feeding it back into the global grid. Never dance alone: just let this music and choreography pass through your bodies and leave its traces, then click "Add as Friend" to make it official.

Figure 6.7: Never dance alone: promoting the "World Dancefloor" (IGN 2013). (Screenshot by the author.)

I revisit the trailer video regularly and watch the comments accumulate, flooding in around the holiday 2014 season and then slowing to a trickle. By 2016, there are about 500 of them. Amid the usual mix of song callouts ("Nick minaj starships!"), endorsements ("I love this game just got it today"), and dismissals ("According to this trailer, only ppl that play this game are girls and gay men"), there's a steady stream of comments that push against the trailer's utopian cosmopolitanism:

I live in India and we aren't gonna get the Xbox One until late 2014. FUCK YOU MICROSOFT!

Nothing showing UK people dancing. Why? Because our houses are so small Kinect can't function lol.

they really think taht japanes people give a fuck about this crap ROFL

i don't think Brazilians need a video game about dancing.

[reply]: I don't the Brazilians depicted can afford a video game, let alone a TV.

Ahahaha so fake . . . real life and people are not this nice

If I got this game and play online my internet quota will be used up as fast as possible >.<

I don't think any Japanese people gonna own an Xbox haha

GTFO of here! You wouldnt dare bring that tv outside in Brooklyn

I lived in Rio and they would have robbed that TV and not start dancing.

[reply 1]: hey those 2 guys did rob that TV , didn't u see how new the tv was.

[reply 2]: Hey, do not talk like that in Brazil is a beautiful country

[response]: I never said Brazil was not a beautiful country. But if there was a TV in the middle of a favela they would rob it. It's just a fact. Plus almost all my friends already have been robed, be it in the street or in their homes.

Racists

lol they dont have clean water .. but they have ps4 . . . wow the priorities . . . :)

FUCK YEAH BRAZILIAN FAVELAS! LET'S DANCE THE POVERTY AWAY!

@*kiri*: The belonging body project promises that dance can collapse the distinctions between the Rio favela, the Tokyo arcade, the Brooklyn stoop, the Mumbai street, and the Paris café—with a little help from technology, implicitly available to everyone. These commenters reject that premise and reassert difference, in terms of economic resources, local race and class ideologies, uneven distribution of consumer goods across global markets, and even the typical dimensions of one's living space.

@*Massumi2002*: Capitalism is the global usurpation of belonging. . . . Belonging per se has emerged as a problem of global proportions. (88)

@*kiri*: Never dance alone: Is it a promise, or a warning? What fate might you suffer if you *do* dance alone? Beware the isolation and precarity of living off the grid. Better to buy your way onto the networked dance floor, if you can afford it.

CIRCULATING: PLAYABLE BODIES BEYOND DANCE GAMES

@*Kolb2013*: Audience participation could be seen as buying into and proliferating the ideas of activation and formation of creative subjects that are so central to post-industrial conceptions of labor. (41)

@*kiri*: In the fall of 2015 two dance videos were making the rounds through social media, leaving a trail of Tweets, Vine remixes, YouTube parodies, blog posts, and comment threads as view counts rapidly mounted into the tens of millions. I watched them both for the first time on the same morning: after spending 10 days traveling abroad, I woke up at 4 A.M. with jet lag and blearily opened my iPad to catch up on the memes I had missed. I found the first video through a post on The Hairpin, where Haley Mlotek wrote, "I haven't been this obsessed with trying to somehow teach myself, through repeated viewings, complicated choreography to a pop song since Britney Spears released 'I'm A Slave 4 U'" (Mlotek 2015). I clicked through to the JustinBieberVEVO channel on YouTube and watched the video for "Sorry," the latest Bieber single. An all-female crew clad in stylishly garish colors, flaming lipstick, and dark sunglasses danced against a stark white background. The choreography and videography emphasized their silhouettes: wide stances opening up expanses of white space between legs, knees knocking out to the sides, sharp pelvic contractions and spinal arches shown in profile, arms reaching out and then sharply yanking back to break at the elbow. At times they seemed to stutter, with rapid sequences of sharply defined poses that invoked a jittery frame rate, while also calling to mind popping, locking, voguing, and J-Setting repertoires. Bieber's own body never appeared in the video. The opening title screen presented his name, in a studiously artless marker-scrawl; at the end, a dancer held up a hand-written poster reading "We ♥ JB," as though this whole production were a fan-produced homage. (The dancers were not credited in the video; I scrolled down to the "About" section and learned that they were members of the New Zealand-based ReQuest and Royal Family dance crews, choreographed by Parris Goebel.) I clicked back to Mlotek's piece, where she reminisced about her adolescent dance tributes to Britney Spears and reflected on the enduring presence of that choreography in her bodily archive:

> I spent many, many afternoons peering carefully at the television screen in my living room, trying to replicate the way her languid, circular movements paired with the jerky, sudden contractions of her forearms. Later that year I was tasked with choreographing a small performance for my high school dance class and I stole most of the movements from the video; last night, while we walked to the subway, I gave a small demonstration of what I could remember for Alex, and she was appropriately embarrassed on my behalf. (Mlotek 2015)

Justin Bieber - Sorry (PURPOSE : The Movement)

JustinBieberVEVO

Subscribe 19,916,396

1,056,765,416

Figure 6.8: Demonstrative bodies in "Sorry," crossing the one-billion-view mark (JustinBieberVEVO 2015). (Screenshot by the author.)

@*kiri*: A comment in a friend's Instagram feed led me to the second video, an eerily perfect counterpart to "Sorry." This time, a lone male body danced in an empty, glowing lightbox. It was the body of the rap star Drake, performing his new single "Hotline Bling," with occasional intercuts of black-clad women posing and dancing in Bond-girl silhouette. "Sorry" presented blazing colors, fashion-spread costuming, glossy smiles, and tightly coordinated ensemble work; "Hotline Bling" showed a man in baggy gray sweatpants performing deep uncoolness. By the time I saw the video, Drake's languidly haphazard dancing had already generated a flood of parodies, including many that drew on videogames and iconic pop culture texts: A Wii tennis racket appears in Drake's hand, his dancing draws disgusted stares from Star Trek characters, and so on (Frank and Alexander 2015). Some people insisted the terrible dancing was a calculated attempt to drive viral circulation; others embraced a "So bad it's good" position. A commenter on one of many "unofficial" YouTube uploads of the video praised Drake for putting his own body on the line rather than perpetuating masculinist fantasies of dominating other bodies:

> I respect him as an artist because he has deliberately made such an intimate song, a fun one. I think its refreshing to see him in this light. Brings back the days of Carlton Banks of Fresh Prince of Bel-air. As stupid as people think he looks, knowing how true the "monkey see, monkey do" saying is, people are going to make this a popular dance real soon, lol! Drake is known for the "smooth gangster anthems", so this is something different that I felt he wanted to do to show people the fun side to his personality. I personally don't wanna hear everyday about being shot, having my vagina busted backward, instructed to twerk til I hurt . . . yall got my point! (comment transcribed from screenshot, November 2, 2015; video deleted from YouTube)

@*kiri*: This commenter draws attention to the intimate affordances of the playable body: how vulnerability invites connection and reciprocity. But the proliferation of "Hotline Bling" parodies and remix videos more often presented displays of domination: showing off one's tech skills and subcultural capital by making Drake dance in a jail cell on the Starship Enterprise, for instance.

"Hotline Bling" and "Sorry" circulate different kinds of body projects, each premised on the mobilization of playable bodies. The "Sorry" dancers function as demonstrative bodies. They are costumed and framed to pop out in silhouette, inviting imitation: If I can let this dance flow through me, I can cross through the magic mirror and dwell in that desirable and accomplished body. The dancers' sunglasses help render them available for imaginary occupation, much like the whited-out facial features of *Just Dance*'s screen dancers. This video also celebrates technique, disciplined mastery, and the potential for breakout moments of individual expression in the context of tightly coordinated ensemble choreography; like *Dance Central*, it invokes the "real dance" authentication process of demonstrating your self-control by mastering someone else's choreography, then demonstrating your

Figure 6.9: Still from a widely circulated "Hotline Bling" parody. This uploader's Instagram caption reads: "Captain Kirk and Spock looking at @champagnepapi like wtf #startrek #drake #hotlinebling #funny #comedy #humor #hilarious" (the_domin8r_82 2015). (Screenshot by the author.)

expressive agency by infusing that choreography with flow and flavor. It will take practice to learn this choreography, but that practice will yield the rewards of fully "owning it," integrating it into one's embodied repertoire.

"Sorry" had accumulated over a billion YouTube views by March of 2016. It models a collective body project of fandom performed through corporeal commitment: performing this choreography is an act of joyful devotion, a way of "giving back" to Justin Bieber through a gesture of intimate reciprocity rather than a commercial transaction, and an opportunity to forge visceral connections to other fans. The terms of this project dictate that if you make your body playable, you will reap rewards in terms of pleasure, intimacy, mastery, and collectivity: Never dance alone. Meanwhile, "Hotline Bling" presents the playable body as action figure; remixers mobilized Drake's body like a virtual black doll, reenacting the familiar story of the black male body as an automaton that can be made to dance on command (Bernstein 2011). Of course, Drake is not just any black male body; he is also a powerful, wealthy celebrity, an attractive target for an emperor-has-no-clothes intervention. Playing with Drake's dancing body is a way of turning the tables, refusing to be choreographed by the pop culture industry, while subjecting a star to the indignities of Autodancing.

Like dance games, "Hotline Bling" and "Sorry" show us playable bodies operating as interfaces for engaging with popular culture, cultivating intimacy, and exploring dynamics of control and consent. Indeed, they function as dance games in their own right, posing dance challenges that "demand a response from a larger community of dancers" in a context of playful, ritualized competition (Bench 2013:129). Those responses can take the form of intimate reciprocity or of power moves—rendering one's own body playable, or asserting control over other bodies.

OUTRO: OUR BODIES, OUR AVATARS

@Bench2009: Media illustrate what we think bodies are and what they can do at any given historical moment. (279)

@Gibbs2010: The body, then, is not so much a medium as a series of media, each of which connects in its own way with technological media. (201)

@kiri: Uploading, disciplining, infringing, autodancing, belonging, and circulating: These projects attest to the flexible capacities of playable bodies, mobilized to perform an ever-expanding repertoire of social and kinesthetic choreographies. The playable body is the body as playback device, capable of reenacting a repertoire that has been stored away in the archive of cumulative embodied experience. It is the body as game, a site for play within the constraints of structuring rules and motivating challenges that may be both arbitrary and highly compelling. It is the body as an instrument with affordances negotiated through material engagement and practiced technique. And it is the body as puppet, an object susceptible to manipulation by numerous agents, forever raising questions about hierarchies of control and ownership.

Dance games ask players to render their bodies playable, but they also offer reassuring evidence of their own limitations as control technologies. Game choreography does not simply stream through players' bodies like the code that animates digital screen dancers. Dance games highlight the quirks, glitches, and idiosyncratic capacities of playable bodies; learning a new routine requires not just consent but active collaboration and repeated practice. Part of the appeal of these games lies in their affirmation that humans are not mass-produced, interchangeable pieces of hardware, pre-loaded with an operating system that will let us run software sold to us by multinational corporations. They show that choreography operates through the mobilization of technique: techniques of moving and attending to others' movements, of listening, of remembering and anticipating. In the course of learning choreography, the playable body is not a receiving or consuming body but a recognizing body, engaged in practicing familiar techniques and feeling out new ones through trial and error.

When dance game players consent to let their bodies be animated by someone else's intentions, they do so with the understanding that this arrangement is a temporary apprenticeship: they can render themselves playable for the sake of learning new techniques and discovering hitherto unknown capacities, then use those resources for their own purposes, exceeding the perceptual capacities of the game systems and moving beyond the artificial confines of their dance floors. That is, dance games secure consent by holding out the possibility that players will ultimately unpin themselves from the demonstrative bodies on their screens and practice "real dance": dance that is unquantifiable, untrackable, imbued with individual flow and flavor, and can only be recognized by other humans.

Embodied performance practices have always circulated across sensory domains, media platforms, and social spheres. Dance games structure that circulation by engineering a new confluence of surveillance technologies, listening and movement practices, and intimate social relations, which work together to materialize the playable body as a choreographic interface. Game designers, choreographers, and living-room dancers have engaged in a complex and sometimes contentious collaboration on this project, finding ways to use emerging technologies and established social media platforms to support the virtual transmission of embodied practice. Their efforts honor and celebrate dance as both joyful play and satisfying labor. At the same time, dance games articulate connections between the precarious vulnerability of social dance situations and that of subjecting one's body to tracking and evaluation by non-human technologies. Motion-sensing interfaces are becoming part of everyday life, and they are at the heart of the virtual reality platforms being rushed to market as I write. As we move forward in this era of playable bodies and intimate media, dance games show us how people draw on their accumulated embodied knowledge in making sense of new technologies—and how that knowledge can be playfully tested, seriously challenged, and ultimately transformed.

PHOTOS ARE DISCARDED AFTER EACH SONG.

Figure 6.10: A *Dance Central* meta-selfie. (Photograph by the author.)

NOTES

INTRODUCTION

1. De Ridder and van Bauwel 2015 offer a discussion of "intimate media cultures" that focuses on practices of intimate storytelling on social media (emphasizing sexual intimacy); Cass et al. 2003 define "intimate media" as personal artifacts, "things that people create and collect to store and share their personal memories, interests, and loves" (220), in analog or digital formats.
2. Later, the *Zumba Fitness* series for the Wii did track hip motion—and *only* hip motion—by requiring that players don a belt with a hip pocket for the Wii Remote (Pipeworks Software 2010).
3. For further discussion of the scholarly literature on virtuality, repetition, and practice, see Miller 2012.

CHAPTER 1

1. Of course, conventional game avatars are not blank slates; they have specific and idiosyncratic capabilities, and there is a rich scholarly literature on how players negotiate relationships with them (e.g., Burrill 2006, Taylor 2006, Miller 2008a, Pearce 2009).
2. While the *Guitar Hero* games paved the way for dance games by encouraging some gamers to develop rock star moves, those games still put a controller in players' hands and emphasized technical virtuosity at the level of fingerwork (Miller 2009, Miller 2012).

CHAPTER 2

1. See Inglese 2016 for a case study of "minstrel legacies" in South Africa and a review of the literature on transnational minstrelsy.
2. The spin-off game *Dance Central Spotlight*—a download-only release for the Xbox One console in 2014—did introduce some "Manly" routines, in response to years of player feedback. This game diverged from the main franchise in many respects and is outside the scope of my study.
3. Readers interested in exploring the literature on games and gender might start with Taylor 2003, Taylor 2006, Stromer-Galley and Mikeal 2006, Royse et al. 2007, Kafai et al. 2008, Pearce 2009, and Shaw 2012.

CHAPTER 3

1. This is not to propose a seamless melding of Massumi's and Ahmed's theories of affect; among other important differences, Massumi makes a sharp distinction between affect and emotion, while Ahmed generally treats them as interchangeable terms.

REFERENCES

Aguirre, Marcos, and Kiri Miller. 2015. Recorded phone interview, August 14.

Ahmed, Sara. 2004. *The Cultural Politics of Emotion*. New York: Routledge.

Alexander, Leigh. 2012. "Harmonix on Gender, Self-Expression in *Dance Central*." http://www.gamasutra.com/view/news/39514/Harmonix_on_gender_selfexpression_in_Dance_Central.php (accessed May 29, 2013).

Amazon.com. 2013a. "Customer Reviews: Dance Central 2—Xbox 360." http://www.amazon.com/Dance-Central-2-Xbox-360/product-reviews/B0050SYYEK (accessed August 1, 2013).

Amazon.com. 2013b. "Customer Reviews: Dance Central—Xbox 360." http://www.amazon.com/Dance-Central-Xbox-360/product-reviews/B004I5EE46 (accessed August 1, 2013).

Amazon.com. 2014. "Customer Reviews—Just Dance: Nintendo Wii." http://www.amazon.com/Just-Dance-Nintendo-Wii/product-reviews/B002MWSY3O (accessed July 20, 2014).

Apatow, Judd, dir. 2007. *Knocked Up*. Universal Pictures.

Auslander, Philip. 1999. *Liveness: Performance in a Mediatized Culture*. New York: Routledge.

Auslander, Philip. 2005. "At the *Listening Post*, or, Do Machines Perform?" *International Journal of Performance Arts and Digital Media* 1(1):5–10.

Austin, Michael, ed. 2016. *Music Video Games: Performance, Politics, and Play*. New York: Bloomsbury.

AverageAsianDude. 2012a. "Dance Central 2—Crew Challenge: Lu$h Crew—Real Love—Hard 100%—5* Gold Stars—2.1+ Millions—YouTube." http://www.youtube.com/watch?v=Ag2o_DRO_I (accessed February 14, 2014).

AverageAsianDude. 2012b. "Dance Central 3—Call Me Maybe—Hard 100%—5* Gold Stars (DLC)" (December 4). https://www.youtube.com/watch?v=XhmLCriOLac (accessed February 21, 2013).

AverageAsianDude. 2013a. "Important Message, please watch" (December 18). https://www.youtube.com/watch?v=Wl1CeQw3SWA (accessed June 11, 2014).

AverageAsianDude. 2013b. "Just Dance 3—Apache (Jump On It) [partial title]" (complete citation details unavailable due to deletion from YouTube; see Chapter 6). https://www.youtube.com/watch?v=57VsVffH5eI (accessed December 28, 2015).

AverageAsianDude. 2014. "Just Dance 2014—Timber—5* Stars (DLC)" (February 11). https://www.youtube.com/watch?v=DYwGj3IN-cE (accessed June 11, 2014).

AverageAsianDude. 2016. "Channel Update and bad news." (January 17). https://www.youtube.com/watch?v=mHOE1FlqRN0 (accessed January 29, 2016).

Balsamo, Anne. 1996. *Technologies of the Gendered Body: Reading Cyborg Women*. Durham, NC: Duke University Press.

Beam, Christopher. 2008. "Epic Win: Goodbye, Schadenfreude; Hello, Fail" (October 15). http://www.slate.com/articles/life/the_good_word/2008/10/epic_win.html (accessed September 8, 2014).

Behrenshausen, Bryan G. 2007. "Toward a (Kin)Aesthetic of Video Gaming: The Case of Dance Dance Revolution." *Games and Culture* 2(4):335–354.

Behrenshausen, Bryan G. 2013. "The Active Audience, Again: Player-Centric Game Studies and the Problem of Binarism." *New Media & Society* 15(6):872–889.

Beleboni, Matheus Giovanni Soares. 2014. "A Brief Overview of Microsoft Kinect and Its Applications." Interactive Multimedia Conference, University of Southampton, Southampton, UK. http://mms.ecs.soton.ac.uk/2014/papers/2.pdf.

Bench, Harmony. 2009. *Choreographing Bodies in Dance-Media*. Ph.D. dissertation, Culture and Performance, University of California at Los Angeles.

Bench, Harmony. 2010. "Screendance 2.0: Social Dance-Media." *Participations* 7(2):183–214.

Bench, Harmony. 2013. "'Single Ladies' Is Gay: Queer Performances and Mediated Masculinities on YouTube." In *Dance on Its Own Terms: Histories and Methodologies*, ed. Melanie Bales and Karen Eliot, 127–151. New York: Oxford University Press.

Bench, Harmony. 2016. "Affective Temporalities: Dance, Media, and the War on Terror." In *Choreographies of 21st Century Wars*, ed. Gay Morris and Jens Richard Giersdorf, 157–179. New York: Oxford University Press.

Berger, Harris M. 1999. *Metal, Rock, and Jazz: Perception and the Phenomenology of Musical Experience*. Hanover, NH: University Press of New England.

Berger, Harris M. 2009. *Stance: Ideas about Emotion, Style, and Meaning for the Study of Expressive Culture*. Middletown, CT: Wesleyan University Press.

Berlant, Lauren. 2008. *The Female Complaint: The Unfinished Business of Sentimentality in American Culture*. Durham, NC: Duke University Press.

Bernstein, Robin. 2011. *Racial Innocence: Performing American Childhood from Slavery to Civil Rights*. New York: New York University Press.

Bishop, Sam. 2009. "Just Dance Review" (December 3). http://www.ign.com/articles/2009/12/04/just-dance-review (accessed July 18, 2014).

Blaine, Tina. 2005. "The Convergence of Alternate Controllers and Musical Interfaces in Interactive Entertainment." http://nime.org/2005/proc/nime2005_027.pdf (accessed November 9, 2010).

Blanco Borelli, Melissa, ed. 2014. *The Oxford Handbook of Dance and the Popular Screen*. New York: Oxford University Press.

Boch, Matt. 2012. Roundtable Panel: "Finding the Soul of your Game." Transcription from audio recording by the author. PAX East Convention, April 6. Boston, MA.

Boch, Matt. 2013. "Gender Assumptions in Mocap." http://criticalpathproject.com/?v=77997447 (accessed February 2, 2016).

Boch, Matt, and Kiri Miller. 2012. Recorded interview, April 6. Boston, MA.

Boellstorff, Tom. 2008. *Coming of Age in Second Life: An Anthropologist Explores the Virtually Human*. Princeton, NJ: Princeton University Press.

Boellstorff, Tom, Bonnie Nardi, Celia Pearce, and T. L. Taylor. 2012. *Ethnography and Virtual Worlds: A Handbook of Method*. Princeton, NJ: Princeton University Press.

Bogost, Ian. 2007. *Persuasive Games*. Cambridge, MA: MIT Press.

Bollen, Jonathan. 2001. "Queer Kinesthesia: Performativity on the Dance Floor." In *Dancing Desires: Choreographing Sexualities On and Off the Stage*, ed. Jane C. Desmond, 285–314. Madison: University of Wisconsin Press.

Born, Georgina. 2012. "Digital Music, Relational Ontologies and Social Forms." In *Bodily Expression in Electronic Music: Perspectives on Reclaiming Performativity*, ed. Deniz Peters, Gerhard Eckel and Andreas Dorschel, 163–180. New York: Routledge.

Bosse, Joanna. 2007. "Whiteness and the Performance of Race in American Ballroom Dance." *Journal of American Folklore* 120(475):19–47.

Bourdieu, Pierre. 1977 [1972]. *Outline of a Theory of Practice*. Translated by Richard Nice. Cambridge: Cambridge University Press.

Bourdieu, Pierre. 1990. *Photography: A Middle-Brow Art*. Translated by Shaun Whiteside. Cambridge: Polity Press.

BowserBike. 2013. "[Just Dance 2] "Hey Ya!" by Outkast—HQ Choreography" (December 6). https://www.youtube.com/watch?v=N_umrFfxakU (accessed February 26, 2016).

Bozon, Mark. 2016. "Wii: The Launch Games" (May 18). http://www.ign.com/articles/2006/05/18/wii-the-launch-games (accessed January 19, 2016).

Bragin, Naomi. 2014. "Techniques of Black Male Re/dress: Corporeal Drag and Kinesthetic Politics in the Rebirth of Waacking/Punkin." *Women & Performance: A Journal of Feminist Theory* 24(1):61–78.

Brinner, Benjamin. 1995. *Knowing Music, Making Music*. Chicago: University of Chicago Press.

Broadhurst, Susan. 2007. *Digital Practices: Aesthetic and Neuroesthetic Approaches to Performance and Technology*. New York: Palgrave Macmillan.

Brown, Simone. 2015. *Dark Matters: On the Surveillance of Blackness*. Durham, NC: Duke University Press.

Buck, Ralph, Sylvie Fortin, and Warwick Long. 2012. "A Teacher 'Self-Research' Project: Sensing Differences in the Teaching and Learning of Contemporary Dance Technique in New Zealand." In *Fields in Motion: Ethnography in the Worlds of Dance*, ed. Dena Davida, 233–254. Waterloo, Ontario, Canada: Wilfrid Laurier University Press.

Burgess, Jean, and Joshua Green. 2009. *YouTube: Online Video and Participatory Culture*. Cambridge: Polity Press.

Burrill, Derek A. 2006. "Check Out My Moves." *Social Semiotics* 16(1):17–38.

Burrill, Derek A., and Melissa Blanco Borelli. 2014. "Dancing with Myself: Dance Central, Choreography, and Embodiment." In *The Oxford Handbook of Dance and the Popular Screen*, ed. Melissa Blanco Borelli, 429–442. New York: Oxford University Press.

Butler, Judith. 1990. *Gender Trouble: Feminism and the Subversion of Identity*. New York: Routledge.

Butler, Judith. 1993. *Bodies That Matter: On the Discursive Limits of "Sex."* New York: Routledge.

Calfin, Mike. 2010. "Dance Central—Lady Gaga's Just Dance—Break it Down mode" (November 16). https://www.youtube.com/watch?v=2qO89zJaCuU (accessed August 11, 2014).

Calvo-Merino, Beatriz, Daniel Glaser, Julie Grézes, Richard Passingham, and Patrick Haggard. 2005. "Action Observation and Acquired Motor Skills: An fMRI Study with Expert Dancers." *Cerebral Cortex* 15(8):1243–1249.

Cargo Collective. 2016. "Cargo—Gallery." http://cargocollective.com (accessed February 25, 2016).

Carr, Patricia. 2011. "KINECT WEIGHT LOSS JOURNEY WEEK 1 WEIGH IN" (May 24). https://www.youtube.com/watch?v=7AYWM6M87js (accessed March 14, 2016).

Cass, John, Lorna Goulden, and Slava Kozlov. 2003. "Intimate Media: Emotional Needs and Ambient Intelligence." In *The New Everyday: Views on Ambient Intelligence*, ed. Emile Aarts and Stefano Marzano, 218–223. Rotterdam, The Netherlands: 010 Publishers.

Cheng, William. 2014. *Sound Play: Video Games and the Musical Imagination*. New York: Oxford University Press.

Chion, Michel. 1994. *Audio-Vision: Sound on Screen*. Translated by Claudia Gorbman. New York: Columbia University Press.

Chun, Wendy Hui Kyong. 2009. "Race and/as Technology; or, How to Do Things to Race." *Camera Obscura* 24(1):7–34.

Chun, Wendy Hui Kyong. 2011. *Programmed Visions: Software and Memory*. Cambridge, MA: MIT Press.

Clements, Ryan. 2010. "Dance Central Kinect Review: The Dance Genre Is Back" (November 3). http://xbox360.ign.com/articles/113/1132366p1.html (accessed June 20, 2014).

Clifford, James. 1988. *The Predicament of Culture*. Cambridge, MA: Harvard University Press.

Clough, Patricia. 2010. "The Affective Turn: Political Economy, Biomedia, and Bodies." In *The Affect Theory Reader*, ed. Melissa Gregg and Gregory J. Seigworth, 206–225. Durham, NC: Duke University Press.

Coleman, E. Gabriella. 2010. "Ethnographic Approaches to Digital Media." *Annual Review of Anthropology* 39:487–505.

Collins, Karen, ed. 2008a. *From Pac-Man to Pop Music: Interactive Audio in Games and New Media*. Burlington, VT: Ashgate.

Collins, Karen. 2008b. *Game Sound: An Introduction to the History, Theory, and Practice of Video Game Music and Sound Design*. Cambridge, MA: MIT Press.

Collins, Karen. 2013. *Playing with Sound: A Theory of Interacting with Sound and Music in Video Games*. Cambridge, MA: MIT Press.

Csikszentmihalyi, Mihaly. 1991. *Flow: The Psychology of Optimal Experience*. New York: Harper Perennial.

Dance Central. 2016. "Dance Central." https://www.facebook.com/dancecentral (accessed February 1, 2016).

DanceCentral.com. 2011a. "Dance Central Fitness Challenge" (October 7). http://www.dancecentral.com/dance-central-fitness-challenge (accessed June 4, 2012).

DanceCentral.com. 2011b. "Requests, Suggestions, & Features Feedback" (February 8). http://www.dancecentral.com/forums/showthread.php?t=1262 (accessed January 14, 2013).

DanceCentral.com. 2012a. "Dancing like a Lady" (May 26). http://www.dancecentral.com/forums/showthread.php?t=8341 (accessed January 14, 2013).

DanceCentral.com. 2012b. "DLC Discussion—Low by Flo Rida" (May 28). http://www.dancecentral.com/forums/showthread.php?t=8354 (accessed June 28, 2012).

DanceCentral.com. 2012c. "Just Dance 4's full setlist" (August 17). http://www.dancecentral.com/forums/showthread.php?t=10143 (accessed September 19, 2012).

DanceCentral.com. 2014. "May Dancer's Spotlight: Meet John" (May 7). http://www.dance-central.com/may-dancers-spotlight-meet-john (accessed May 22, 2014).

Davida, Dena, ed. 2012. *Fields in Motion: Ethnography in the Worlds of Dance*. Waterloo, Ontario, Canada: Wilfrid Laurier University Press.

De Ridder, Sander, and Sofie van Bauwel. 2015. "Youth and Intimate Media Cultures: Gender, Sexuality, Relationships, and Desire as Storytelling Practices in Social Networking Sites." *Communications* 40(3):319–340.

DeFrantz, Thomas F. 2004. "The Black Beat Made Visible: Hip Hop Dance and Body Power." In *Of the Presence of the Body: Essays on Dance and Performance Theory*, ed. Andre Lepecki, 64–81. Middletown, CT: Wesleyan University Press.

DeFrantz, Thomas F. 2012. "Unchecked Popularity: Neoliberal Circulations of Black Social Dance." In *Neoliberalism and Global Theatres*, ed. Lara D. Nielsen and Patricia Ybarra, 128–140. New York: Palgrave Macmillan.

DeFrantz, Thomas F. 2014. "Hip-Hop Habitus v.2.0." In *Black Performance Theory*, ed. Thomas F. DeFrantz and Anita Gonzalez, 223–242. Durham, NC: Duke University Press.

Demers, Joanna. 2006. "Dancing Machines: 'Dance Dance Revolution,' Cybernetic Dance, and Musical Taste." *Popular Music* 25(3):401–414.

Desmond, Jane C. 1997. "Embodying Difference: Issues in Dance and Cultural Studies." In *Meaning in Motion: New Cultural Studies in Dance*, ed. Jane C. Desmond, 29–54. Durham, NC: Duke University Press.

Desmond, Jane C., ed. 2001. *Dancing Desires: Choreographing Sexualities on and off the Stage*. Madison: University of Wisconsin Press.

Dewey, Caitlin. 2014. "The Only Guide to Gamergate You Will Ever Need to Read" (October 14). https://www.washingtonpost.com/news/the-intersect/wp/2014/10/14/the-only-guide-to-gamergate-you-will-ever-need-to-read/ (accessed February 2, 2016).

Dixon, Steve. 2007. *Digital Performance: A History of New Media in Theater, Dance, Performance Art, and Installation*. Cambridge, MA: MIT Press.

Dodds, Sherril. 2001. *Dance on Screen: Genres and Media from Hollywood to Experimental Art*. New York: Palgrave.

Dodds, Sherril. 2014. "Values in Motion: Reflections on Popular Screen Dance." In *The Oxford Handbook of Dance and the Popular Screen*, ed. Melissa Blanco Borelli, 445–454. New York: Oxford University Press.

DRAGNARON. 2012. "Sexy and I know it—LMFAO—Hard 100% Flawless—Dance Central 3" (October 19). https://www.youtube.com/watch?v=0F4rf8LsEEM (accessed February 27, 2016).

Driscoll, Kevin. 2013. "Soulja Boy and Dance Crazes." http://spreadablemedia.org/essays/driscoll/#.UYFBD4Li7QQ (accessed May 1, 2013).

Dyer, Mitch. 2012. "Dance Central 3 Video Review" (October 15). http://www.ign.com/videos/2012/10/15/dance-central-3-video-review (accessed February 1, 2016).

Entertainment Software Rating Board. 2016. "Dance Central." http://www.esrb.org/ratings/Synopsis.aspx?Certificate=29594&Title=Dance+Central (accessed February 3, 2016).

Fine, Gary Alan. 1983. *Shared Fantasy: Role-Playing Games as Social Worlds*. Chicago: University of Chicago Press.

Fischer-Lichte, Erika. 2008. *The Transformative Power of Performance: A New Aesthetics*. Translated by Saskya Iris Jain. New York: Routledge.

Fish, Stanley. 1980. *Is There a Text in This Class? The Authority of Interpretive Communities*. Cambridge, MA: Harvard University Press.

Fisher, Jennifer, and Anthony Shay, eds. 2009. *When Men Dance: Choreographing Masculinities across Borders*. New York: Oxford University Press.

Foster, Susan Leigh. 1992. "Dancing Bodies." In *Incorporations*, ed. Jonathan Crary and Sanford Kwinter, 480–495. New York: Zone Books.

Foster, Susan Leigh. 1995. "An Introduction to Moving Bodies: Choreographing History." In *Choreographing History*, ed. Susan Leigh Foster, 3–21. Bloomington: Indiana University Press.

Foster, Susan Leigh. 1998. "Choreographies of Gender." *Signs* 24(1):1–33.

Foster, Susan Leigh. 2009. "'Throwing Like a Girl'? Gender in a Transnational World." In *Contemporary Choreography: A Critical Reader*, ed. Jo Butterworth and Liesbeth Wildschut, 52–64. New York: Routledge.

Foster, Susan Leigh. 2011. *Choreographing Empathy: Kinesthesia in Performance*. New York: Routledge.

Foucault, Michel. 1988. "Technologies of the Self." In *Technologies of the Self: A Seminar with Michel Foucault*, ed. Luther H. Martin, Huck Gutman and Patrick H. Hutton, 16–49. Amherst: University of Massachusetts Press.

Frank, Allegra, and Julia Alexander. 2015. "Drake's 'Hotline Bling' Memes Bring Hip-Hop and Gaming Fans Together" (October 30). http://www.polygon.com/2015/10/30/9645972/drake-hotline-bling-meme-video-games-wii-tennis (accessed November 5, 2015).

FreeStyleGames. 2009. *DJ Hero*. Activision.

Fritsch, Melanie. 2016. "Beat It! Playing the 'King of Pop' in Video Games." In *Music Video Games: Performance, Politics, and Play*, ed. Michael Austin. New York: Bloomsbury.

Galloway, Alexander R. 2012. *The Interface Effect*. Malden, MA: Polity Press.

Galloway, Alexander R., and Eugene Thacker. 2007. *The Exploit: A Theory of Networks*. Minneapolis: University of Minnesota Press.

GameTrailers.com. 2010. "Dance Central Video Game, Review" (November 4). http://www.gametrailers.com/video/review-dance-central/707175#comments (accessed April 11, 2011).

Garcia, Luis-Manuel. 2011. *"Can You Feel It, Too?": Intimacy and Affect at Electronic Dance Music Events in Paris, Chicago, and Berlin*. Ph.D. dissertation, Music, University of Chicago, Chicago, IL.

Gaston, Martin. 2010. "Just Dance 2 Review" (October 21). http://www.videogamer.com/wii/just_dance_2/review.html (accessed July 20, 2014).

Gates, Henry Louis Jr. 1988. *The Signifying Monkey: A Theory of African-American Literary Criticism*. New York: Oxford University Press.

Gee, James Paul. 2004. *Situated Language and Learning*. New York: Routledge.

Gee, James Paul. 2006. "Learning by Design: Good Video Games as Learning Machines." In *Digital Media: Transformations in Human Communication*, ed. Paul Messaris and Lee Humphreys, 173–186. New York: Peter Lang.

Gee, James Paul. 2008. "Learning and Games." In *The Ecology of Games: Connecting Youth, Games, and Learning*, ed. Katie Salen, 21–40. Cambridge, MA: MIT Press.

Geertz, Clifford. 1988. *Works and Lives: The Anthropologist as Author*. Stanford, CA: Stanford University Press.

Gibbs, Anna. 2010. "After Affect: Sympathy, Synchrony, and Mimetic Communication." In *The Affect Theory Reader*, ed. Melissa Gregg and Gregory J. Seigworth, 186–205. Durham, NC: Duke University Press.

Gibson, Ellie. 2010. "Just Dance: Gonna Be Surprisingly OK" (January 19). http://www.eurogamer.net/articles/just-dance-review (accessed August 1, 2014).

Gillespie, Tarleton. 2010. "The Politics of 'Platforms.'" *New Media & Society* 12(3): 347–364.

Gimlin, Debra L. 2001. *Body Work: Beauty and Self-Image in American Culture*. Berkeley: University of California Press.

Glasser, AJ. 2010. "Dance Central Review" (November 4). https://web.archive.org/web/20111203001108/http://www.gamepro.com/article/reviews/217165/dance-central-review/ (accessed June 9, 2014).

Goodridge, Janet. 2012. "The Body as a Living Archive of Dance/Movement: Autobiographical Reflections." In *Fields in Motion: Ethnography in the Worlds of Dance*, ed. Dena Davida, 119–143. Waterloo, Ontario, Canada: Wilfrid Laurier University Press.

Grimshaw, Mark. 2012. "Sound and Player Immersion in Digital Games." In *The Oxford Handbook of Sound Studies*, ed. Trevor Pinch and Karin Bijsterveld, 347–366. New York: Oxford University Press.

Grodal, Torben. 2003. "Stories for Eye, Ear, and Muscles: Video Games, Media, and Embodied Experience." In *The Video Game Theory Reader*, ed. Mark J. P. Wolf and Bernard Perron, 129–155. New York: Routledge.

Guterl, Matthew Pratt. 2013. *Seeing Race in Modern America*. Chapel Hill: University of North Carolina Press.

Hahn, Tomie. 2007. *Sensational Knowledge: Embodying Culture through Japanese Dance*. Middletown, CT: Wesleyan University Press.

Hamera, Judith. 2007. *Dancing Communities: Performance, Difference, and Connection in the Global City*. New York: Palgrave Macmillan.

Hamilton, Kirk. 2012. "On Playing *Dance Central 2* While Male" (January 13). http://kotaku.com/5876059/on-playing-dance-central-2-while-male (accessed March 10, 2014).

Hardt, Michael, and Antonio Negri. 2000. *Empire*. Cambridge, MA: Harvard University Press.

Harmonix Music Systems. 2005. *Guitar Hero*. Red Octane.

Harmonix Music Systems. 2007. *Rock Band*. MTV Games.

Harmonix Music Systems. 2010. *Dance Central*. MTV Games.

Harmonix Music Systems. 2011a. "Dance Central 2 Behind the Scenes—Characters & Crews" (September 30). http://www.youtube.com/watch?v=rPUg9oXaiSo (accessed January 15, 2013).

Harmonix Music Systems. 2011b. "Dance Central 2 Behind the Scenes—Choreography" (July 11). https://www.youtube.com/watch?v=9A7r4NwAZPs (accessed May 5, 2015).

Harmonix Music Systems. 2011c. "Dance Central Sketchbook: Meet Mo & Emilia" (February 2). http://www.harmonixmusic.com/blog/dance-central-sketchbook-meet-mo-emilia/ (accessed August 17, 2015).

Harmonix Music Systems. 2011d. "Episode 55—Rock the Matt Boch Talk Doc" (November 3). www.rockband.com/community/podcast/episode055 (accessed January 18, 2013).

Harmonix Music Systems. 2012. "Preview Video: 'Low' by Flo Rida" (May 28). http://www.dancecentral.com/preview-low (accessed June 28, 2012).

HarmonixMusic.com. 2013. "Dance Central Song/Choreographer List" (June). http://forums.harmonixmusic.com/discussion/238352/dance-central-song-choreographer-list (accessed February 15, 2016).

Haye, Julia. 2011. "10, 9, 8 . . . Lawsuit? The Blow Up Over Beyoncé's 'Countdown' Choreography" (October 18). http://www.lawlawlandblog.com/2011/10/10_9_8lawsuit_the_blow_up_over.html (accessed January 27, 2013).

Hazzard-Gordon, Katrina. 1990. *Jookin': The Rise of Social Dance Formations in African-American Culture*. Philadelphia: Temple University Press.

Hoggins, Tom. 2010. "Dance Central Review" (November 12). http://www.telegraph.co.uk/technology/video-games/8128990/Dance-Central-review.html (accessed July 20, 2014).

Holmes, Mannie. 2015. "Alfonso Ribeiro Explains How the Carlton Dance was Invented on 'The Fresh Prince of Bel Air'" (August 19). http://variety.com/2015/tv/news/fresh-prince-of-bel-air-alfonso-ribeiro-carlton-dance-1201570543/ (accessed February 9, 2016).

Horst, Heather, Becky Herr-Stephenson, and Laura Robinson. 2010. "Media Ecologies." In *Hanging Out, Messing Around, and Geeking Out*, ed. Mizuko Ito, 29–78. Cambridge, MA: MIT Press.

IGN. 2011. "Rayman Raving Rabbids Wii Trailer" (May 19). https://www.youtube.com/watch?v=ZTXMjYve048 (accessed February 1, 2016).

IGN. 2013. "Just Dance 2014—Gamescom Trailer" (August 21). https://www.youtube.com/watch?v=PLCapQu-oPE (accessed September 24, 2014).

Inglese, Francesca. 2016. *Coloured Moves and Klopse Beats: Minstrel Legacies in Cape Town, South Africa*. Ph.D. dissertation, Ethnomusicology, Brown University, Providence, RI.

Isbister, Katherine. 2016. *How Games Move Us: Emotion by Design*. Cambridge, MA: MIT Press.

Isbister, Katherine, and Kristina Höök. 2009. "On Being Supple: In Search of Rigor without Rigidity in Meeting New Design and Evaluation Challenges for HCI Practitioners."

In *Conference on Human Factors in Computing Systems: Proceedings of ACM CHI 2009.* Boston, MA: Association for Computing Machinery. http://www.katherineinterface.com/chi_ 2009.pdf.

Ito, Mizuko, Sonja Baumer, Matteo Bittanti, danah boyd, Rachel Cody, Becky Herr-Stephenson, Heather Horst, Patricia G. Lange, Dilan Mahendran, Katynka Z. Martínez, C. J. Pascoe, Dan Perkel, Laura Robinson, Christo Sims, and Lisa Tripp. 2010. *Hanging Out, Messing Around, and Geeking Out.* Cambridge, MA: MIT Press.

JD3Autodance. 2011. "Autodance: Jim" (October 7). https://www.youtube.com/watch?v=pVRVwS7NHhw (accessed March 15, 2016).

Jenkins, Henry. 2006. *Convergence Culture: Where Old and New Media Collide.* New York: New York University Press.

Jenkins, Henry, Sam Ford, and Joshua Green. 2013. *Spreadable Media: Creating Value and Meaning in a Networked Culture.* New York: New York University Press.

Jones, Steven E. 2008. *The Meaning of Video Games: Gaming and Textual Strategies.* New York: Routledge.

Jones, Steven E., and George K. Thiruvathukal. 2012. *Codename Revolution: The Nintendo Wii Platform.* Cambridge, MA: MIT Press.

Just Dance UK. 2010. "JustDance2 Backstage part 3: Meet the dancers" (October 1). https://www.youtube.com/watch?v=QX0CzE3FUes (accessed November 14, 2015).

JustinBieberVEVO. 2015. "Justin Bieber—Sorry (PURPOSE: The Movement)" (October 22). https://www.youtube.com/watch?v=fRh_vgS2dFE (accessed March 15, 2016).

Juul, Jesper. 2005. *Half-Real: Video Games between Real Rules and Fictional Worlds.* Cambridge, MA: MIT Press.

Juul, Jesper. 2010. *A Casual Revolution: Reinventing Video Games and Their Players.* Cambridge, MA: MIT Press.

Kafai, Yasmin B., Carrie Heeter, Jill Denner, and Jennifer Y. Sun, eds. 2008. *Beyond Barbie and Mortal Kombat: New Perspectives on Gender and Gaming.* Cambridge, MA: MIT Press.

Kassabian, Anahid. 2013. *Ubiquitous Listening: Affect, Attention, and Distributed Subjectivity.* Berkeley: University of California Press.

Kat Rina. 2011. "Dance Central -N.E.R.D Lapdance (Hard) 5 Star Gold 95%" (May 17). http://www.youtube.com/watch?v=kPFr27b86tE (accessed January 14, 2013).

Khoury, Joakim. 2012. "Ubisoft Just dance 3—Autodance." http://cargocollective.com/joa-kimkhoury/Ubisoft-Just-dance-3-Autodance (accessed February 23, 2016).

Kilner, J. M., and R. N. Lemon. 2013. "What We Know Currently about Mirror Neurons." *Current Biology* 23:R1057–R1062.

Knoblauch, William M. 2016. "*Simon:* The Prelude to Modern Music Video Games." In *Music Video Games: Performance, Politics, and Play,* ed. Michael Austin. New York: Bloomsbury.

Kolb, Alexandra. 2013. "Current Trends in Contemporary Choreography: A Political Critique." *Dance Research Journal* 45(3):29–52.

Konami Corporation. 1998. *Dance Dance Revolution.* Konami.

Kozel, Susan. 2012. "Embodying the Sonic Invisible: Sketching a Corporeal Ontology of Musical Interaction." In *Bodily Expression in Electronic Music: Perspectives on Reclaiming Performativity,* ed. Deniz Peters, Gerhard Eckel and Andreas Dorschel, 61–70. New York: Routledge.

Kraut, Anthea. 2009. "Race-ing Choreographic Copyright." In *Worlding Dance,* ed. Susan Leigh Foster, 76–97. Basingstoke, UK: Palgrave Macmillan.

Kuipers, Giselinde. 2014. "Ethnographic Research and Cultural Intermediaries." In *The Cultural Intermediaries Reader,* ed. Jennifer Smith Maguire and Julian Matthews, 52–63. Los Angeles: Sage.

Lahav, Amir, Tal Katz, Roxanne Chess, and Elliot Saltzman. 2012. "Improved Motor Sequence Retention by Motionless Listening." http://www.ncbi.nlm.nih.gov/pubmed/22434336 (accessed June 25, 2012).

Lahav, Amir, Elliot Saltzman, and Gottfried Schlaug. 2007. "Action Representation of Sound: Audiomotor Recognition Network While Listening to Newly Acquired Actions." *Journal of Neuroscience* 27(2):308–314.

Lakes, Joi Michelle. 2005. "A Pas de Deux for Choreography and Copyright." *New York University Law Review* 80:1829–1861.

Landay, Lori. 2012. "The Mirror of Performance: Kinaesthetics, Subjectivity, and the Body in Film, Television, and Virtual Worlds." *Cinema Journal* 51(3):129–136.

Lange, Patricia G. 2008. "Publicly Private and Privately Public: Social Networking on YouTube." *Journal of Computer-Mediated Communication* 13(1):361–380.

Latty2cute. 2012. "Dance Central 2—Milkshake—Hard 100%—Kelis" (February 24). http://www.youtube.com/watch?v=4l57qgYmpr0 (accessed February 11, 2013).

Lave, Jean, and Etienne Wenger. 1991. *Situated Learning: Legitimate Peripheral Participation.* Cambridge: Cambridge University Press.

Leonard, David J. 2005. "To the White Extreme: Conquering Athletic Space, White Manhood, and Racing Virtual Reality." In *Digital Gameplay: Essays on the Nexus of Game and Gamer*, ed. Nate Garrelts, 110–129. Jefferson, NC: McFarland.

Lewis, Anne. 2014. "Just Dance 2015 Is Out Now!" (October 21). http://blog.ubi.com/just-dance-2015-launch/ (accessed January 19, 2016).

Liraella. 2012. "An Amazing Game for an Exercise Beginner!" (November 20). http://www.amazon.com/review/ROFSJY0EIVRI5/ref=cm_cr_pr_cmt?ie=UTF8&ASIN=B002I0K3Z2 (accessed January, 14 2013).

MacCormick, John. 2011. "How Does the Kinect Work?" http://users.dickinson.edu/~jmac/selected-talks/kinect.pdf (accessed August 27, 2014).

MacDonald, Keza. 2014. "How Just Dance Conquered the World" (January 17). http://www.ign.com/articles/2014/01/17/how-just-dance-conquered-the-world (accessed February 12, 2014).

Magelssen, Scott. 2014. *Simming: Participatory Performance and the Making of Meaning.* Ann Arbor: University of Michigan Press.

Makuch, Eddie. 2013. "Kinect Sales Reach 24 Million" (February 12). http://www.gamespot.com/news/kinect-sales-reach-24-million-6403766 (accessed May 21, 2013).

Manning, Susan. 2004. *Modern Dance, Negro Dance: Race in Motion.* Minneapolis: University of Minnesota Press.

Marcus, George E. 1995. "Ethnography in/of the World System: The Emergence of Multi-Sited Ethnography." *American Review of Anthropology* 24:95–117.

Marks, Aaron, and Jeannie Novak. 2009. *Game Audio Development.* Clifton Park, NY: Delmar.

Marks, Laura U. 2002. *Touch: Sensuous Theory and Multisensory Media.* Minneapolis: University of Minnesota Press.

Marriott, Michel. 2004. "The Color of Mayhem" (August 12). http://tech2.nytimes.com/mem/technology/techreview.html?res=9502E6DE163FF931A2575BC0A9629C8B63 (accessed June 19, 2006).

Marx, Gary T. 1988. *Undercover: Police Surveillance in America.* Berkeley: University of California Press.

Massumi, Brian. 2002. *Parables for the Virtual: Movement, Affect, Sensation.* Durham, NC: Duke University Press.

Mauss, Marcel. 1992 [1934]. "Techniques of the Body." In *Incorporations*, ed. Jonathan Crary and Sanford Kwinter, 455–477. New York: Zone Books.

McGraw, Hugh, ed. 1991. *The Sacred Harp, 1991 Revision*. Bremen, GA: Sacred Harp Publishing Company.

McRobbie, Angela. 1993. "Shut Up and Dance: Youth Culture and Changing Modes of Femininity." *Cultural Studies* 7(3):406–426.

Meyer, Moe. 1994. "Introduction: Reclaiming the Discourse of Camp." In *The Politics and Poetics of Camp*, ed. Moe Meyer, 1–22. New York: Routledge.

MightyMeCreative. 2011a. "Dance Central 2 NEWS—Interview with DC Choreographer Ricardo @ PAX Prime '11" (September 2). https://www.youtube.com/watch?v=CkrF8o-tiuo (accessed January 14, 2013).

MightyMeCreative. 2011b. "'PON DE REPLAY' Dance Central Hard Gameplay 100%—MightyMeCreative" (March 31). https://www.youtube.com/watch?v=bzIQLvhFHvc (accessed March 15, 2016).

Miller, Karl Hagstrom. 2010. *Segregating Sound: Inventing Folk and Pop Music in the Age of Jim Crow*. Durham, NC: Duke University Press.

Miller, Kiri. 2004. "'First Sing the Notes': Oral and Written Traditions in Sacred Harp Transmission." *American Music* 22(4):475–501.

Miller, Kiri. 2007. "Jacking the Dial: Radio, Race, and Place in *Grand Theft Auto*." *Ethnomusicology* 51(3):402–438.

Miller, Kiri. 2008a. "The Accidental Carjack: Ethnography, Gameworld Tourism, and *Grand Theft Auto*." *Game Studies* 8(1). http://gamestudies.org/0801/articles/miller.

Miller, Kiri. 2008b. "Grove Street Grimm: *Grand Theft Auto* and Digital Folklore." *Journal of American Folklore* 121(481):255–285.

Miller, Kiri. 2008c. *Traveling Home: Sacred Harp Singing and American Pluralism*. Urbana: University of Illinois Press.

Miller, Kiri. 2009. "Schizophonic Performance: *Guitar Hero, Rock Band*, and Virtual Virtuosity." *Journal of the Society for American Music* 3(4):395–429.

Miller, Kiri. 2012. *Playing Along: Digital Games, YouTube, and Virtual Performance*. New York: Oxford University Press.

Miller, Kiri. 2013a. "Dance Central Research Project." http://surveymonkey.com/s/dcresearch.

Miller, Kiri. 2013b. "Virtual and Visceral Experience in Music-Oriented Video Games." In *The Oxford Handbook of Sound and Image in Digital Media*, ed. Carol Vernallis, Amy Herzog and John Richardson, 515–531. New York: Oxford University Press.

Miller, Kiri. 2017. "Virtual and Visceral Ethnography." In *Out of Bounds: Ethnography, Music, History*, ed. Ingrid Monson, Carol J. Oja, and Richard K. Wolf. Cambridge, MA: Harvard University Press.

Miller, Kiri, Sumanth Gopinath, and Jason Stanyek. 2014. "Forum on Transcription: Conversation 5." *Twentieth Century Music* 11(1):145–152.

Millington, Brad. 2009. "Wii Has Never Been Modern: 'Active' Video Games and the 'Conduct of Conduct,'" *New Media & Society* 11(4):621–640.

Mlotek, Haley. 2015. "Britney Spears, 'I'm a Slave 4 U'" (October 28). http://thehairpin.com/2015/10/britney-spears-im-a-slave-4-u/ (accessed November 5, 2015).

Muñoz, José Estéban. 2001. "Gesture, Ephemera, and Queer Feeling: Approaching Kevin Aviance." In *Dancing Desires: Choreographing Sexualities on and off the Stage*, ed. Jane C. Desmond, 423–442. Madison: University of Wisconsin Press.

Nakamura, Lisa. 2002. *Cybertypes: Race, Ethnicity, and Identity on the Internet*. New York: Routledge.

Nardi, Bonnie A. 2010. *My Life as a Night Elf Priest: An Anthropological Account of World of Warcraft*. Ann Arbor: University of Michigan Press.

Negishi, Kaima. 2013. "From Surveillant Text to Surveilling Device: The Face in Urban Transit Spaces." *Surveillance & Society* 11:324–333.

Nettl, Bruno. 1983. *The Study of Ethnomusicology: Twenty-Nine Issues and Concepts.* Urbana: University of Illinois Press.

Nintendo. 2013. "Consolidated Sales Transition by Region" (April 23). http://www.nintendo.co.jp/ir/library/historical_data/pdf/consolidated_sales_e1303.pdf (accessed June 17, 2014).

Noland, Carrie. 2009. *Agency and Embodiment: Performing Gestures/Producing Culture.* Cambridge, MA: Harvard University Press.

O'Connor, Erin. 2007. "Embodied Knowledge in Glassblowing: The Experience of Meaning and the Struggle Towards Proficiency." *Sociological Review* 55(s1):126–141.

Only Music Gaming. 2015. "Dance Central: Crank That (Easy) Music by Soulja Boy HD Gameplay Video DC " (November 26). https://www.youtube.com/watch?v=QkcWxUi2aRg (accessed February 26, 2016).

Ortner, Sherry. 1984. "Theory in Anthropology since the Sixties." *Comparative Studies in Society and History* 26(1):126–166.

Pakes, Anna. 2009. "Knowing through Dance-Making: Choreography, Practical Knowledge and Practice-as-Research." In *Contemporary Choreography: A Critical Reader*, ed. Jo Butterworth and Liesbeth Wildschut, 10–22. New York: Routledge.

Parkin, Simon. 2010. "The Science of Just Dance: What Made a Throwaway Party Game on Wii a Modern Warfare-beater?" (August 6). http://www.eurogamer.net/articles/2010-08-04-the-science-of-just-dance-article (accessed August 1, 2014).

Parviainen, Jaana. 2012. "Seeing Sound, Hearing Movement: Multimodal Expression and Haptic Illusions in the Virtual Sonic Environment." In *Bodily Expression in Electronic Music: Perspectives on Reclaiming Performativity*, ed. Deniz Peters, Gerhard Eckel, and Andreas Dorschel, 71–81. New York: Routledge.

Pearce, Celia. 2009. *Communities of Play: Emergent Cultures in Multiplayer Games and Virtual Worlds.* Cambridge, MA: MIT Press.

Peters, Kathrin, and Andrea Seier. 2009. "Home Dance: Mediacy and Aesthetics of the Self on YouTube." In *The YouTube Reader*, ed. Patrick Vonderau and Pelle Snickars, 187–203. Stockholm: National Library of Sweden.

Pham, Minh-Ha T. 2015. "Visualizing 'The Misfit': Virtual Fitting Rooms and the Politics of Technology." *American Quarterly* 67(1):165–188.

Pipeworks Software. 2010. Zumba Fitness: Majesco Entertainment.

Pitts, Russ. 2012. "Making Gangnam" (November 26). http://www.polygon.com/2012/11/26/3656984/making-gangnam-style-harmonix-dance-central-psy (accessed February 9, 2013).

Polanyi, Michael. 2015 [1958]. *Personal Knowledge: Towards a Post-Critical Philosophy.* Chicago: University of Chicago Press.

Raykoff, Ivan, and Robert Deam Tobin, eds. 2007. *A Song for Europe: Popular Music and Politics in the Eurovision Song Contest.* Burlington, VT: Ashgate.

Redhead, Steve, Derek Wynne, and Justin O'Connor, eds. 1997. *The Clubcultures Reader: Readings in Popular Cultural Studies.* Oxford: Blackwell.

Reilly, Jim. 2011a. "The Best Selling Games of 2010" (January 14). http://www.ign.com/articles/2011/01/14/the-best-selling-games-of-2010 (accessed January 19, 2016).

Reilly, Jim. 2011b. "Just Dance 2 Sales Pass 5 Million" (January 11). http://www.ign.com/articles/2011/01/11/just-dance-2-sales-pass-5-million (accessed May 21, 2013).

riffraff67. 2012. "Dance Central 3 "Call Me Maybe" DLC (Hard) 100% Gold Gameplay" (December 6). https://www.youtube.com/watch?v=lfCfd6cqHKQ (accessed 30 May 2013).

RiffraffDC. 2012. "Dance Central 3 Collabo "Beware of the Boys" (Hard) 100% Gold Gameplay" (December 24). https://www.youtube.com/watch?v=4PmrM7HhwYs (accessed February 26, 2016).

rosroskof. 2011. "Dance Central—Lapdance (Hard) May 17 DLC" (May 17). http://www.youtube.com/watch?v=kPFr27b86tE (accessed January 14, 2013).

Royse, Pam, Joon Lee, Baasanjav Undrahbuyan, Mark Hopson, and Mia Consalvo. 2007. "Women and Games: Technologies of the Gendered Self." *New Media & Society* 9(4):555–576.

Ryan, Marie-Laure. 1999. "Cyberspace, Virtuality, and the Text." In *Cyberspace Textuality: Computer Technology and Literary Theory*, ed. Marie-Laure Ryan, 78–107. Bloomington: Indiana University Press.

Salen, Katie, and Eric Zimmerman. 2004. *Rules of Play: Game Design Fundamentals.* Cambridge, MA: MIT Press.

Salkind, Micah. 2016. *Do You Remember House? Mediation, Memory, and Crossover Community-Making in Chicago House Music Culture.* Ph.D. dissertation, American Studies, Brown University, Providence, RI.

Schechner, Richard. 1985. *Between Theater and Anthropology.* Philadelphia: University of Pennsylvania Press.

Schloss, Joseph G. 2006. "'Like Old Folk Songs Handed Down from Generation to Generation': History, Canon, and Community in B-boy Culture." *Ethnomusicology* 50(3):411–432.

Schneider, Rebecca. 2011. *Performing Remains: Art and War in Times of Theatrical Reenactment.* New York: Routledge.

Serafin, Stefania. 2014. "Sonic Interactions in Multimodal Environments: An Overview." In *The Oxford Handbook of Interactive Audio*, ed. Karen Collins, Bill Kapralos and Holly Tessler, 234–246. New York: Oxford University Press.

Shaw, Adrienne. 2012. "Rethinking Game Studies: A Case Study Approach to Video Game Play and Identification." *Critical Studies in Mass Communication* 30(5):347–361.

Shusterman, Richard. 1999. "Somaesthetics: A Disciplinary Proposal." *Journal of Aesthetics and Art Criticism* 57(3):299–313.

Simonett, Helena. 2001. *Banda: Mexican Musical Life across Borders.* Middletown, CT: Wesleyan University Press.

Smith, Jacob. 2004. "I Can See Tomorrow in Your Dance: A Study of *Dance Dance Revolution* and Music Video Games." *Journal of Popular Music Studies* 16(1):58–84.

Smith, Jamin. 2010. "Dance Central Review" (November 4). http://www.videogamer.com/xbox360/dance_central/review.html (accessed June 28, 2012).

Smith Maguire, Jennifer. 2008. "The Personal Is Professional: Personal Trainers as a Case Study of Cultural Intermediaries." *International Journal of Cultural Studies* 11(2):211–229.

Smith Maguire, Jennifer. 2014. "Bourdieu on Cultural Intermediaries." In *The Cultural Intermediaries Reader*, ed. Jennifer Smith Maguire and Julian Matthews, 15–24. Los Angeles: Sage.

Smule. 2009. *I Am T-Pain.* Mobile app.

Sobchack, Vivian. 1992. *The Address of the Eye: A Phenomenology of Film Experience.* Princeton, NJ: Princeton University Press.

Stahl, Matt. 2013. *Unfree Masters: Recording Artists and the Politics of Work.* Durham, NC: Duke University Press.

Stanton, Erica. 2011. "Doing, Re-doing and Undoing: Practice, Repetition and Critical Evaluation as Mechanisms for Learning in a Dance Technique Class 'Laboratory.'" *Theatre, Dance and Performance Training* 2(1):86–98.

Staples, William E. 2014. *Everyday Surveillance: Vigilance and Visibility in Postmodern Life*, 2nd ed. Lanham, MD: Rowman & Littlefield.

Sterne, Jonathan, and Mitchell Akiyama. 2012. "The Recording that Never Wanted to Be Heard and Other Stories of Sonification." In *The Oxford Handbook of Sound Studies*, ed. Trevor Pinch and Karin Bijsterveld, 544–560. New York: Oxford University Press.

Stillman, Barry C. 2002. "Making Sense of Proprioception." *Physiotherapy* 88(11):667–676.

Stromer-Galley, Jennifer, and Rosa Leslie Mikeal. 2006. "Gaming Pink: Gender and Structure in The Sims Online." In *Digital Media: Transformations in Human Communication*, ed. Paul Messaris and Lee Humphreys, 197–210. New York: Peter Lang.

Sutton-Smith, Brian. 1997. *The Ambiguity of Play*. Cambridge, MA: Harvard University Press.

Taylor, Diana. 2003. *The Archive and the Repertoire: Performing Cultural Memory in the Americas*. Durham, NC: Duke University Press.

Taylor, T. L. 2003. "Multiple Pleasures: Women and Online Gaming." *Convergence* 9(1):21–46.

Taylor, T. L. 2006. *Play between Worlds: Exploring Online Game Culture*. Cambridge, MA: MIT Press.

Taylor, T. L. 2014. *Raising the Stakes: E-Sports and the Professionalization of Computer Gaming*. Cambridge, MA: MIT Press.

the_domin8r_82. 2015. "the_domin8r_82 on Instagram." https://www.instagram.com/p/9WYrKOQElM/ (accessed March 15, 2016).

Thompson, Chanel, and Kiri Miller. 2015. Recorded phone interview, August 19. Boston, MA.

Thornton, Sarah. 1996. *Club Cultures: Music, Media and Subcultural Capital*. Hanover, NH: Wesleyan University Press.

Troup, Christina. 2010. "Dance Central Review: A Rhythm Game That's Definitely Not for Wallflowers" (November 3). http://www.1up.com/reviews/dance-central-review (accessed June 20, 2014).

Ubisoft. 2006. *Rayman Raving Rabbids*. Ubisoft.

Ubisoft. 2009. *Just Dance*. Ubisoft.

Ubisoft. 2011. "Just Dance 3—The Making-of—Part 1: Evolution" (November 21). https://www.youtube.com/watch?v=lERo8UZsqLs (accessed February 11, 2013).

VGChartz. 2016. "Game Database." http://www.vgchartz.com/gamedb/ (accessed January 19).

Waksman, Steve. 1999. *Instruments of Desire: The Electric Guitar and the Shaping of Musical Experience*. Cambridge, MA: Harvard University Press.

Watkins, Megan. 2010. "Desiring Recognition, Accumulating Affect." In *The Affect Theory Reader*, ed. Melissa Gregg and Gregory J. Seigworth, 269–285. Durham, NC: Duke University Press.

Weheliye, Alexander G. 2002. "'Feenin': Posthuman Voices in Contemporary Black Popular Music." *Social Text* 20(2):21–47.

Wenger, Etienne. 1998. *Communities of Practice: Learning, Meaning and Identity*. New York: Cambridge University Press.

Whalen, Zach. 2004. "Play Along—An Approach to Videogame Music." *Game Studies* 4(1). http://www.gamestudies.org/0401/whalen.

Wilson-Bokowiec, J., and M. A. Bokowiec. 2006. "Kinaesonics: The Intertwining Relationship of Body and Sound." *Contemporary Music Review* 25(1):47–57.

zacha83. 2009. "Sugar Hill Gang: Apache (Jump On It)" (October 23). https://www.youtube.com/watch?v=1fd9qP-sHbQ (accessed February 9, 2016).

Zimmerman, Eric. 2004. "Narrative, Interactivity, Play, and Games: Four Naughty Concepts in Need of Discipline." In *First Person: New Media as Story, Performance, and Game*, ed. Noah Wardrip-Fruin and Pat Harrigan, 154–164. Cambridge, MA: MIT Press.

INDEX

Note: Figures and tables are indicated by italic "*f*" and "*t*" following the page number. Endnote material is indicated by italic "*n*" and chapter number in parentheses "(1)" following page number.

game design, 7, 9, 14, 48, 64, 68, 111, 120,
124, 136, 152, 165
See also interactive audio; *specific consoles;
specific games*
game industry, 64, 69, 75, 76–77
See also specific companies
GamePro.com, 49
game production, 19–20
Gamergate, 75
game sound design. *See* interactive audio
GameTrailers.com, 45
Gaston, Martin, 36
gender-as-choreography (S. Foster),
77–78, 85
gendered association, in dance gameplay,
63, 71–72
gender norms (Butler), 77
gender politics, in *Dance Central*, 74–88
Gibson, Ellie, 10–11
Gillespie, Tarleton, 11
Glasser, AJ, 49, 50
Goebel, Parris, 205
Grand Theft Auto, 22
Grand Theft Auto: San Andreas, 65
Granger, Florian, 37–38, 41, 52
gray-market entrepreneurship, 195–197
Grimshaw, Mark, 101
Grodal, Torben, 7, 102
Guitar Hero, 12
business model for, 80–81
comparison to dance gameplay, 7, 8, 14,
36, 40, 96, 107, 114, 121, 123, 143,
211n2(1)
design and development of, 97–98, 100
as predecessor of dance games, 93–94
schizophonic performance in, 9–10

Hahn, Tomie, 25–26
Hairpin, The (website), 204
Hamera, Judith, 25–26, 117
Hamilton, Kirk, 56–57, 58
haptic images/visuality (Marks), 34
Harmonix Music Systems, 96–97
advertising focus, 186
business model for, 80–81
choreographer recruitment, 151, 152–154
choreographic copyrights, 169
copyright infringement, 195
as diversity advocate, 64, 69
game design features, 94, 123, 124–125

history of, 9, 12, 42
marketing campaigns, 13, 189–190
motion-capture systems, 44–45, 45f
See also specific games
HCI theories. *See* human-computer
interaction (HCI) theories
Hernandez, Francisca "Frenchy," 152, 153,
161–163, 165, 190
hip-hop, 13, 47, 53, 65, 66, 68, 99, 108,
125–140, 147–148, 154, 172, 180–181
See also specific artists and songs
hired body (S. Foster), 167
Hoggins, Tom, 36, 49–50, 53
Holm, Hanya, 168
Horgan v. MacMillan (1986), 168
human-computer interaction (HCI)
theories, 117–118
See also dance games as transmission
systems

identity tourism (Nakamura), 19, 46, 66, 79
IGN.com, 36, 52
Inasi, Arthur, 49
Incredible Bongo Band, 125, 130
information distribution, within dance
games, 19
intellectual property, 168–175, 195–197
interactive audio
in dance gameplay, 28, 93, 94–95, 97,
101–102, 107–108, 111–112
history of, 8
in music games, 94
perceptible effects test for, 101–102
See also kinesthetic listening
interactivity
of code and player's bodies, 20
fitness technologies and, 46–47
Grodal on, 100, 102
Zimmerman on cognitive/
meta-interactivity, 106
See also surveillance technologies
interfaces
dance games as transmission systems and,
115–118
DDR innovation and, 8
enculturation of body as, 2–3, 6–7
musical instruments and, 18–19, 25, 111
in music games, 9–10
playable bodies as interfaces with popular
culture, 111, 142, 204–208, 209

Noland, Carrie, 63, 77
notation
    copyright and, 169
    in dance transmission, 121–122
    in orchestral music, 121–122
    shape-note, 23, 23f
    in video, 169
    See also Dance Central

O'Connor, Erin, 116
Oladehin, Kunle, 153–154
1up.com, 52
"On Playing Dance Central 2 While Male"
    (Hamilton), 56–57
Outkast
    "Hey Ya!," 15f

Panjabi MC
    "Beware of the Boys," 57f
paratext (Jones), 148
Parkin, Simon, 38, 40, 41
participatory culture (Jenkins), 3, 16,
    18, 20
PAX East (Penny Arcade Exposition), 17,
    96–97, 136
pedagogy/teaching/learning
    choreographic labor in dance games and,
        150, 153, 159, 162–164, 172–173
    choreography, kinesthetic lag and game
        pedagogy, 120–125
    dance skill-and-drill rehearsal, 121, 124,
        136, 163
    game audio, 100–101
    game video, 122
    Magelssen on simming, 129, 142
    research methodology, 19
    somatic prospecting in, 63
    studio dance pedagogy, 115, 118–120,
        122, 124, 142
    See also dance games as transmission
        systems; headings at Dance Central;
        headings at Just Dance; kinesthetic
        listening; specific choreographers
people of color. See performativity and
    embodied difference; specific groups
performance, as vital acts of transfer
    (D. Taylor), 19
performativity and embodied
    difference, 61–91
    introduction, 61–64

butching up vs. cross-gender
    performance, 82–85
dance games archive and, 64–74
Dancing Like a Lady forum thread, 79–82
gender and sexuality discourse on
    YouTube, 85–88
gender politics in Dance Central,
    63–64, 74–88
identity categories and, 62–66
race and gender in player reviews/
    interviews, 70–74
screen dancers, 66–70, 73–74, 81
summary conclusion, 88–91
Perlot, Matt, 68–69
Perry, Katy, 5, 74
persuasive games (Bogost), 35, 88
Pham, Minh-Ha, 46–47
Pickett, Wilson
    "Land of 1000 Dances," 67
Pitbull
    "Timber," 192, 193f
Pitts, Russ, 44–45
playable body, defined, 118, 208
playable dance, defined, 142
playing along (Miller), 96
playlists, 94
    See also specific artists; specific games
PlayStation, 4, 8
PlayStation 4, 199, 201
PlayStation Move, 12
popular dance, defined, 141
practical knowledge theories, 115–116, 117
    See also dance games as transmission
        systems
practice
    in performance studies, 20
    repetition and impact on quality of
        experience, 22–24
    See also communities of practice; dance
        games as transmission systems;
        embodied practice
presentational dance, defined, 141
private dance lessons. See surveillance
    technologies
private/public tensions. See surveillance
    technologies
proprioception, 34, 58, 96–103, 107
Psy
    "Gangnam Style," 169
public privacy, 54–59

seeing-and-being-seen. *See* surveillance technologies

Segregating Sound (Miller), 65

self-surveillance technologies, 46–47

sensational knowledge (Hahn), 25–26

sexual orientation. *See* performativity and embodied difference

The Shadows, 125

shame, 32, 35, 50–54, 65, 79, 132

shape-note notation, 23, 23*f*

shared objects of embodiment (Bench), 103, 106

sheet music industry, 64–65, 80

shovelware, use of term, 10

simming (Magelssen), 129, 142

Simon, 7–8

Smith, Jamin, 36, 124

Smith, Will, 131–132

Smith Maguire, Jennifer, 150–151

social dance, defined, 141–142

sociality of emotions (Ahmed), 103

social media platforms
  casual games for, 10
  dance communities of practice on, 17, 18–20, 25, 32, 56, 81, 106, 107, 111, 116, 117, 182–183
  See also interviewees; intimate media and body projects; Twitter; YouTube

social risk. *See* vulnerability/social risk

somatic prospecting, 63

Soria, Spikey, 153–154, 161–163

Soulja Boy
  "Crank That," 136–141

sound design. *See* interactive audio

Spears, Britney, 165
  "I'm A Slave 4 U," 204, 205

spectatorship, 38

Spice Girls, 165

Spillman, Gregoire, 40, 51

Stanton, Erica, 177

studio dance pedagogy, 115, 118–120, 122, 124, 142

Sugarhill Gang, 133
  "Apache (Jump on It)," 125–126, 130, 132*f*, 134–136, 135*f*

surveillance technologies, 27, 31–59
  introduction, 31–35
  element of shame in, 50–54
  flailing and embarrassment, 35–38
  kinesthetic vision and, 34

motion-sensing aspects of, 16, 19, 23–24, 209
and public privacy, 54–59, 55*f*, 56*f*, 57*f*
social affordances and, 47–50
trust and control, 38–47
See also self-surveillance technologies

surveys. *See* qualitative survey of players

synchresis (Chion), 7

synesthesia, 58

Takamoto, Naoko, 152–154, 161–162

Taylor, Diana, 19, 115

Taylor, T. L., 18, 35, 66

teaching. *See* pedagogy/teaching/learning

technique
  defined, 115–116, 208
  in relational infrastructure, 25–26
  See also dance games as transmission systems

techniques of the body (Mauss), 35

Thiruvathukal, George K., 4

Thompson, Chanel, 17, 190
  choreographic labor, 150–151, 153, 154, 156–162, 157*f*, 164, 165, 166–167, 170–171, 172, 173–175, 176
  on karaoke analogy, 96
  on recognition, 69, 90
  reviews of choreography, 105
  studio dance pedagogy, 119
  Twitter handle, 160

training, in relational infrastructure, 25–26

transcription
  kinesthetic, 28, 99, 107–108, 111–112, 115, 122, 141
  of musical works, 93, 98, 111

transduction. *See* kinesthetic listening

transduction technologies, 95

transmission. *See* dance games as transmission systems

twinbladestaff. *See* interviewees

Twitter, 17, 88, 119, 155*f*, 160, 174, 179, 183

Ubisoft, 67
  advertising focus, 51, 186
  Autodance and JDTV alliance with, 199–200
  copyright infringement, 195, 196–197
  game design features, 5, 124–125
  See also specific games

Usher, 49, 154